leading

<u>the</u> way

leading
the way

strategies
for managing
the school

edited by Mandy Tunica

contributors
Ken Curran, Robyn Johnston, Gary Johnston, Cath Laws,
Julie McCowage, Terry O'Brien, Susie Sharman, Kay Williams

MACMILLAN

First published 1995 by
MACMILLAN EDUCATION AUSTRALIA PTY LTD
107 Moray Street, South Melbourne 3205

Associated companies and representatives
throughout the world

National Library of Australia
cataloguing in publication data

Tunica, Miranda
Leading the way.

ISBN 0 7329 2023 X.

1. School management and organization. 2. Primary school administration.
I. Title.

372.12

Typeset in Futura and Stone Informal by Superskill Graphics, Singapore

Printed in Hong Kong

Edited by Scharlaine Cairns, Charlie C. Editorial P/L.
Designed by Raul Diche
Cartoons by Nik Scott
Cover design by Kim Roberts

ACKNOWLEDGEMENTS

The authors and publishers are grateful to the following for permission to reproduce copyright material:

Australian Council for Educational Administration for extracts from *The Practising Administrator*, Vol. 14, No.1, 'Marketing your School: finding things out' by Kenneth Stott; Ken Curran, Principal Coogee Public School, for *Proforma for program submissions* and *Principal's Financial Management Checklist*; Michelle Hugonnet/CEO, Sydney, for *Determining Assessment Purposes and Priorities*; SCA for extract from *Journal of Applied Communication Research* Vol. 8 'An Investigation of Proportional Time Spent in Various Communication Activities by College Students' by Barker et al; Department of School Education, N.S.W., for extracts from OASIS.

Diagrams, charts: Professor Ken Eltis, Dean of Education, University of N.S.W., page 61; Dr R. Harrold, page 91; Robert McAlpine/Beverly Hills Girls High School, pp. 103, 104, 105, 109, 110; Mayfield Publishing Co., page 81; Terry O'Brien, pp. 102, 223, 229-238; Taylor & Francis Publishers, page 91 (bottom).

While every care has been taken to trace and acknowledge copyright, the publishers tender their apologies for any accidental infringement where copyright has proved untraceable.

Contents

Preface

Schools have always been subject to change — be it in policy, curriculum, or assessment and reporting. They have responded to political and community demands for programs designed to meet the needs of students in a multicultural society and have addressed the specific needs of girls, Aborigines, and talented and gifted students as well as those with learning difficulties. At the same time, they have been actively involved in the technological revolution, acquiring and translating to their students a range of computer skills. Additionally, they have taken up a range of societal problems by introducing such courses as drug education, sex education and road safety education. As if this was not enough, national economic problems of recession and unemployment have had significant effects on schools, where family problems have been carried into the classroom. Teachers are now finding themselves acting as welfare workers or counsellors — roles often beyond their expertise.

It is a tribute to the professionalism and extraordinary ability of the teaching service that such wide ranging changes have been taken on board and implemented so effectively. Teachers are generally concerned, committed and flexible and, while each change has placed further strains on their workloads and increased their stress levels, they have shown a fine capacity to adjust and adapt. The widely disseminated view that arose from government commissioned reports and media coverage indicating there existed a demonstrated lack of public confidence in public education has, however, had an adverse effect on their morale.

The wide scale organisational changes in education in the 1990s have had far reaching implications for schools and their leaders. Whereas other changes could be justified on the basis of educational need, the changes wrought by the economic rationalism of the last decade have resulted in changed roles for school leaders. The central plank of governmental policy during this period has been devolution of power and responsibility from centralised bodies to schools. Principals who attained their positions through their demonstrated abilities as educational leaders have had to acquire new skills, understandings and behaviours as they wrestle with issues of global budgeting, computerised finance packages, human resource development and management programs, marketing and sponsorship, staff selection and school councils. Increased accountability and community scrutiny, although challenging and timely, have added to the pressure, anxiety and stress. Many school leaders firmly believe that the emphasis has been wrongly placed on management rather than education — on the product rather than the process — on competition rather than cooperation and collegiality. The instigators of the changes would argue that the current reforms and restructuring of education systems will lead to better outcomes for students, staff, parents and communities. This may well be true — only time will tell. Efficient management of school resources does not necessarily equate with educational excellence!

This book was designed to support school leaders in their new roles. No attempt has been made to justify or rationalise the purposes of such changes, rather we decided to put together a practical resource book with a range of ideas, examples, suggestions, case studies and surveys and proformas that can be used by schools when they are implementing the required policies and programs. Although much of the text and examples are drawn from NSW experience and the requirements for government schools, the ideas can be readily adapted to suit other systems and institutions. Except in the opening chapter, where change is examined in its economic and political context, the contributors, who are all experienced in their fields, have concentrated on providing practical, realistic advice on the ways in which these changes can be introduced and management skills and techniques developed.

As editor, I proposed the focus areas but made no attempt to influence the opinions or conclusions of the individual contributors, whose ideas do not necessarily reflect those of each other, the editor, or the organisation in which they work. While making allowance for the variety of leadership styles and the differing school contexts, the contributors all agree on the need for consultation and collaboration with staff and community to ensure commitment to the change process.

Since writing this book, more changes have occurred in NSW government schools — particularly in the area of financial management. Although some of the procedures and practices have changed, the general principles remain the same.

Many people have supported me in the preparation of this book and I am particularly grateful to the contributors for their patience and forbearance; to Bronlyn Schoer for her constructive advice; to Pat Hoban and Sue Cusbert for their continuing interest in the project and their out of hours secretarial support; to those at the Catholic Education Office, Southern Region for their willingness to share their ideas; and to the school leaders and executives, such as Robert McAlpine and Ron Hurley, who have been prepared to allow us to incorporate some of their proformas into the various chapters. Finally, I would like to thank my family, who, by now, are all thoroughly tired of the venture!

Mandy Tunica

About the Authors

Mandy Tunica (BA M.Litt) has over thirty years experience in education. She held an executive position in a high school when she was seconded, first to the Macquarie University Teacher Education Program, and later to regional consultancy. In 1981, she was appointed to the Inspectorate, a position she held for ten years. After the restructuring of the Department of School Education, Mandy was appointed to the position of Cluster Director. Since her 'retirement', she has been lecturing part-time at several universities as well as working in her own consultancy business. She was the coordinating editor and senior author on this project.

Ken Curran holds an MA in Psychology and is currently Principal of Coogee Public School. He has had experience in schools in the NSW western region and Sydney metropolitan area. He has a particular interest in Student Welfare issues and in applying Human Resource principles to school administrative and financial management.

Gary Johnston holds a BA, MEd and Dip Ed from the University of Sydney. He currently works in the Training and Development Directorate in the NSW Department of School Education. He is responsible for the provision of policy advice on issues in pre-service teacher training, teacher induction, and teacher development and retraining. Gary was a teacher and school executive member in city and country high schools before lecturing in teacher education at the University of Sydney. Prior to taking up his current position, he was an inspector of schools in a city region, with responsibility for teacher development. In this role, he was responsible for developing and conducting induction and professional development programs for primary and secondary school Principals.

Robyn Johnston, MA Dip Ed, is currently a lecturer in Communication Studies at the University of Technology, Sydney. Robyn was a teacher in NSW secondary schools and in TAFE colleges, prior to her taking up appointments in higher education. Robyn's teaching includes graduate and undergraduate programs in interpersonal, group and organisational communication. Robyn also has a particular interest in staff training and development. She is actively involved in professional associations and frequently provides consultancy advice in areas related to communication, training and development to a range of industries in both the public and private sectors.

Cath Laws holds a Master of Education and has been Principal of small schools in NSW. She is currently working with Principals, executive, teachers and administrative staff in an Education Resource Centre, assisting in training and development of staff in rapidly changing educational times.

Julie McCowage (Dip Ed, Grad Dip) has taught in a range of NSW primary schools. She was in an executive position when she was seconded to the local Education Resource Centre to work as curriculum consultant, developing and presenting a variety of training and development programs. Earlier in her career, Julie worked for a newspaper in Italy and, in 1990, she gained a Public Relations Certificate.

Terry O'Brien has a Bachelor of Arts in English and History, a Diploma of Education and a Master of Educational Administration. She has had fifteen years experience as a teacher and head teacher. Terry has worked for three years as a curriculum consultant with the Department of School Education, and for four years as a Principal Education Officer for the NSW Board of Studies. She is currently the Principal of Penshurst Girls High School in Sydney.

Susie Sharman, BA, Dip Ed and registered psychologist, has fifteen years of experience as a teacher and counsellor in Queensland and in rural and metropolitan NSW.

Kay Williams, MA (UNSW) and MBA from the Australian Graduate School of Management, held a range of senior positions in Guidance and Special Education before being appointed Assistant Director in this area. She then held the position of Staff Inspector in the Policy Unit and later in the Industrial Relations Directorate, before leaving the NSW Department of Education to establish her own consultancy business specialising in training, development and research.

CHAPTER 1

Managing Change: the Principal as an agent of change

Kay Williams

'Education responds to both social demands and individual aspirations
. . . controversies about educational policies are in fact controversies about
man's individual and collective present and future wants.'[1]

Change is inevitable. The processes of life and growth demand appropriate change. History recounts it. Education prepares young people for it. Schools teach the skills, attitudes and values required for young people to develop into adults contributing to our society. Since society changes, schools must constantly review and reassess their roles and curricula. As the pace of change increases in our complex modern world, so the demands on schools to synthesise, assess and respond increase.

Changes in social, natural, economic and political environments throughout the last decade have impinged upon governments and schools. Governments have responded in terms of their expectations of the public sector in general, and of schools in particular. There are three key pressures that have affected Principals as public sector managers: economic rationalism, neo-liberalism and corporate management.

---

[1] Kogan, Maurice (1978), *The Politics of Educational Change*, Manchester University Press, Manchester, pp. 16–17.

Economic Rationalism

The Pressures

Economic rationalism in government has affected schools. Governments have increasingly assumed that social welfare planning and services ought to be secondary to and a consequence of economic planning.[2] It follows that the opening up of the education sector to market forces has been influential in determining policy and direction at the school level.

This trend is exemplified in a study by one of Australia's economic rationalist think tanks, the Centre of Policy Studies at Monash University funded by the Federal government. The study put forward its own agenda for educational reform without making any real attempt to consider the social and educational issues involved. Schools, it asserted,[3] have three purposes:

● to 'impart knowledge and skills'
● to 'inculcate habits, attitudes and values (in old fashioned language, to "build character")'
● to 'test and certify the performance of students'.

...economic rationalism has affected schools...

These functions may be referred to as the '*cognitive*, the *socialisation* and the *screening* functions respectively'.

---

[2]   Pusey, M. (1992), 'Economic Rationalism', in *Canberra: a nation changes its mind,* Cambridge.
[3]   Freebairn, J., Porter, M., and Walsh, C. (1987), *Spending and Taxing: national economic priorities,* Melbourne Centre for Policy Studies, Melbourne, pp. 95–6.

Its reform agenda involved a criticism of activities that encourage an 'appetite for education by promoting among so-called disadvantaged groups a softening of the curriculum and of performance requirements, and by the payment of means-tested allowances to senior secondary and tertiary students'. The entitlement to public education is challenged (thereby invoking scarcity as an incentive) and choice as to the *quality* or *variety* is limited (promoting competition among suppliers). Without substantiation, the study's authors alleged low quality service (a questionable claim in terms of whole-sector comparisons with, for example, the USA) and a lack of accountability by teachers (who are portrayed as largely self-interested). They asserted that private education is not inferior to public and is less costly to government. This led them to deduce that:

- government expenditure on public education should be reduced
- teachers and schools should be made more accountable to parents and students, thereby breaking the power of education systems and unions and allowing education to be determined largely by *private choices and private initiatives*.[4]

These notions are reflected more broadly in an article by Andrew Hay,[5] the then President of the Australian Chamber of Commerce. The article identifies some of the pressures for change from such interest groups as the Business Council of Australia and the Chamber of Commerce and Industry of Victoria. It concludes:

> 'The Australian education system must become more market orientated, with greater freedom for schools to operate independently of education bureaucracies and the teacher unions.'

...more market orientated...

4   Ibid, pp. 110–111.
5   Hay, Andrew (1988), 'A Market Approach to Education', *The Professional Administrator*, Vol. 40, no. 3, May–June, pp. 4–8.

It will be seen, then, that education policy has been influenced by the following significant economic assertions:

- the free market is the best distribution mechanism for goods and services (including public sector goods such as education)
- competition promotes excellence and the survival of the fittest. (Good schools will prosper, poor schools will close, pupils will be challenged to compete for success.)
- 'global' budgets will allow the expression of preferences. (Local schools can decide how to apply allocated lump sum funds.)

The Implications

Questions of equity or social justice, the redress of disadvantage, and the existence and advantages of cooperative behaviour are, of course, not addressed in a free market policy.

Australian education has not been alone in this surge of claims for a market-based service. The USA (under Reagan), the UK (under Thatcher), and the New Zealand school systems had all been subjected to such change earlier. Australia was, however, different in terms of the centralised nature and size of the systems that the changes sought to disband. In a large country with a small population and an already relatively low expenditure on public sector infrastructure, large systems developed that have produced economies of scale, enabling standards to be maintained. It remains to be seen whether the same levels of education can now be delivered to those in less favoured geographic and socio-economic areas as are delivered in favoured areas, and whether the education dollar can spread as far under a devolved system. There is already evidence that the widening gap between rich and poor in society will be reflected in a comparable gap in their capacities to access quality public sector services, including education.

...the widening gap between rich and poor...

Further, in an increasingly pluralistic society such as ours, the erosion of the capacity of educational systems to deliver a socialising process that forges commonly accepted standards and values and the development of one that promotes and fosters individualism, may be at cross-purposes with our need to grow as a united community.

Neo-liberalism

The Pressures

The principal implications for the education sector are:

- that neo-liberal government seeks to be small and non-interventionist, and to withdraw from direct provision of services that can be supplied by the private sector (or can be privatised).
- that individual liberty and choice (rather than community action and responsibility) are central.
- that personal responsibility and striving for personal gain will promote excellence and merit.

The Implications

The traditional problem of striking an appropriate balance, in our two-party system, between enterprise and individuality on the one hand and community action and personal responsibility on the other, confronts school administrators with the problem of fostering unity in diversity and instilling values of the common good along with the promotion of individuality. In Australian society, public schools have traditionally exercised a significant role in fostering social cohesion. As our society becomes increasingly diversified, and as individualism is increasingly promoted, the need for schools to foster understanding, acceptance and cooperation becomes increasingly important, not only for the better management of schools, but also for the good of society in developing future citizens who can live together in harmony.

Corporate Management

The Pressures

The third major impact on public sector management, and on the government's exercise of control over both State and non-government education systems has been the embracing of the principles of corporate management. The public sectors of almost all governments, State and Federal, have been restructured accordingly.

The Implications

Sometimes referred to as 'the new managerialism', corporate management structures have been used by governments to forge new relationships between two of the traditionally independent arms of government under the Westminster system: the parliament and the bureaucracy. These changes have, moreover, been made with little regard for the sort of distinction that Mintzberg[6] draws between professional and machine bureaucracies (see Appendix A, 'The School as an Organisation', p. 215). Because of their importance, it is appropriate to spend a little more time examining them.

...the Westminster system...

The four principal characteristics of corporate management are discussed in the following paragraphs.

Strong Centre Control and Direction

This requires the establishment of a corporate planning process that ensures strong central control over the organisation's broad direction and performance by a series of corporate, strategic and implementation plans. These plans further specify performance indicators across the range of the organisation's activities by specifying required outcomes that will be measured as evidence of the plans' success or lack of it.

Output Orientation

In the public sector, this strategic planning function becomes the vehicle whereby ministerial control is retained and ministerial accountability for the bureaucracy's performances is exercised. Strategic control (exercised by control over outcomes) thereby replaces traditional bureaucratic methods of control by direct supervision (control over process) as the means of guaranteeing performance. Notions of 'risk management' and 'acceptable levels of risk' are established to determine how much control Ministers can afford to devolve, and over what issues since, ultimately, ministerial responsibility remains (at least in theory).

---

6   Mintzberg, Henry, (1979), *The Structuring of Organisations*, Prentice Hall, New Jersey, pp. 325–54.

Education systems have traditionally invested resources in incremental improvements to *processes*, i.e. the quality of teaching and learning. The problem of defining *outputs*, the difficulty of measuring them, the long time-frames within which cause and effect emerge, and the difficulty of assigning causes to effects, have all led in the past to a view that an emphasis on best possible quality of process was the best way of maximising educational outcomes.

The present specification of outputs in organisations where outputs are not readily definable — in particular the human service area — has led to concern that the search for output measures may distort the processes of education towards those ends that may be measurable, but that may not be evidence of a successful education process.

The emphasis on outputs assumes that organisation performance over time can be measured in terms of whether outputs improve, quantitatively or qualitatively. Again, this presupposes some control over standardising *inputs* (creating a problem that, again, weakens the power of outputs to drive human service management).

Managers are encouraged to promote improved productivity by providing rewards for improved efficiency and cost effectiveness. The critical concern for schools in this case is whether changes in outputs *can* be effectively measured, and whether the outputs are true indicators of the things that one is attempting to measure.

...providing rewards for cost effectiveness...

This focus has also tended to regard the public primarily as taxpayers (funding education) and consumers (being educated), having a predominantly economic stake in education, as assessed by the extent to which schools can deliver people with marketable skills in the most cost-effective manner. The danger in such a perspective arises when broader personal and social goals (such as preparing individuals to become happy, self-actuating adults, able to cooperate for the greater good of the community) are overlooked.

Devolution of Management Responsibility

Much has been written about 'devolution of authority' in education in recent years. This is an attractive term to professionals who, as Mintzberg[7] notes, typically seek to exercise as much autonomy as possible in carrying out their jobs.

In the case of corporate management, however, the rhetoric of 'let the managers manage' is well understood (in the context of central policy making and control) as meaning those in control should have the freedom to apply resources in order to achieve ends centrally specified (outcomes). It does not mean, as professionals frequently assume, those in control should have the freedom to determine what the outcomes will be. It is simply the principle of freedom to experiment in the allocation of resources of different types (people, equipment, work environments, etc.) to meet centrally defined outcomes.

In such a model, innovation and initiative are encouraged through entrepreneurialism and competition, and rewards and sanctions are apportioned according to how well designated outputs are achieved.

Devolved Budgeting Processes

Part of this devolution of responsibility involves devolution of decisions about which resources will be purchased in order to achieve specified outputs. Program budgeting becomes the main management tool for imposing control while devolving responsibility. Schools can now expect to receive, in cash, the money previously allocated to them through the supply of teachers, administrators and equipment (often bulk purchased). Now they will have the responsibility of determining the distribution of this money into each sector.

Difficulties can arise when school-based purchasing does not provide the level of market power necessary to negotiate discounts that a central purchasing authority can muster, where the necessary level of financial management skills is absent, or where schools fail to recognise that they exercise these choices in the context of established industrial and legal requirements for which they have not previously had to take responsibility.

Program budgeting systems incorporate reporting mechanisms that hold managers to account for their actions, and usually also involve central monitoring, review and audit provisions (including efficiency and effectiveness reviews). The extent of this control-by-budget can sometimes lead to an ends–means inversion where meeting budgeting requirements is addressed at the expense of meeting pupils' educational needs.

The Application of Corporate Management Principles to Education

Corporations in the private sector usually exist to market a service that people can choose to buy or reject. The discipline of the market determines that efficient organisations survive and inefficient organisations collapse because people cease to buy their products. This process is dependent on the capacity of people to form opinions about the desirability (utility) to them of what they are buying, the capacity to reject or accept available products, the yardstick of profitability to force decisions about the corporate activity, and the ability to measure individuals' performances in terms of their contribution to this profitability.

---

[7] Ibid.

In transferring the corporate model to the public sector, undoubtedly some public sector organisations are better suited than others to emulate its activities. From a study of Mintzberg's distinction between 'professional' and 'machine' bureaucracies, we can see that the difficulties in successfully applying the model to a professional bureaucracy, such as education, are far greater than those of applying it to the management of a machine bureaucracy, such as a water board or department of roads. These differences also exist in the private sector, where the model has much greater congruence in its application to, for example, the running of a hotel or hotel chain, or the production of consumer goods of various kinds, than it does to the management of a large legal practice or a private welfare agency.

These difficulties can be demonstrated if we take the example of a large bakery and compare the effectiveness of the mechanisms used to gauge efficiency and effectiveness and compare this situation with 'production' within the school context.

...'production' within the school context...

In a bakery, the quality and quantity of loaves produced are measurable outputs. If the number of loaves increases while resource and production costs remain the same, then productivity has been increased. This may be because cheaper flour has been bought or because a quicker way of baking, involving less electricity and fewer person hours, has been developed. In these cases, the costs per loaf have decreased and we can say that efficiency has improved. On the other hand, the bakery may produce the same number of loaves for the same price, but the taste, texture or other measurable features of the bread may have improved. This may have occurred because a better quality flour has been purchased for the same price as the former flour, or the cooking process has been modified in some way. In this case, while costs remain the same, the quality of production has improved, and so effectiveness has increased.

Critical to the judgement of efficiency and effectiveness is the capacity to measure qualitatively and quantitatively the outputs (the bread) but also the inputs (one of which is the quality of the flour). If, for example, the flour used varied from batch to batch and its quality was not known, it would not be possible to say whether the changes in bread quality were the result of better management by the baker or chance variation. Similarly, if during the bread-making process other people were making changes to the dough or adjusting the ovens in a manner unknown to the baker, then it could not be confidently asserted that management of the process was responsible for any improvements or defects in the quality of the bread.

In a machine bureaucracy, such as a large bakery, it can be seen that it is highly likely that one can aspire to at least sufficient control over the measurement of outputs and sufficient knowledge of the inputs and process to link changes in outputs to changes in efficiency and effectiveness.

When, however, we transfer this analogy to the professional bureaucracy of the school, and we explore one element, say, the third grade reading process, we can see the problems inherent in using performance indicators to measure success.

Even if we are satisfied that we have adequate capacity to measure reading performance, how can we claim that class 3A in one year, with a certain pattern of results, has been better taught than class 3A the previous year with a lesser score in reading? Perhaps the skills of the children have been differently developed by their second grade teacher. Perhaps the innate abilities of the groups differed. We could control for these variations by measuring the group at the start of the year and again at the end. But we are dealing with growing human beings. How can we assess the impact of irregular maturation rates on different children? How can we know which children are being encouraged to read or are even being taught at home to assist their learning? How many have access to a municipal library that is running programs to encourage reading? How many are doing extra practice at home? How many children are disturbed by trauma in the home? Should we take into account absences or family trauma that could affect adjustment and learning? How might we determine, under these circumstances, the nature and extent of the teacher's contribution? Even if we take measures and make statistical adjustments for all such events, would the findings be worthwhile in terms of the time and resources they consume?

...immeasurable values...

The complexity of the professional bureaucracy is only glimpsed in this example of the problems of attributing responsibility for change involving a readily measurable skill (reading, ability, with its dimensions of word knowledge, fluency, oral skills, comprehension, vocabulary, etc.). When we look to the broader dimensions of learning goals, including social development and self-actualisation, we become aware of the difficulty of, first, measuring change and, secondly, attributing that change to the school process. To take the further step of using performance on a year-by-year basis as an indicator of the effectiveness of the management of the process, and to reward the performances of teachers and Principals accordingly, is to act on a basis of very tenuous validity. This is not to say that we should not attempt to measure outputs but, rather, that we should recognise such measures as far from rigorous, often misleading, and readily challengeable, no matter what statistical modifications we may use to control external variables.

Of course, we could propose other sorts of measures — client satisfaction could be one. Again, the relationship between what has occurred in the classroom and what students or parents, at any time, are able to evaluate raises new questions.

Much useful work has, admittedly, been done in the area of performance indicators as guides to schools in assessing their programs. The point here is that the interpretation of these processes is necessarily mediated by informed professional opinion, and that this is an essential characteristic of the professional bureaucracy. The assumption that strategic control can be exercised by statistical processes leads to an inadequate model for the professional bureaucracy. Such professional organisations must be managed in ways that, while they draw on understandings in corporate management, do not wholeheartedly embrace them.

Other Control Devices

Finally, in looking at how corporate management models function, two other devices for control need to be considered — the use of organisational structure and restructuring as a control device, and the use of media in marketing the organisation and developing its relationship with its environment.

Restructuring

The introduction of corporate management techniques typically requires the dismantling of organisational structures based on the supervisory model, and the establishment of middle management centres of responsibility with functions delineated by program targets outlined in the corporate/strategic plan. Such centres are usually self-contained units with clear sets of duties and program targets for which managers are held accountable through performance targets. Education Resource Centres or sub-regional offices are examples.

Central agencies, despite the talk of devolution, take on a new and more prominent role in directing 'top-down' management reforms and reinforcing both central control and local accountability.

Detailed central control of staffing and financial inputs is supplanted by the monitoring of outputs and, hence, productivity.

Finally, change in the culture of the organisation towards these ends is frequently achieved by an initial process of destabilising job security. Individual jobs are restructured and employees are required to apply for positions in a process that seeks to ensure their level of commitment to the new culture. An elite management group is usually created at the strategic apex, where management skills are valued above technical and professional ones. There is an assumption that these skills can be applied regardless of organisational context, and a clear distinction is made between managers and non-managers. In the public sector, this has been effected by the creation of a 'senior executive service'.

A feature is the frequently made assumption that management practices are 'content-free'. That is, that the art of management can be practised independently of a knowledge of and training in the technical skills employed by the operating core.

..content free management...

While there is some ground for this assertion in terms of machine bureaucracies, Mintzberg's analysis[8] would challenge this assumption in respect of the management of professional bureaucracies. The essential issue to note is that it can be expected that management of professionals by senior managers who do not share their professional role socialisation can be expected, in the long run, to be a significant barrier to the effective management of those professionals, because of the specific sort of management skills and behaviours required in a professional bureaucracy.

The Media and Relationships with the Environment

A further feature of a corporate management approach necessitating analysis is the way large firms and industries use the media to proactively shape the organisation's environment.

Initially, in organisations, the public relations function was seen as a means to enhance the relationship between the organisation and its environment — to develop an understanding of the organisation through information-giving and to, thereby, promote goodwill. As strategic planning advanced, it became apparent that, instead

---

[8]   Ibid.

of simply managing relationships, firms might use their public relations structures strategically and proactively to create the sort of climate that was favourable to the organisation's interests, and in which its operations would be facilitated.

The concept of *issues management* emerged.[9] The techniques of marketing available to public relations departments were applied to creating a climate of opinion advantageous to the strategic directions that organisation wished to take. The employment of political lobbyists, the funding of directed research, and the use of opinion polling coupled with the development of media campaigns to shape public opinion towards the organisation's corporate interests were all used to create an environment favourable to the organisation. Of course these techniques were not new, as the reader of *Nineteen Eighty-Four*[10] or *Brave New World*[11] will attest. They did, however, enter into the strategic planning processes of corporations, and are increasingly in the process of being transferred into the public sector. Noam Chomsky's recent film, *Manufacturing Consent*, explores some of the implications of this development.

The use of practical strategies to shape public opinion is, of course, a practice which is attractive to governments confronted with the difficulties of managing a community of divergent interest groups and needing to gain and maintain support for its policies.

What has been noticeable in the education sector is an increasing resort to opinion-shaping techniques to support determined policy, rather than the traditional research-based debate engaged in by the profession about desirable change. Both sorts of activity have always existed, but the indication of a change in balance might be signalled by an exploration of two specific examples from the NSW Education system:

- Following its restructure under *Schools Renewal*,[12] the 'Community Relations Unit' was renamed 'Media and Marketing'.
- The introduction of new selection procedures for school executive teachers was termed 'Merit Selection', despite research evidence that the new selection processes employed were less valid than the process being discarded (see the table on the next page).

Predicting Potential

What is the correlation between using various selection methods to predict job success and actual performance? On the next page are the results of five studies, using correlation 1.00 as perfect correlation. It is worth noting that 'job knowledge', includ-

[9]   See Heath, Robert L. and Nelson, Richard Alan (1986), *Issues Management: corporate public policy making in an information society*, Sage, Beverley Hills, p. 19: '*An uncertain operating climate has fostered the growing acceptance of issues management by business executives who, through trial and error, are learning that they must shape as well as respond to the regulatory and social conditions affecting their corporations.*'

[10] George Orwell.

[11] Aldous Huxley.

[12] Scott, Brian (1990), 'School-centred Education: Building a more responsive State school system', *The Management Review*, NSW Education Portfolio, Milsons Point.

ing work samples and assessment, have the highest correlation — whereas references and interviews have low correlations.[13]

Validity Coefficients for Predicting Potential[14]

Predictors	Herriot (1987)	Dunnette (1972)	Reilly and Chao (1982)	Hunter and Hunter (1984)	Schmitt (1984)
Cognitive ability	0.27	0.55 0.45	–	0.53	0.248
Work sample	0.38	–	–	0.44	0.378
Job knowledge	–	0.51	–	0.78	–
Biographical data	0.24	0.34	0.38	0.37	0.243
Assessment centres	0.41	–	–	0.63	0.407
Personality tests	0.15	–	–	–	0.149
Interviews	0.14	–	0.23	0.14	–
References	–	–	0.17	0.26	–

Managing the Professional Bureaucracy

Henry Mintzberg identifies the following problem areas associated with professional bureaucracies.[15]

● The professional bureaucracy is unique among the five forms (simple structure, professional bureaucracy, machine bureaucracy, divisionalised form and adhocracy — see Appendix A, 'The School as an Organisation', page 215) in that it is democratic, disseminating power to its professional workforce, and necessarily providing them with extensive autonomy (allowing them to seek to perfect their skills).

---

[13] The research evidence on various selection procedures suggests that interviews and use of references are among the least valid selection processes for predicting potential. The most valid procedures involve the use of stipulated work environments, known as assessment centres, that evaluate the performance of individuals actually doing the sort of tasks required to perform the job. Such centres are resource intensive and, thus, costly to maintain — which accounts for their limited use except for senior management positions. The traditional inspection process for promotion in schools was of course similarly costly, and the decision to depart from it may well have had economic advantages. The point to be made, however, is that the changes in NSW were marketed to both the profession and to parents and the community at large as 'the introduction of Merit Selection', implying that existing procedures were at least less meritorious, an assertion which flies in the face of the research evidence.

[14] From a paper presented by Jane Watts at a Westpac Human Resources Management Conference in Sydney (1990). The table is derived from the work of Professor Gillian Stamp, England, 1964.

[15] Mintzberg, Henry, op. cit, pp. 371–9.

- There is virtually no effective control over the work except through professional training and sense of responsibility.
- A professional bureaucracy presents problems of supervision. In the machine type, this is accomplished by standardising work processes and outputs. As we have seen, this is a loose coordinating mechanism at best when applied to the professional type, and can be effectively coordinated only by the standardisation and development of the skills of professionals (hence education's traditional focus on teacher training and development).
- The problem of coordination means that management requires what Mintzberg describes[16] as 'the continual reassessment of contingencies imperfectly conceived, in terms of programs artificially distinguished'. The complex process requires the informed judgement of professionals, supervised and managed by those senior professionals with more experience yet remaining receptive to new insights.

...informed judgement of professionals...

- Typically, this dependence on professional discretion makes it difficult to deal with incompetence and lack of conscientiousness. Discretion also enables some professionals to ignore the needs of clients and/or their organisation. Loyalty to the profession may blind them to the need for loyalty to the organisation (especially if they see these as in conflict). Clients may be seen as secondary to the professional practice itself. Irresponsible behaviour may be difficult to control. All such problems point to the importance of collegiality in a supervising relationship that establishes norms of expected behaviour on the one hand and encourages the pursuit of excellence on the other. In a professional bureaucracy, excellence must be *encouraged* and *fostered*. It cannot be *regulated* into existence.
- Because of the nature of professional practice, professional bureaucracies tend to be conservative and slow to innovate. This presents special challenges at a time of rapid change in the organisation's environment. Divergent thinking and innovation have to be particularly fostered.

---

[16] Ibid, p. 373.

● These inherent difficulties of coordination, discretion and innovation make professional bureaucracies vulnerable to takeover by stakeholders outside the profession. Mintzberg[17] says:

> 'What responses do the problems of coordination, discretion and innovation evoke? Most commonly, those outside the profession — clients, non-professional administrators, members of society at large and their representatives in government — see the problem as resulting from a lack of external control of the professional and his profession. So they do the obvious: try to control the work with one of the other coordinating mechanisms. Specifically, they try to use direct supervision, standardisation of work processes, or standardisation of outputs.'

In the recourse to corporate management strategies, we can see the resort to standardisation of outputs as more appropriate to a machine bureaucracy. The message for school administrators is that this is an adequate control for enhancing professional practice and, at the school level, must be accompanied by — and should not displace — traditional means of professional supervision.

Mintzberg[18] makes four further points on this issue:

● 'The fact is that complex work cannot be effectively performed unless it comes under the control of the operator who does it'.
● 'Technocratic controls only serve to dampen professional conscientiousness'.
● Controls also upset the delicate relationship between the professional and his client, a relationship predicated on unimpeded personal contact between the two.
● The incentive to perfect, even to innovate — the latter weak in the best of times in a professional bureaucracy — can be reduced by external controls.'

In the management of change in the present era, then, Principals have a particular responsibility to incorporate the new demands on schools into the organisation in such a way that the essential requirements for managing professionals are supplemented rather than distorted in the processes that are established at school level.

...controls upset the relationship between professional and client...

---

[17] Ibid, p. 376.
[18] Ibid, pp. 377–8.

Mintzberg[19] asks:

> 'Are there then no solutions to a society concerned about its professional bureaucracies? Financial control of (them) and legislation against irresponsible behaviour are obviously necessary. But beyond that, must the professional be left with a blank check (sic), free of public accountability? Solutions are available, but they grow from a recognition of professional work for what it is. Change in the professional bureaucracy does not sweep in from new administrators taking office to announce major reforms, nor from government technostructures intent on bringing the professionals under control. Rather, change seeps in, by the slow process of changing the professionals — changing who can enter the profession, what they learn in its professional schools (ideals as well as skills and knowledge), and thereafter how willing they are to upgrade their skills. Where such changes are resisted, society may be best off to call on the professionals' sense of responsibility to serve the public, or, failing that, to bring pressures on the professional associations rather than on the professional bureaucracies.'

The Principal and the Change Process

Where does this leave the Principal in determining how to manage change in schools?

So far we have primarily concentrated on external pressures for change because it is these which, over the past decade, have generated the most dramatic pressures on school administrators. There are, of course, also pressures for change that arise from the body of practice in the developing profession — research findings, the exploration of new methodologies relevant to changing curricula, and student behaviours, expectations and needs, all generate pressures from *within* schools.

At the school level, the management of change will involve:

● the absorption of external pressure for change from the environment and the stakeholders (see Appendix B, 'Stakeholders and Other Influences', page 219)
● identifying that change mandated by those in a position to exercise control over the organisation
● identifying needs for change arising from within the body of professional knowledge and the experiences of teachers in the school in applying this knowledge.

To respond to these pressures and to achieve cohesion in the organisation require attention, on the one hand, to the quality of relationships among the staff — the nature of the organisation as a team of people — and, on the other hand, to the processes of implementing change. While, of course, the two are interrelated, the first issue is concerned with morale in the school and the way in which *people* are managed. The second is concerned with what occurs when we seek to change established behaviours by implementing new programs to meet new goals. It is helpful to make some observations on these two areas, before looking at managing the whole process of change.

---

[19]   Ibid, p. 379.

Managing Climate

From Mintzberg's[20] observations it follows that, in managing a professional bureaucracy, it is important to develop an organisation culture or climate that fosters the exercise of professional responsibility and a striving for excellence.

The culture of any organisation is a product of the values, morés and codes of behaviour adopted by the organisation. The climate of a professional bureaucracy should be characterised by professionals with a commitment towards the organisation and their profession, and a willingness to strive for and expend effort in developing professional skills and excellence in practice. Such behaviour is generated when individuals are empowered by a sense of control over their own destinies and a sense that their work is recognised by the organisation.

These factors are well known to teachers familiar with the body of knowledge about enhancing learning outcomes in students. They are equally important to Principals and other school executives in developing a school organisation that promotes excellence in teaching through appropriate staff management. All teachers need to be supported by their supervisors to develop a sense of vocation characterised by commitment to excellence in professional practice, and a sense of job satisfaction that comes from adequate professional preparation, the availability of support and advice, and the ability to develop pride in achievement.

Managing Organisation Climate and Morale	
Culture	Values Morés Codes
Climate	Trust Commitment Effort/Striving Control over own destiny Recognition of worth
For the individual	Sense of vocation Job satisfaction

---

[20]   Ibid.

Change in organisations, particularly rapid change, can adversely affect organisational morale. The school Principal's role in managing the climate of the organisation is critical to the quality of teaching in the school.

Morale[21] depends upon:

- a shared sense of vision
- a clear understanding of purpose
- a commitment to excellence/professionalism
- a sense of empowerment from:
  — control over own destiny
  — belief in the worth of the job
  — conviction about own capacity to succeed
  — commitment to the organisation.
- a feeling of being valued by significant others (who maybe peers, students, parents or supervisors).

The strategies of the corporate management process, particularly in relation to the development of corporate plans, provide Principals with an opportunity to initiate activities that bring staff together towards the development of a shared vision and a clarity of purpose. As such they can become critical tools for building morale.

Any externally imposed planning processes can, of course, be problematic. Certain aspects are non-negotiable and certain requirements may not be acceptable to or be valued by some or most staff. The Principal's task here is to develop a consensus about what must be done and (within this constraint) to look, with the staff, to what can and should be done in developing a vision and plan for the school. In this process, one is reminded of the prayer:

> 'God grant me the serenity to accept the things I cannot change,
> the power to change the things I can,
> and the wisdom to know the difference.'

Notwithstanding the imposition of external controls (that are always, in one form or another, a feature of schools that are accountable to their stakeholders) the art of managing within the organisation requires agreement on the identification and incorporation of these non-negotiables as a starting point — but only a starting point — from which schools will go on to develop a vision that incorporates the aspirations of well-trained staff, aware of the standards required for professional practice and accepting the responsibility for its implementation.

Managing the Change Process

Once the school has developed an understanding of its purpose or mission and a view of the sort of organisation it wishes to become, the planning process will help develop a model of the school's activities.

---

[21] **Morale** n. Moral condition; conduct, behaviour, discipline, cheerfulness, zeal (*Oxford Dictionary*.)

Where the implementation of these plans requires change in the way in which the school operates, and depending on whether such change is externally or internally driven, much can be learnt from the longitudinal studies by Matthew Miles, and his associates[22] throughout the 1980s, on the implementation of change in schools in New York City and the District of Columbia, USA.

Miles argues that leaving old patterns and entering the new involves a process of transition that can be characterised on three dimensions, each of which must be addressed by managers:

Leaving the old		Entering the new
Loss	→	Commitment
Unlearning	→	New Learning
Uncertainty and anxiety	→	Stabilisation and coherence

As people prepare to leave old behaviours behind, they experience a sense of loss of the known, and need to replace it by developing a commitment to the new. Awareness and acceptance of the need for change, together with involvement in developing the blueprint for change, helps generate such commitment.

People need to unlearn old skills and learn new ones that will serve them better. In moving from the centralised, hierarchical structure to a devolved system they will leave behind behaviours of dependency and the capacity to blame others up the line for inadequacies. They will move to new behaviours that involve a readiness to take up initiatives offered and accept responsibilities for decision making. Learning such skills may require formal training as well as the development of new structures within which this decision making can occur at the school level.

...loss of the known...

---

22   See Miles, M. B. in Miles, M. B. (ed.) (1964) *Innovation in Education*, Teachers' College Press, Columbia University, New York; also Miles, M. B., Saxl, Ellen and Lieberman, Ann, 'What Skills do Educational "Change Agents" Need? An Empirical View', *Curriculum Enquiry*, Vol. 18, no. 2, pp. 157–93; McLaughlin, M. W. (1987) 'Learning from Experience: lessons from policy implementation, *Educational Evaluation and Policy Analysis*, Vol. 9, no. 2. See also Majone, G. and Wildavsky, A. (1977) 'Implementation as Evolution', *Policy Studies Review*, no. 2, pp. 103–7.

Individuals differ in their capacity to accommodate change. The nature of change can generate uncertainty and anxiety because the future is unfamiliar. Managers need to acknowledge that these states can raise fears about change which are real and require time and developing familiarity with the new in order for individuals to again develop a sense of stability and empowerment that comes from understanding and accepting the new order.

...capacity to accommodate change...

Matthew Miles[23] has identified a series of stages characterising the process of successful change in schools. To underscore the developmental nature of change, he characterises the change process as *evolutionary planning* and identifies five stages that need to be recognised and managed:

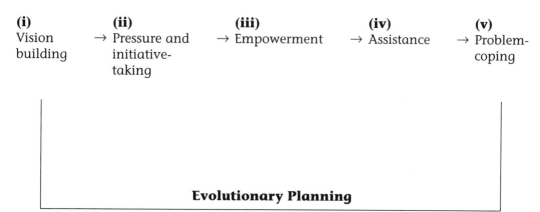

(i) Vision building	**(ii)** → Pressure and initiative-taking	**(iii)** → Empowerment	**(iv)** → Assistance	**(v)** → Problem-coping

Evolutionary Planning

Vision Building
In this phase, staff need to be provided with a vision of what the organisation is striving to become, and a clear understanding of its goals. Participation in the development of this phase strengthens both understanding and commitment.

---

23   Miles, M. B. (1964), op. cit.

Pressure and Initiative-taking

Since individuals will differ in their willingness to move from the status quo, this phase involves the initiation of actual change through strong leadership that exerts pressure for change by demonstrating and seeking commitment to the change process. It also involves taking decisive action towards implementing the vision by such techniques as identifying and supporting those individuals who are prepared to 'give it a go' and experiment with or model programs that embody the changes required.

Empowerment

This phase involves the provision of opportunities and incentives for all people within the organisation to take action to implement the vision, or move towards its goals. People will be encouraged to emulate successful initiatives emerging from Stage (ii) above. This stage of the process also requires action to develop those new skills necessary to implement the change. By this phase, all staff will be increasingly feeling the expectations to develop new behaviours consistent with agreed goals and directions. The climate of expectation of change in professional practice as the norm for behaviour will in itself bring pressure on most individuals to move towards the change.

Assistance

This phase involves practical assistance and support for all staff as they develop and implement new procedures and programs. As well as direct assistance from supervisors and formal education programs, much will be learnt from the experience of colleagues in the process. It is, therefore, essential that frequent professional dialogue between colleagues is encouraged and facilitated through such structures as staff report-backs, team teaching, problem solving meetings, and the like.

Problem-coping

Finally, provision needs to be made to identify and address problems as they arise and to examine their implications for revising the vision, policy or implementation strategy under which the program operates. The practical lessons learnt from implementation will be providing messages about whether the changes work to improve learning and which methods work best. This knowledge needs to be fed back into the learning process.

From his research, Miles[24] has identified the following characteristics of change in schools (that are consistent with the inferences that can be drawn from Mintzberg's[25] observations about professional bureaucracies):

- *Change must be implemented, not adopted.* That is, its goals must be taken up and *used* by individuals in an organisational context to be effective.
- *Policy makers cannot make mandatory what matters.* The focus for successful change should be on the behaviour of those implementing new policy, not on the policy statements themselves.
- *Both pressure* (in the form of mandating and inducements) *and support* (capacity-building and system-changing) *are necessary*, and neither is effective alone.

---

[24]   Ibid.
[25]   Mintzberg, Henry, op. cit.

- *Change is a problem of the smallest unit* (e.g. schools, subject departments or individuals). Implementation is dominated by the processes, motives and incentives at the local level.
- *Implementation is evolutionary.* Problems are never 'solved' but have regular back-effects on policy and administration. The process is one of bargaining and mutual transformation, not 'execution' of a plan.
- *Variability is the rule* — uniformity the exception.
- *Change is incremental* — lags are typical.

A Checklist to Assist in Managing Change

From the foregoing discussion it is clear that, as Principals have always known, managing change in a school (as in any professional bureaucracy) is complex. However, the preparatory checklist on the next page will be useful to Principals embarking on a program of change.

Having examined your answers to the questions in the checklist, return to Miles' steps in the process of change on page 22, and develop an outline plan and timetable for the process. The involvement of staff in developing the plan is essential in generating commitment.

Conclusion

It is essential that Principals and teachers, as professionals involved in education, should concern themselves with response to change. Schooling is a process that the State imposes on all individuals aged from five to fifteen years. The development of relevant educational services in a changing society is critical to the well-being of the State's future citizens and, hence, of the State itself. Failed experiments can have an adverse effect on both the individual and the country. Inadequate education is costly to redress and we cannot 'recall the products' for repair. If we are to respond in an informed way, we must first develop a frame of reference that lets us place demands for change into a proper perspective.

This requires of us that we:

- understand the nature of schools as organisations
- understand how different sorts of organisations differ and why
- are able to determine the nature of the pressures for change
- are able to make decisions about how to respond to these pressures.

It is only by the development of such a perspective that we are able to assess, evaluate and decide on appropriate action, with higher levels of confidence concerning the outcomes and their effects on students and on the nature of education in our community. Educators as professionals have a special responsibility to contribute to the debate about change from the viewpoint of their professional discipline. They are partners with parents and the wider community and its elected leaders, but only the teachers have the benefit of the professional training and practice necessary to contribute to the debate and to influence its outcomes in the best interests of their students and society at large.

Checklist

1 Who are the key stakeholders involved in implementing the required changes?

2 What changes will each group need to make in:
● attitudes?
● values?
● awareness?
● needs?
● behaviour?

3 Who are the key individuals in each group?

4 Are they likely to be:
● strongly supportive?
● uncommitted?
● strongly resistant?

5 What will it take to gain their commitment?

6 Who could pilot or model some aspects of the change?

7 By what strategies can I apply pressure towards change?
● When?
● Where?
● How?

8 How can I support those implementing change?

9 How can I demonstrate my commitment to the changes required?

10 What mechanisms are to be established to:
● evaluate the trial?
● examine any broader implications that emerge?

11 What mechanisms can I establish to revise the planning process in the light of these experiences?

12 How can I encourage others to adopt the procedures being modelled by those implementing change, or to integrate them in some way into their own practice?

13 How can I foster a climate of professional sharing?

14 What resources will I need to bring to bear?
● materials?
● exercise?
● support?

CHAPTER 2

Managing Human Resource Development

Gary Johnston

Introduction

The importance of ongoing development of staff, and the value to be gained by organisations from such development, is being recognised increasingly by leaders in many organisations throughout Australia. Such recognition has resulted as organisational leaders realise that, with the increasing pace of change and the knowledge explosion confronting citizens of the late 20th century, initial vocational or professional training is insufficient to ensure ongoing organisational effectiveness and the achievement of desired and necessary outcomes. There is also an increasing recognition that organisations, as well as the individual staff in those organisations, need to be able to renew or revitalise themselves and learn from past organisational successes and failures. In other words, organisations need to become learning entities.

As school leaders, Principals have significant responsibilities in ensuring the ongoing development of individual staff members as well as continual renewal of the school organisation. Such development and renewal has been necessitated in schools throughout Australia as a result of changing curricula, policy initiatives of governments, changing school populations, staff turnover and an ageing teaching population. This responsibility for providing development opportunities has also increased as schools have gained more autonomy and school leaders have a greater role in the selection, assessment and career development of staff.

This chapter attempts to present Principals and aspiring Principals with some techniques for establishing effective development strategies for their schools and their staffs. It examines the dimensions of human resource development and organisational development. It provides guidelines for establishing effective Human Resource Development (HRD) programs in schools and presents an overview of recent research on teacher preparation and development. Also included are a number of proformas and checklists that can be used in developing and managing an effective HRD policy and program.

What is Human Resource Development?

Before the 1970s, in many education systems, there was a view that when teachers entered the profession they were fully trained to perform the tasks associated with teaching. Teachers as professionals were expected to 'keep up to date' through professional reading, membership of professional associations and by undertaking further qualifications at higher education institutions. There were few other formal opportunities for the further professional growth and development of teachers. There were virtually no readily available opportunities for other members of staff working in schools. Significant change started to occur in the 1970s, when governments provided funding for extensive 'inservice education' of teachers.

A Plethora of Labels and What they Mean

Over the years, various terms have been used to describe the professional development activities undertaken by teachers and other school staff. Terms such as 'inservice education' and 'professional development' have been applied to programs and courses designed for teachers. 'Staff development', 'training and development' and 'personal development' were other terms designed to encompass all staff involved in the education system — clerical, administrative, ancillary and teaching staff.

...training...

In more recent times, the term 'human resource development' has been used in industry and in some education systems.

Most writers agree that 'human resource development', or alternative terms, describe activities designed to improve the current or future performance of employees by increasing, through learning activities, the employees' abilities to perform their jobs. These activities should aim to achieve some or all of the following:

- increase employees' knowledge
- increase employees' skills
- change employees' attitudes

The American writer Nadler (1984),[1] tried to define more precisely the difference between the terms *training*, *development* and *education*. He offered the following distinctions:

- *Training*: learning activities that aim to enhance a person's current job performance.
- *Education*: learning activities aimed at preparing a person for some future job.
- *Development*: learning activities aimed at personal growth without any direct relationship to current or future job performance.

There have been lengthy debates about the possible distinctions between education and training, and the inclusiveness of terms such as 'training' and 'development' and 'human resource development'.

...staff development...

---

[1]   Nadler, L. (1984), *Handbook of Human Resource Development*, John Wiley and Sons, New York, 1.1ff.

In school education systems, the terms 'inservice education', 'professional development', and 'staff development' have been used to encompass learning activities for executive, administrative, clerical, ancillary and teaching staff, as well as for parents and community members.

In school systems the learning activities referred to as 'human resource development' are those involving the executive, teaching and ancillary staff of schools, and parents and community members.

Who Should Benefit?

In the debate about the terms used, there has at times been a lack of clarity about who was and is to benefit from the learning activities provided to people involved with school systems.

One pervading view since the 1970s, when such activities became widespread in school systems, was that development activities were designed to benefit primarily the individuals involved. This view supported a model of training and development provision in which individual teachers, groups of teachers, parents and community members requested the right to attend 'inservice courses' from a 'menu' of courses provided by a central or regional inservice provider. The focus of such development was, therefore, on the individual who participated in staff development. It was the responsibility of the individual undertaking staff development to apply new understandings in his or her school and use newly gained skills. Frequently, however, as has been noted in evaluation of many training studies from a range of organisations, constraints arising from the employees' organisation could mitigate against the application of newly gained skills. Hence the benefit of training for the individual and the potential benefits following implementation of new approaches in the school were minimised.

In more recent times, leaders of school education systems have taken the view that such training and development activities should benefit both the organisation (the school, the region and the system) and the individuals involved (teacher, parent, school assistant or Principal).

At the same time, there has been recognition that for change or renewal to occur in schools, as in other organisations, there is a need for school or organisational development as well as individual development. When an organisational development focus is adopted, learning activities focussing on the school as a whole rather than the individual teachers in the school are central.

The term 'organisational development' was first used by researchers in the field of behavioural science in the late 1960s. Organisational development activities involve responding to change and the need for change in the organisational context. Organisational development strategies aim to change beliefs, attitudes, values and the structures of organisations so that they can better adapt to new technologies, challenges and the dizzying rate of change itself. Such strategies often include developing mechanisms that allow organisations to continually monitor their capacity for self-renewal and evaluate their capacity to adapt to the changing environment.

As educational leaders, Principals must manage the human resource development function to ensure that both the organisation (the school and, therefore, the pupils and the system) and the individual staff members benefit from the learning activity being undertaken.

It follows, therefore, that in managing school HRD programs, Principals need to ensure that the range of human resource development activities involving the school staff and its parent and community members meet both the needs of individuals and those of the organisation (school and system), and benefit both the individual and the organisation.

The Characteristics of Effective HRD Programs

Many writers have researched the characteristics of effective training and development programs. Most agree that effective programs:

- are designed to meet the identified needs of individuals and groups of individuals or the organisation as a whole
- are planned organisational activities rather than spur of the moment, ad hoc events
- further the goals of the organisation while also providing an opportunity for individuals to adjust to work life, adapt to new demands of the organisation or the system, and grow and develop.
- are learning experiences and activities from which permanent change results.

Effective HRD programs in schools can encompass:

- the induction of staff new to the profession and new to the school
- training and development activities conducted within and outside the school relating to, for example, curriculum changes and implementation, the teaching/learning process, interpersonal skills, management of people and physical and financial resources, and leadership skills for individuals and groups of staff members.
- remedial activities for individual teachers
- career planning activities for individual teachers seeking promotion.

Training and development activities can take place during staff meetings, executive meetings, student-free days, grade and faculty meetings, and individual counselling sessions, as well as at formal HRD courses within and outside school time. Training and development activities may include completion of programs of study at higher educational institutions, through professional associations, through visits to other schools or organisations, or some form of job rotation or responsibility-sharing under supervision.

HRD Programs Based on Needs

While a diverse range of activities can become part of a training and development program the effectiveness and relevance of such training for both the individual and the organisation for which the Principal is responsible should be determined by the existence of a need in the organisation for such activities.

As the list of characteristics of effective training and development activities presented above suggests, there are a number of steps that need to be carried out before any HRD activity takes place.

Critically the Principal of a school must ensure that:

- a needs assessment/analysis is conducted to establish the training needs of the individuals or groups of individuals in the school. This is sometimes called a training needs analysis (TNA)
- a school HRD plan is developed as a result of the needs analysis.

What is a Training and Development Needs Analysis?

Training needs assessment has been defined as the 'systematic study of a problem or innovation, incorporating data and opinions from various sources in order to make effective decisions or recommendations about what should happen next'.[2]

Such a definition highlights several issues:

- training needs may result from an existing problem, or may emerge from the introduction of a new process, or an innovative curriculum, or a need that will occur in the immediate future
- needs analysis should involve gathering data systematically from more than one source, i.e. decisions should not be made on the basis of one person's idea
- needs analysis does not always show a traditional training course as a solution to problems.

Training needs analysis may reveal an array of diverse needs. Sometimes the needs will reflect the various audiences of your school, e.g. curriculum needs from specific faculties, or needs resulting from positions of responsibilities (executive staff requiring leadership training, ancillary staff needing computer training, new staff needing induction). On other occasions, needs analysis may reveal a more general need to review school policies or total school programs, e.g. new approaches to multicultural needs, talented child policies, or assessment procedures.

The needs identified can often be seen as falling into the following categories:

- individual versus school (or faculty/work area)
- reactive needs (existing weaknesses needing a remedy) versus proactive needs (preparation of employees to handle anticipated future changes both within the school, the system, and the community, e.g. new information system, and competency approaches to education)
- training versus development versus education needs.

---

2 Rossett (1987), *A Training Needs Assessment*, Educational Technology Publications, New Jersey.

Data gathered during a training needs assessment should assist in the identification of poor performance, causes of poor performance and potential performance problems in the future and, thereby, allow for decisions to maximise the effectiveness of HRD planning. Needs assessment should identify if performance problems are the result of:

- lack of skill or knowledge
- lack of practice
- lack of incentives including lack of both positive and negative feedback about performance, or by rewarding good work with extra work!
- obstacles created by the school organisation
- lack of motivation of individual staff members.

...lack of motivation...

Exercise: Forces for change — the need for training

All schools are subject to a variety of internal and external forces for change. All of these forces have implications for training and development of staff. These forces of change give rise to symptoms indicating the need to change in organisations. These symptoms indicate a gap between what *is* (current performance) and what *should be* (performance required to meet the changed circumstances).

It should be stressed that the gap between 'what is' and 'what should be' is often based on perception and is, therefore, not necessarily objective. It may be the perception of individual teachers, or of an individual executive, of particular aspects of the school's work.

Issues for Reflection

♦ *As you reflect on the concept of a training and development needs analysis, complete the following table from the point of view of your school. Remember that the forces for change you identify may be system wide or specific to your school, and may be arising from within or outside your school and its community.*

Forces for Change: a training and development needs analysis exercise

Example

Forces for change	Symptoms of the need for change	HRD implications
● Introduction of a new syllabus or curriculum.	● Few members of staff familiar with new curriculum.	● Staff development days. ● Support for request to attend inservice days.
● Introduction of accrual accounting.	● No executive staff member with understanding of procedures.	

...no executive staff with understanding of procedures...

Training Needs Analysis Flowchart

Conducting a human resource development needs analysis in a school, as in any other organisation, is a multi-phase process. Often, each phase will require investigating different sources of information. The following flowchart illustrates these processes.

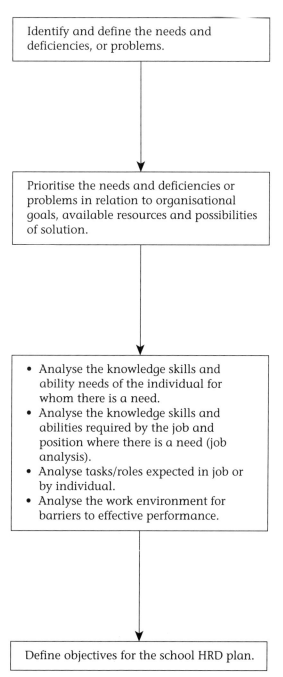

Dos and Don'ts in Conducting HRD Needs Analysis

Step	Do	Don't
1 Define the problem, need or deficiency.	Define the need in terms of behaviour, e.g. John has difficulty building a team of staff to collaborate on a task.	State the need in terms of a perceived solution, e.g. John needs a leadership development course.
2 Prioritise the need/ problem in relation to organisational goals and available resources.	Ask yourself which need or priority should be met or solved first to provide the greatest benefit to the school.	Ignore organisational analysis or a review of available resources.
3 Identify/analyse: • knowledge, skills abilities required to carry out job/ position. • Knowledge, skills and abilities required by individuals • tasks associated with jobs. **4** Consider: work environment factors that may be barriers to effective work performance.	**Analyse these steps simultaneously (i.e. 3 and 4).** Ensure the job analysis takes a person orientated and task orientated approach, i.e. consider knowledge/skills/abilities/ motivation required by individual to perform the job as well as identifying the tasks associated with the job. Decide: • how information is to be collected, e.g. survey, interview, observation. • other sources of information.	Use only one or two sources of information.
5 Develop objectives for school HRD plan.	Analyse data gathered to ascertain needs to be addressed in school HRD plan. Focus on objectives/ outcomes to be achieved by HRD plan.	Ignore individual needs in developing objectives. Select training or alternate strategies until objectives have been clearly established.

Needs Analysis Techniques

A range of techniques can be used to identify the training needs of a school. In small schools observation of staff at work and discussion with staff will be possible and appropriate for identifying training needs. In larger schools, techniques including surveys, questionnaires, group discussion as well as sample observations and discussion with supervisors may be necessary.

...observations of staff at work...

The techniques involved sometimes will involve examining the jobs and tasks for which various staff members have responsibility (job analysis), assessing the individuals carrying out those jobs (person analysis) and also, very importantly, examining the environment in which staff are working.

...examining the environment in which staff are working...

Job Analysis

Job analysis involves gathering information about job requirements. The table on the next page lists some common methods used in job analysis.

Job Analysis Methods	
Method	**Comments**
1 Analysis of job description.	Job descriptions usually outline typical duties and responsibilities of a particular position or type of position. Job descriptions are not meant to be all inclusive but can be helpful in identifying the knowledge, skills and abilities needed to perform the job.
2 Development and analysis of job and tasks (task analysis).	Making a list of the specified tasks required for each job and analysing them can assist in making judgements about the knowledge, skills and abilities required by the job and identifying the 'skill gaps' of current incumbents.
3 Observation of a person undertaking the job.	This technique may assist in identifying knowledge, skills and abilities needed to perform the job, especially when the job is not familiar or there are unusual circumstances related to the job.
4 Conducting interviews with or surveying: ● job holders ● supervisors ● higher management.	Interviews with job incumbents, supervisors and senior staff will provide the most detailed information. Structured and unstructured surveys and questionnaires can be used to gather data. Job incumbents are the best source of information about their jobs but they might not accurately represent their jobs, because of the perception of the reasons for the analysis or because of the organisational climate in which they work.

Staff Analysis

Staff analysis involves gathering data about the skills knowledge and abilities of job holders. This process is important for determining the number of staff members requiring specific types of training and development. It is also vital in cases where a development program is being designed involving remediation. Such information will allow a comparison to be made between the requirements of the job and the current knowledge, skills and abilities of each job incumbent.

Staff Analysis	
Method	**Comments**
1 Analysis of information from performance reviews.	Analysis of supervisor's/work reports and performance reviews will provide information about areas of strength as well as the knowledge, skills and abilities needing improvement.
2 Interviews/questionnaire.	Interviews and questionnaires allow the individual staff members to be involved in assessing their own training needs. This is important because individuals are the only ones who know what they believe they need to learn. Questionnaires or surveys can be easily structured to target particular characteristics or groupings of staff in the organisation.
3 Distribution and analysis of attitude surveys.	Used individually, such surveys can provide useful information about the morale, motivation and job satisfaction of each staff member, analysis of this data may lead to alternative development activities.
4 Critical incident technique.	This technique involves recording either observations or perceptions of staff or supervisors concerning critical incidents in which participants have been successful or unsuccessful in carrying out aspects of their job or specific tasks. Repeated evidence of tasks not being carried out successfully, or staff indicating lack of success in an area indicates the possible need for a staff development exercise.
5 Focus group discussions.	Small group discussions of up to ten staff members, from either the same disciplinary area or diverse disciplinary areas, in which a number of key questions regarding areas for staff development are discussed. Common areas of concern or need can be recorded.

(Table continued on next page)

(Staff Analysis table continued.)

Method	Comments
6 Peer coaching systems.	Peer coaching is often associated with 'mentor' and 'buddy' systems to provide mutual supported assistance particularly to inexperienced colleagues. This one-to-one discussion between peers can assist in identifying training and development needs for individual staff members.

Work Environment Analysis

The requirements of the job (knowledge/skills/abilities), the abilities or inadequacies of the individual, and the skill gap between what the job requires and the current skill of the person are critical factors in a person's performance in a particular job. There are, however, other factors that influence work performance that need to be examined when assessing a school's training needs. Additional information needs to be gathered when assessing the training needs in schools if training is to achieve real outcomes that benefit the organisation.

For example, is there a deficiency in performance, or application of newly gained skills or knowledge because:

- staff do not have the opportunity to use such skills or knowledge
- school or faculty structures make implementation difficult
- school policies mitigate against application
- supervisors or other staff members are either disinterested or discourage application
- the school lacks adequate resources
- Individuals receive little recognition for attempting anything that is new.

...the school lacks adequate resources...

Consider also whether the performance problem is the result of poor motivation on the part of staff members. Obviously the motivation to apply or even seek new skills or understandings varies for individuals. What can be motivating and rewarding for one staff member in fact may seen as a sanction or a demotivator for another.

It is important to gain an understanding of staff members' perceptions of some of the work environment barriers that limit improved performance. Surveys, questionnaires and interviews involving individuals or groups of employees can provide useful information for those responsible for staff development about these motivational aspects of the work environment.

Encouraging staff to reflect on these work environment/motivational issues can also assist staff in reassessing the causes of their own behaviour and may sometimes lead to the identification of simple solutions for what were major problems. Such data gathering can also provide the basis for supervisors and school leaders to develop more appropriate management approaches.

Barriers to effective performance created by the work environment will often relate to the structure of the work flow, the nature of supervision, the need for additional and/or different resources to perform the tasks of the job, and the need for innovative reward mechanisms.

In summary, managing the school human resource development function requires the development of an HRD policy and program that is based on the real needs of the staff within a school. This requires that time and energy is given to training needs identification and analysis. At the same time the school leader needs to be responsive to changes in the school's external environment and demands at a system level, to ensure that the staff development policy is relevant. These responsibilities have become more pressing as more authority and accountability is being devolved to the school level of educational systems.

Case Study: The work environment at Twyford Road Public School

Twyford Road Public School is a large primary school in a growing coastal town. The school is well regarded in the community and has a long and proud history, having recently celebrated its centenary. The nature of the school's community has been changing rapidly in recent years with an influx of young families from the city. The school's enrolment has increased from 200 to nearly 500 over the last five years. The new parents, while pleased with the school, have sought greater diversity in the school's curriculum and extra curricula activities.

The school has a staff of 24 including a Principal, a deputy Principal, 17 teaching staff and 5 administrative staff. The Principal, Bill Johns, has been at the school for 12 years (eight years as Deputy Principal and four as Principal). Nine of the teaching staff and three of the administrative staff have been at the school for long periods, including one teacher who has been on the staff for 22 years.

In curriculum terms, the school has emphasised the teaching of the 'basics' and has a traditional teacher-centred approach to classroom practice. Some of the more recently appointed teachers have tried to introduce student-centred, inquiry based approaches to teaching and learning, particularly in curriculum areas such as Science and Technology. This has led to some conflict among the staff. Bill Johns has pointed out to the staff that the parents generally support the school's emphasis on traditional methods of teaching.

The overall organisation of the school is also fairly traditional. Student seating in classrooms is arranged in rows, teachers retain the same classroom year after year, and there is little rotation of staff across the grades. Sport is a significant part of school life and the Principal promotes the sporting achievements of students at assemblies and in reports to parents. There is, however, little emphasis on personal development and health education apart from the sex education talks given to Year 6 students and their parents each year by an outside agency.

School-based training and development activities usually focus on explanations of new policies and syllabuses issued by the education system. Some of the staff attend the regular training and development activities conducted at the nearest education resource centre, 40 km away. The general reaction of staff attending these activities has been that, though the ideas and approaches presented were interesting, they were not really relevant to Twyford Road. In some cases, staff who have tried to implement new ideas and to persuade their colleagues to do so have been regarded as the 'enemy within' by some members of the staff.

...the enemy within...

Bill Johns has reminded the staff that, while it is important to look at new approaches to teaching and learning, it must be remembered that the community supports the school's emphasis on the teaching of the 'basics', its good discipline and its encouragement of sporting success. He recently told the staff at a staff meeting to remember the old adage 'when you are on a good thing, stick to it.'

Issues for Discussion

♦ *What are the main barriers to effective teaching performance created by the work environment at Twyford Road Public School?*

♦ *If you succeeded Bill Johns as Principal, what steps would you take to ensure the effectiveness of the school's training and development activities?*

Types of Training for the Self Managing School

In recent years many education systems and/or sectors have devolved power, authority and resources to schools in a bid to create self-managing schools. Such devolution has produced schools with new powers (including power, authority and resources for human resource development of the school's staff and community members) but also new needs. As Caldwell and Spinks[3] suggest:

> 'The self managing school will require a range of knowledge, skills and attitudes not demanded in schools which have worked within a framework of centrally determined policies, plans and budgets and with few requirements as far as accountability is concerned.'

A number of recent reports have noted the need for new types and methods of training and development for teachers and for a redefinition of what constitutes effective training and development, and development delivery.

The Commonwealth Schools Commission report of 1988, *Teachers Learning: Improving Australian Schools through Training and Development*, illustrated this point. This report was critical of current inservice training and development activities. It indicated that current programs:

● do not address the direct needs and concerns of participants
● are 'one-off' activities that do not have any follow up
● provide no follow up support for ideas and practices introduced or for activities
● contain topics not well connected to the priorities of schools and teachers.

The report concluded that there was a lack of longer term systematic planning of activities and programs to encourage effectiveness. Research evidence points to the fact that the 'one-off' inservice training and development activity is the least effective, both for the individual and the school.

In a similar vein, the nature and sufficiency of what has constituted professional development of teachers (particularly that which occurs away from schools — one-day or two-day courses or voluntary post graduate study at Higher Education institutions) has been questioned by Costello (1991). In an article on government policy and

---

[3] Caldwell Brian J. and Spinks J. M. (1989), *The Self Managing School*, Falmer Press, London, pp. 20–1.

the training and development of teachers, Ray Costello a former General Secretary of the Australian Teachers Federation, attempts to redefine the notion of professional development of teachers:

> 'The term professional development is taken . . . to mean the process of growth in competence and maturity through which teachers add range, depth and quality to the performance of their professional task . . .
>
> Teachers are greatly assisted in their professional development by additional training or by undertaking developmental opportunities away from their regular jobs. But these experiences are not the essence of professional development, important though they can be in stimulating it . . . the centrality of the work teachers do (is) . . . the focus of consideration for professional development.'[4]

The Nature of Inservice Training and Development of Teachers

While there has been a call for new approaches to the ongoing development of teachers and a recognition of the importance of focussing such development on the real needs of schools, there is evidence to suggest that the teaching staffs of schools have a wide range of development opportunities.

The following information taken from *Teachers in Australian Schools: a 1989 profile*[5] (based on a survey of 600 Australian teachers) by the Australian College of Education, provides school teachers with details of the diversity of opportunities that can be used as part of a school's HRD program. Among other things, this survey sought information about teacher training and development. The findings of the survey in the areas of teacher training and development are summarised in the following paragraphs.

Initial Training and Qualification
- The vast majority (78%) of respondents had completed three or more years of initial training.
- Nearly half (47%) had a pass degree or higher qualification.
- Nearly a quarter (22.8%) were upgrading their qualifications at higher education institutions during the two years before the survey.

Inservice Training and Development
- While 40.6% of respondents indicated that the source of inservice education was their own school, 19.4% indicated regional offices as the source, 11.9% said teacher or education centres and 14.2% said professional associations.
- Between $\frac{1}{4}$ and $\frac{1}{3}$ of teachers had attended inservice training and development activities for three days or less. The survey showed that 35% of admin-

---

4 Costello, R. (1991), 'Government Policy for Professional Develoment of Teachers,' in Hughes P. (ed.) *Teachers' Professional Development*, ACER, Hawthorn, Victoria, p. 131.
5 Logan, L., Dempster, N. Berkeley, G., Howell, M., Warray, M., Department of Education, (1990) University of Queensland.

istrators and 11.3% of classroom teachers attending training and development activities of 10 days duration or longer.
- Just over half of all training and development activities attended by respondents was in school time.
- Very few (less than 3%) of training and development activities attended by respondents were organised by higher education establishments.

Types and Contents of Current Inservice Training and Development Activities

There are four main types of inservice training and development:

- whole school activities designed to review an aspect of the school's program, e.g. student welfare policy, or the introduction of new procedures or policies developed by educational systems
- faculty or subject based activities relating to the curriculum and/or school organisational matters, e.g. introduction of a new syllabus or student assessment procedures
- 'one-off' activities external to the school, usually of one day's duration or less, where representatives for a school attend an activity outside the school so as to bring new information back to the school
- multi-phased activities conducted either at the school or outside it to provide training or retraining of individuals in specialist areas, e.g. teaching English as a second language or educational leadership. Such programs are sometimes jointly conducted with tertiary institutions and usually involve face-to-face training activities, school based action research and completion of projects or assignments.

Common Topics of School Based Training and Development Activities
- Subject content
- Curriculum design and development principles and practices
- Teaching processes
- Student assessment and evaluation.

Evaluation and Review

Having established on HRD policy and program, it is important to review and evaluate the extent and effectiveness of school-based HRD programs. The means of evaluating training and development programs should be clearly set out at the time of planning the HRD program and when preparing each training and development activity. Evaluation should take place at a number of levels.

Program evaluation may encompass a review of the extent of the HRD activities in the school and may be focussed on obtaining information about the distribution of development activities among the staff, and the types of activities attended by staff, in order to have an overall picture of the needs of staff. Evaluation may focus on the effectiveness of various activities within the total HRD program. The following dimensions could be evaluated following every training initiative.

- *Reaction*: How did staff members respond to the program? Did they find it useful? Did they enjoy it?
- *Learning/change*: What did participants learn, how did they gain from attending?
- *Application*: Have any of the new skills or learnings been applied in the school?
- *Organisational* (school) results: Has the learning had an impact on organisational outcomes? Has the school changed/improved?

The Principal may not be responsible for conducting the evaluation. This may be the work of a committee within the school. However, the Principal should ensure that review and evaluation information is gathered to assist in setting the directions for future development work. The questionnaire on the facing page will help in this evaluation process.

School Based Management of HRD Activities

The management of school based training and development activities involves both short-term and long-term planning and coordination, and ongoing procedural management for the conduct of activities.

Even when a school has a human resource development committee, the Principal has overall responsibility for ensuring the educational quality and cost effectiveness of those activities, the equity of access for staff, and that such activities meet the identified needs of individuals and the goals of the school and/or the educational system.

Monitoring the activities provided as part of the HRD program and reporting to sector and or government authorities on use of funds also are the responsibility of Principals.

...monitoring HRD activities...

HRD Review Questionnaire

Name _____

Position

Principal ☐

Exec. staff member ☐

Classroom teacher ☐

School administrative ☐

Parent/Community ☐

Other (specify) _____ ☐

1 How many hours of inservice training and development have you attended in the last year? _____

2 How many hours in school time? _____

3 How many hours out of school time? _____

4 Where did you attend these activities?
(Rank order of frequency.)

- at school
- at a local education/teachers' centre
- at a regional location
- at other location outside the region

5 Who organised the activities you attended?
(Rank order of frequency.)

- school staff
- district or regional staff
- professional association
- State office staff
- university staff

6 What was the content of the training and development activities?
(Rank order of frequency, and do not rank any aspect not attended.)

- effective teaching practice subject content
- job skills (e.g. computing skills)
- administrative processes
- management practices (e.g. supervision, leadership)
- school leadership programs
- financial management
- other (specify)

7 What was the estimated total cost of activities attended?
(Include average cost of release relief for teaching duties in estimating costs of the training and development activity.) $ _____

A School Human Resource Development Committee

It is important that all staff have some degree of ownership of a school based training and development plan. An effective way to achieve this is through the establishment of a school HRD committee. In establishing such a committee, the following factors should be taken into account.

Membership of a School HRD Committee

The committee should be representative of staff groupings in the school and should be balanced in its membership so that the views of all staff can be canvassed. One way of achieving a sense of staff ownership of the committee is to call for nominations or arrange for an election of committee members. As large committees can become unwieldy, the school HRD committee should not have a large membership. (The ideal size for small working groups is between 5 and 7.) This membership can be extended by allowing for subcommittees to organise particular activities.

Composition of the Committee

In determining the size and balance of membership the following factors should be considered:

- the need for a convenor with delegated authority from the Principal to release staff to attend training and development activities

... a convenor with delegated authority from the Principal...

- the need for executive staff and teaching staff to be represented. It is preferable if the representatives of the teaching staff are drawn from different areas of the school's work, including consideration of the needs of specialist teachers, e.g. teacher librarians, ESL teachers and part-time staff
- school administrative staff must be represented
- depending on the nature and context of the school, it may be appropriate to have a community or parent representative to provide a perspective on the needs and role of parents in whole school development activities
- it is useful to recognise that HRD activities are responsible for generating change involving individuals or the school more generally. Members of the school HRD committee, in fact, need to be able to act as 'change agents' within the school. The most successful change agents in any organisation are usually those who have commitment to the area of change. They act as 'cheer leaders' of the change process. At the same time these change agents must be credible and connected to various constituencies within the school, as much of their work will involve liaison with and eliciting support from others, particularly in whole school HRD initiatives.

Responsibilities of the School HRD Committee

A School HRD committee should be given a 'Terms of Reference' statement, clearly establishing its responsibilities (including the budget available for training and development activities). The following provides a sample set of terms of reference for a school HRD committee.

Human Resource Development Committee Duties and Responsibilities
- Coordinating the conduct of a schoolwide training and development needs analysis.
- Allocating notional budgets to priority training and development areas identified by the needs analysis or by the educational sector.
- Planning and coordinating the application process for support to attend training and development activities.
- Receiving and processing applications from staff to undertake training and development activities.
- Organising school based training and development activities, including the provision of whole school activities (e.g. School Development Days or Curriculum Days).
- Facilitating faculty or grade development activities and special programs, such as beginning teacher induction programs.
- Approving the release of teachers to attend training and development activities and of funds available for release/relief of teachers.
- Monitoring and reporting, on a regular basis, to the Principal regarding levels of expenditure.
- Evaluating the educational effectiveness and cost effectiveness of activities provided.
- Ensuring equity of access of staff to training and development activities in accordance with equal employment opportunity (EEO) principles.

Budgeting for a School Based HRD Program

In establishing a budgetary system for the school's HRD program there are a number of processes to be considered. The following list provides suggestions of some of those processes:

Budget Processes for School-based HRD
- Determine the sources of funding for all school related HRD activities.
- Establish a total budget for HRD activities.
- Create notional budgets for major sector and/or school HRD priorities or areas of activities.
- Budget for total costs including award rates for travel, workers compensation, insurance cover for guest lecturers and infrastructure costs (such as word processing/printing for materials).
- If appropriate, establish rates of payment according to sector advice for:
  — individuals conducting activities
  — staff of the school or sectors presenting courses or programs outside normal working hours
  — consultants and staff from other organisations or educational sectors presenting courses.
- Establish a chart of accounts, using dissections or sub-dissections, for all HRD activities.
- Establish procedures, consistent with sector and/or school audit requirements, for the monitoring of cash flows, payment of accounts, purchase of equipment and services, and the payment of overtime, travel expenses and allowances
- Ensure that taxation procedures are followed consistent with the pay as you earn (PAYE) taxation legislation where appropriate.

The budget processes proforma on the next page will assist in establishing notional budgets for sector and school human resource development priorities.

Monitoring and Reporting on HRD Activities

Why Monitor and Report on the HRD Function in Schools?

There are a number of reasons why all organisations, including schools, should monitor and report on training and development activities. These reasons include:

- government requirements, e.g. Training Guarantee legislation
- equity provision of training and development activities under EEO legislation
- quality assurance to report on the effectiveness of activities in contributing to quality student outcomes
- accountability for expenditure to school authorities, educational sector or governments, as required.

Budget Processes for School Training and Development Activities

Total budget for activities $ _____

Funding Sources:
- Educational sector grants $ _____
- Funds from school or community fundraising $ _____
- Funds from sale of resources $ _____

Major sector and/or school priorities in training and development for 199_ , and notional budgets

Priority	Notional budget
_____	$ _____
_____	$ _____
_____	$ _____
_____	$ _____
_____	$ _____
_____	$ _____
_____	$ _____
_____	$ _____

Cost factors to be used by organisations in determining budgets for activities

Teacher relief $ _____ per teacher per day

Travel rates _____ cents per km for use of a private car.

Meal costs   Breakfast $ _____   Lunch $ _____   Dinner $ _____

Morning/afternoon tea $ _____

Overtime rates (per hour) for clerical staff

Evenings $ _____   Saturday $ _____   Sunday $ _____

Speakers' rates
- Per hour for educational sector staff, after hours $ _____
- Per hour for staff from other organisations e.g. universities, private providers. $ _____

Equipment
Printing $ _____   Stationery supplies $ _____

Hire of equipment (e.g. video) $ _____   Other $ _____

This accountability requirement includes requirements under the Training Guarantee Act that:

- requires employers to spend a percentage of their payroll (salary costs) on structured training and development costs
- allows both on and off the job training and development activities to be counted as part of the training expenditure
- requires that activities must be part of a structured training program that aims to develop, maintain or improve employment-related skills of employees.
- requires a training program to consist of one or more training activities that could include conferences, seminars and on-the-job training. A program may be developed for one employee or for a group of employees and it may be intended to impart a single skill or a range of knowledge, skills and competencies.

Which Training and Development Activities Should be Monitored or Reported?

In designing monitoring or reporting mechanisms for school based HRD, the following factors should be considered.

- the number of people who participate in training and development activities
- the number of hours of training and development activities undertaken by each individual
- the total expenditure in training and development activities
- the participation by EEO groups — female staff, Aboriginal staff, staff with disabilities and staff from non-English speaking backgrounds
- whether the training and development activities are conducted on or off the job, e.g. school, district, cluster or State level, and within or outside normal working hours.

...outside normal working hours...

EEO Statistics: Some Definitions

In some States and Territories Equal Employment legislation requires that data are collected on the training and development provided to EEO target groups. For the purposes of collecting such data, the following definitions of EEO target groups may be helpful.

Aboriginal Staff
This category refers to any person of Aboriginal or Torres Strait descent who identifies as Aboriginal or Torres Strait Islander and is accepted as such by the community with which he/she is associated.

Staff with Disabilities
This category refers to any person who has a loss or reduction of any functional ability, as a result of a physical impairment, that is expected to last two years or more.

Staff from Non-English Speaking Background
This category refers to a person for whom English is not the first language, or who has one or both parents for whom English is not the first language.

Reporting on School Based HRD Activities

In order to monitor and effectively evaluate training and development activities conducted at school level, data should be collected concerning the participation of individual staff and community members. Such data should be summarised each term or semester, in order to review the provision of training and development activities in relation to school and educational sector priorities. The proformas on the following pages are designed to assist in this process.

Conclusion

This chapter has presented the argument that it is critical to conduct a training and development needs analysis as the basis for effective management of a school based training and development program for staff and community members. Such a needs analysis must analyse the knowledge, skills and values/attitudes required by the school and the individual staff and community members of the school.

Such analysis should look at the jobs staff perform, the work environment of the school and the needs of individual staff and community members. The needs of EEO groups should be given particular consideration. The chapter further advocates that the management of school based training and development programs should be conducted by a school HRD committee on which a range of staff and community members are represented. Such a committee should be accountable to the Principal for monitoring, evaluating and reporting on financial expenditure and the educational effectiveness of the training and development activities undertaken.

The case study that follows on page 54 will assist you to reflect on issues involved in the effective management of school based training and development activities.

Monitoring/Evaluating/Reporting

Individual Participant Evaluation Sheet for School Training and Development Activities

1 Name _____ **School position** _____
(e.g. classroom teacher,
parent, school assistant)

Date of activity _____ **Time of activity** From _____ to _____ am/pm

School/sector priority area _____

Cost of activity Course fees $ _____ Relief/release $ _____

Travel $ _____ Accommodation $ _____

2 Are you a member of any of the following EEO groups?

● female staff

● Aboriginal staff

● staff with disabilities

● staff from non-English speaking background

3 Evaluation comments
Comment on the following aspects of the training and development activity
you attended.

a What were the major outcomes of the activity for you personally and for
the teaching and learning in this school?

_____

_____

_____

_____

_____

b What were the aspects of the activity that you gained most or least from?

_____

_____

_____

c Would you recommend that other members of the school community
attend this activity and why?

_____

_____

_____

Summary Sheet

Monitoring and Reporting on School Training and Development Activities

This sheet can be used to summarise data from individual evaluation sheets regarding training and development activities held over a number of months or a term in a school.

Number of activities held/attended _____

Sector/school priorities addressed:

_____

_____

_____

Period of the activities:From _____ To _____
(Date)   (Date)

Total number of participants _____

Participation data:

Group	Number of participants	Number of hours		Total expenditure
		In school hours	Out of hours	
Teaching staff				
School executive				
School administrative staff				
Parent/community representatives				
TOTALS				

(Sheet continued on next page.)

(Summary sheet continued.)

EEO report:

EEO group	Number of participants	Number of hours		Total expenditure
		In school hours	**Out of hours**	
Female staff				
Aboriginal staff				
NESB staff				
Staff with disabilities				

Case Study: School based human resource development at Luxford High School

Luxford High School is a large secondary school, with 63 teaching staff and 12 administrative staff. The teaching staff of the school includes an executive of 14, including the Principal Ms Jane Spencer and two Deputy Principals with responsibility for curriculum and administration and for training and development of staff and performance management. There are ten heads of subject departments. For the year 1991, the school had a human resource development budget of $22 000, and was allocated two student free days for use in whole school development activities. At Luxford High School, one of these days was used as a 'curriculum day' where whole school curriculum issues were discussed and members of each subject department were provided with time for planning and program development in a particular subject area. School administration staff did not attend either of these days. In 1991, this day was devoted to multicultural education perspectives in the curriculum. The other day was used to hold a district development day coordinated by staff of the local school support centre and the district superintendent. The focus of this day was the implementation of a school improvement program in the district.

Whole school staff meetings are held after school once a month. These meetings are chaired by the Principal or one of the Deputy Principals. They usually deal with administrative matters of school organisation. Occasionally a guest speaker from another school or the local school support centre is invited to address the staff on a new policy issued by the education sector.

The Deputy Principal responsible for training and development and performance management, John Brack, manages the school's training and development budget and coordinates staff attendance at training and development activities. He usually consults with the Principal on major decisions, but not with other members of the executive.

The school submitted to the district superintendent its report on training and development expenditure for 1991. The report indicated that the principal, Jane Spencer, had attended four activities including a national Principals' conference interstate, a major conference on post-compulsory education and a State conference of Principals, for a total expenditure of $4000. The 12 members of the executive had attended 32 activities for a total expenditure of $1400 — major expenditure items including the attendance of six members of the executive at a major State conference/workshop on curriculum change, leadership and management, and a two-day planning and development meeting for the whole executive held on a Friday and Saturday. Thirty-seven of the 59 classroom teachers attended one or more activities, conducted at school or the local school support centre and regional locations, at a total cost of $2400. A major activity was a resume writing workshop for staff interested in promotion, conducted by a private consultant for $500. Twenty staff attended this workshop. Parent and community members were funded to attend six activities at a cost of $400. Two members of the school administrative staff attended activities on school budgeting and computer skills, at a cost of $200. The school had a balance of $1000 in its HRD budget account at the end of the year.

Twenty-two teaching staff and 10 school administrative staff did not attend any activities, apart from those conducted on student free days. Some members of the staff had complained that John Brack, the Deputy Principal responsible for school based HRD activities, did not encourage staff to apply for training and development activities and tended to favour particular individuals. The Principal, Jane Spencer, expressed confidence in John's coordination of the program and indicated that if any staff member wished to attend any activity all they need do was ask John if they could attend.

Issues for Discussion

♦ *What are the major strengths and weaknesses of the HRD program in operation at Luxford High School?*

♦ *What change if any should Jane Spencer, as Principal, make to the management of the program?*

CHAPTER 3

Managing Curriculum Change

Terry O'Brien

What is Meant by 'Curriculum'?

Issues for Reflection

♦ *What does the term 'curriculum' mean to you? List all the things you understand 'curriculum' to represent on a piece of paper, headed 'What* **curriculum** *means to me'.*

Before you can manage curriculum and curriculum change, you must decide what you actually understand 'curriculum' to be — what aspects of schooling are encompassed by this word. Although the word is used in many ways (e.g. 'the New South Wales curriculum', 'the school curriculum', 'the junior curriculum', or 'the History curriculum') most educators agree that it is a fairly comprehensive term that covers far more than a list of subjects in a school prospectus. In fact it covers the *how* as well as the *what*. Subsumed within the broader context of 'curriculum' are the formalised courses of study, as well as the conscious planning that attempts to determine learning outcomes, and the structures that facilitate that learning. Garth Boomer described his understanding of 'curriculum' as follows:

'. . . for most people outside education, curriculum is synonymous with "syllabus" or "course" and signifies work required in a particular subject rather than the *total* educational offerings of a school or institution . . .

when I use the term "curriculum" I mean everything from *design of the system plans and rules and school plans and rules to the realisation of extended teaching units in individual subjects and classrooms, spanning evaluation/assessment.* That is, I have a big view of curriculum . . . Taken fundamentally as what children formally do and learn in schools, curriculum is the be-all and end-all of education. It is what all the other areas of education, buildings and facilities, resources, personnel, staff training and consultancy support, serve.'[1]

...a big view of curriculum...

Apart from the obvious interpretation of 'curriculum' as referring to course content and organisation, teaching approach and the related student activities, the term also encompasses practicalities, such as the arrangements made in schools for students and their learning and development, as well as broader aspects related to teacher development, policy and research, assessment and reporting.

The curriculum is a strategically important management tool. Not only does it provide a response to the mission statements of the system and the school, it also implements curriculum requirements by translating them into teaching activities and student outcomes, it forces the school's resources to flow in specified directions, and it represents a series of decisions about what will be important for tomorrow.

What Does a Manager of Curriculum at School Level Do?

Good curriculum managers direct their skills of organisation, communication, planning and motivation towards collaborative achievement of the curriculum goals of the school within the State and the system. Managing curriculum involves coordination of human and other resources, with the main focus always being the quality of learning and student outcomes.

---

[1] Boomer, G. (1988) 'Some Challenges and Achievements in Australian Curriculum', *Unicorn*, Vol. 14, no. 4, p. 242.

Curriculum management incorporates a variety of tasks relating to the supervision and monitoring of the curriculum — its development, its implementation, its results, its assessment and its reporting.

The following list, though long, is not exhaustive. Neither is it in any fixed order. Decide which items you think are part of curriculum management.

- Establishing curriculum priorities and implementation plans that are consistent with the school's mission.
- Developing curriculum policies for the school, in collaboration with staff, school council and school community.
- Reading and analysing relevant curriculum documents, so as to develop teaching/learning programs consistent with the mandatory curriculum requirements of the Board of Studies and the system, e.g. The Department of School Education.
- Ensuring continuity and balance (e.g. past strengths and new needs, general and vocational education, technology and humanities).
- Preparing the way for curriculum change.
- Coordinating staff and community in discussions of the implications of latest curriculum documents and pedagogy.
- Organising the development of a whole-school curriculum implementation strategy plan, that includes prioritising and a timeline, as well as delegated responsibility for the various tasks.
- Providing support for new syllabuses and maintenance support of old.
- Ensuring the curriculum meets the needs of students — *all* students.
- Relating classroom practice to intended student outcomes by coordinating the development of teaching/learning programs in accord with the objectives and outcomes of the curriculum documents and school policies.
- Ensuring adequate resources are provided to support the school's teaching programs.
- Ensuring teaching methods take different needs into account.
- Identifying and coordinating staff development needs for groups and individuals in relation to curriculum and curriculum development.
- Facilitating flexible and accelerated progression.
- Establishing assessment and reporting procedures.
- Providing review procedures to evaluate school policies, programs, practices and staff expertise.

All of these items are, in fact, part of curriculum management.

Issues for Reflection

◆ *Examine the list above again. If there are any other aspects of curriculum management that you think should have been included, make a note of them.*

Curriculum Maintenance or Curriculum Change?

The changing nature of society, schools and students guarantees that curriculum management is a continuous process. Existing successful practice will require maintenance, but some aspect of curriculum development work or curriculum change is likely to be going on in a school at all times. The management of curriculum is, therefore, more than the development of a set of strategies to support the status quo, to monitor and update resources and to refine practice. Managing the curriculum also involves understanding the change process. This chapter relates those understandings gained from Chapter 1 to the management of curriculum change specifically.

Where do I Start?

Where you begin in the management of curriculum change depends on where you are at present. One way of determining this is by reflecting on existing practice through a personal curriculum analysis, followed by a whole school curriculum audit. You need to know where you are now before you can decide where you are going and how you will get there. The whole process of curriculum change management is shown in the following diagram. The process shown in the diagram can be applied to an individual project or a whole school curriculum change.

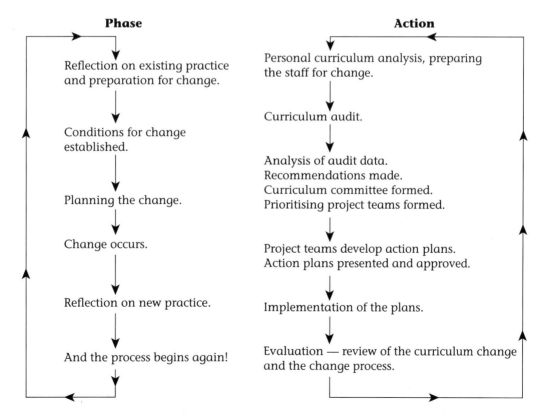

Phase	**Action**
Reflection on existing practice and preparation for change.	Personal curriculum analysis, preparing the staff for change.
	Curriculum audit.
Conditions for change established.	Analysis of audit data. Recommendations made. Curriculum committee formed. Prioritising project teams formed.
Planning the change.	
Change occurs.	Project teams develop action plans. Action plans presented and approved.
Reflection on new practice.	Implementation of the plans.
And the process begins again!	Evaluation — review of the curriculum change and the change process.

Reflecting on Existing Practice

What do I Look for in my Personal Analysis of the Curriculum?

The first aspect of your reflection relates to the purposes of the curriculum. Many of these purposes are predetermined for us by the government of the day and by the expectations of the community in general. Other purposes relate to specialities of your own school as well as its student needs and its community expectations.

Issues for Reflection

♦ *Think for a moment about what you believe the overall purpose of education and, hence, curriculum to be before reading on.*

The mental list you compiled, as instructed above, may have included:

● passing on the cultural heritage, socialisation, inculcation of moral values, and appreciation of learning for its own sake.
● skill training, e.g. inculcation of basic skills and selected information, developing education skills (such as problem solving and decision making), preparation for work and the world beyond school.
● change, e.g. social engineering via cross curriculum perspectives.

For education to lead to individual success in the 1990s, it should provide three passports into the post-industrial society.

...three passports into post-industrial society...

These are:

- an academic passport (which is the traditional role of education) emphasising the development of literacy and numeracy, and the acquisition of knowledge to enable a person to play a meaningful and self-fulfilling role in society
- a vocational passport which focusses on education necessary for work, in a world of rapid technological change
- an enterprise passport. An enterprising individual has a positive, flexible and adaptable disposition towards change . . . an enterprising person has the capacity to initiate creative ideas . . . develop them and see them through in a determined manner . . . is an effective communicator, negotiator, influencer, planner and organiser.[2]

The following is a summary of the goals to emerge from an analysis carried out in 1988 by the Primary Schools Advisory Committee. Also included are the implications for schools.[3]

Goals		Schools must be concerned with the need to:
● Social maintenance	→	ensure the transmission of traditional views, values, roles, skills
● Social development adjustment	→	produce acceptable members of society and respond to economic needs
● To be socially critical	→	help change society by producing individuals who analyse and reflect on the existing society and are equipped to change it for the better
● Academic development	→	emphasise traditional disciplines and aim to produce rational and autonomous individuals
● To be student-centred	→	emphasise personal development of individuals, accept differences. The development of happy, well adjusted individuals with positive self esteem is a prime focus.

As a manager of curriculum you will need to do your research. You will need to have a good understanding of national curriculum initiatives and keep up to date with your professional reading.

Teachers on your staff may be trying to sustain or restore the past. It will be up to you to convince them that the curriculum must change to improve our youth's prospects for the future.

The following proforma is a useful way of ordering your reflections on the curriculum.

---

[2] Ball, C. in a paper written for OECD Centre for Educational Research and Innovation (CERT), quoted in Ellyard, P. 'Education for the 21st Century' in Independence, June 1990, Vol. 15, no. 1, pp. 17–20.

[3] Eltis, K. J. (1989), Into the 90s: understanding the curriculum issues, Sydney Association for Educational Administration, published proceedings of a one-day workshop.

Reflecting on the Curriculum	
Part 1: What do I believe to be the overall purposes of education?	**Part 4**: What aspects of the curriculum at my school meet these purposes?
Part 2: List the mandatory requirements.	**Part 5**: **a** List any mandatory requirements currently not being met. **b** Is there a mechanism in place to periodically monitor mandatory requirements and ensure they are met? **c** Are there any new mandatory requirements about to come on line?
Part 3: What should be the particular curriculum focusses for my school in the light of its: ● specialist nature? ● range of students? ● student strengths? ● student weaknesses? ● community's nature? ● community expectations and aspirations?	**Part 6**: What aspects of the curriculum at my school meet these special needs?

Mandatory Requirements

There are a number of non-negotiable requirements that have impact on curriculum in your school. These include the Education Legislation, Board of Studies requirements for patterns of study, Examination and Assessment requirements, and planned experiences. You should have a personal set of all the necessary documents. (Part 2 of the proforma for 'Reflection on the Curriculum' provides space to list all these mandatory requirements.)

School Requirements

There are a number of concerns relating to curriculum that, in the context of school-centred education, must be decided at school level. The school must balance local needs against national agendas and central requirements.

Think about your own school for a moment. Consider:

- the specialist nature of the school, e.g. comprehensive, technology, high non-English speaking background
- the school's perceived purpose
- the type of students who go there — the full range
- special needs and strengths of the whole student population
- the nature of the local community
- the community's expectations of the school.

These things should be reflected in the *Mission Statement* of the school.

Ask yourself if you are catering adequately for all the curriculum purposes of your school. Are there some areas in which more should be done? Are there needs that have been overlooked? Should new priorities be established? How will these be reflected in the curriculum, both overall and in its various components?

Intention versus Reality — the Diagnosis

Gather a set of all school-specific documents relating to the curriculum offered currently at your school. Gain an overview.

Refer to the proforma, 'Reflecting on the Curriculum' on the facing page. Use it as a checklist.

Part 1
Consider the overall purposes of education especially in the light of the future. Is the curriculum realistically facing the needs that the students will have in the world beyond school? Is it anticipating the future, rather than merely reacting to it as it arrives? (These considerations will enable you to complete Part 4 of the proforma.)

Part 2
Consider the mandatory requirements. Is the school meeting the mandatory require-ments? Is there a mechanism in place to monitor this regularly? Are there any new mandatory requirements about to come on line? (These considerations will enable you to complete Part 5 of the proforma.)

Part 3
Consider the school. Does the curriculum reflect the school's perceived purpose? Is the curriculum responding to student needs? Is the curriculum responding to community expectations? (These considerations will enable you to complete Part 6 of the proforma.)

Review
Once you have completed the proforma, examine Part 5 of the completed sheet.

Are there any mandatory requirements not being met? Before you proceed with any other curriculum auditing/initiatives, **you must amend this**.

If no mechanism is in place to monitor mandatory requirements; you must set up a mechanism to do this immediately.

If there are new mandatory requirements about to come on line, implementation plans for this must be a top priority in any curriculum planning.

What Next? — Prepare your Staff for Change

We have already discussed your vision of the school's curriculum. However, if this vision is to be realised, you must share it and expand upon it with the teachers on your staff. The following diagram[4] emphasises the importance of people preparation in the lead up to achievement of the vision ideals through successful needs analysis (the audit), implementation and evaluation.

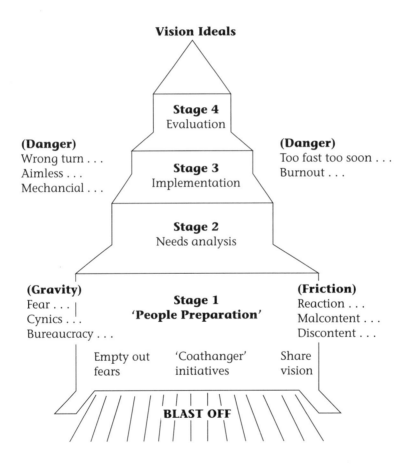

Vision Ideals

Stage 4
Evaluation

(Danger)
Wrong turn . . .
Aimless . . .
Mechancial . . .

Stage 3
Implementation

(Danger)
Too fast too soon . . .
Burnout . . .

Stage 2
Needs analysis

(Gravity)
Fear . . .
Cynics . . .
Bureaucracy . . .

Stage 1
'People Preparation'

(Friction)
Reaction . . .
Malcontent . . .
Discontent . . .

Empty out
fears

'Coathanger'
initiatives

Share
vision

BLAST OFF

---

4   Marsh, C. (1988), *Spotlight on School Improvement*, Allen and Unwin, Sydney, p. 39.

A Series of Staff Development Sessions

Provide a Rationale for Curriculum

The introduction of curriculum development to your staff should include input from you (as a manager of curriculum and an educational leader) on latest trends and initiatives that they may wish to consider, a reminder of the nature of the school population and a reminder of mandatory requirements. (You could present some of the material from the section of this chapter entitled 'Reflecting on Existing Practice', on pages 60–63). This is the time to point out to staff just how much control schools actually have over the school curriculum.

How much Control does a School have over Curriculum?

This can be determined by the following staff meeting exercise.[5]

Divide the audience into small groups. Issue each group with a copy of the incomplete chart from Appendix C, 'Who Controls the Curriculum?' (see page 220). In groups, identify as many factors as possible that influence control over education, and place these on the chart.

Allow 10 minutes discussion. Display an overhead transparency of the handout and call for answers to fill in the blanks.

Ensure that all of the following are included:

- teacher
- formal assessment requirements
- textbook publishers
- student needs
- the economic situation
- media
- university entrance requirements
- Minister for Education

- parents
- system, e.g. Dept of Education
- Board requirements
- syllabus contents and outcomes
- Acts of Parliament
- national agenda
- job needs
- market forces, i.e. student subject selections

Ask participants to nominate any of these factors that are totally non-negotiable obligations currently influencing curriculum and curriculum change in schools. Since the majority of the factors listed have elements that must be decided at school level, you should bring the audience to the conclusion that schools have a great deal of control over their curriculum.

Invite the Whole Staff to Reflect on Existing Curriculum Practice

Issue copies of the proforma 'Reflecting on the Curriculum' (page 62) to all staff members and take them through their exercise as outlined in the section of this chapter entitled 'Reflecting on Existing Practice' (pages 60–63).

---

[5] This exercise has been adapted from one in the NSW Department of School Education, Human Resource Development Directorate (1991), 'Module 2 — Understanding the Context of Curriculum Management' from *Managing the Curriculum*, (Unit of The Certificate in School Leadership and Management), p. M2—3 and Handout 2.1.

This could be followed by some exploratatory discussion based on questions such as:

- What kind of people do we want our students to become?
- Should a curriculum set high standards for teaching or only for learning?
- To what degree do teachers identify with or have 'ownership' of the curriculum in a school?
- What influences the curriculum we offer?
- Are we managing the curriculum we offer by effective staffing, or is staffing controlling the curriculum?

...what kind of people do we want our students to be?...

Introducing the Curriculum Audit

A curriculum audit will enable you to develop a knowledge of all the factors that contribute to curriculum, and share ownership of future curriculum and curriculum development programs. The problem that initiated the audit might be a specific issue (e.g. investigating assessment and reporting practice) or a general analysis of curriculum across the school, to ensure that it has remained relevant.

Most models of curriculum development begin with a form of diagnosis of needs. At the top of the facing page is a diagram of a model of the curriculum process.[6]

---

[6] Model after A. and H. Nicholls, in Print, M. (1987), *Curriculum Development and Design*, Allen and Unwin, Sydney, p. 30.

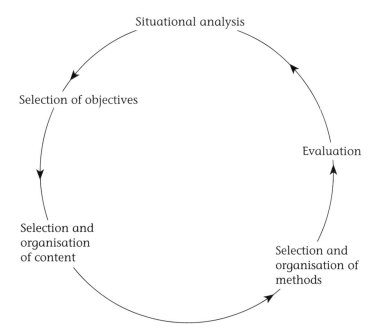

The curriculum audit is more than an exercise in consultation. The curriculum audit will enable you to discover what others regard as the curriculum strengths and problems. It will enable diagnosis of needs. The problems you have perceived are part of this situation too but, through the audit, you will be able to learn what other participants in the situation see as their options for dealing with them, as well as encourage ownership of future solutions.

A curriculum audit will enable you to examine the particular school context in which the curriculum takes place and collect information about the current situation. The factors that relate to this context are analysed — students, student needs and expectations, students' homes and backgrounds, their parents' aspirations and expectations, the school, its learning climate, its staff, its facilities, its resources and equipment. The results are then incorporated into subsequent planning for and development of curriculum. Thus, it is vital that information is collected from a wide range of sources.

Typical methods for collecting information include informal discussion with students, teachers and parents; brainstorming; analysis of existing school documents, results and requirements; interviews; inventories and questionnaires.

Staff should be able to suggest sources of information and methods of collection, and a curriculum committee should be formed to undertake the task.

Let the Audit Begin

What Should be in the Audit?

The audit team should, first, find ways to check that what is already believed about the school environment, students, teachers, etc. is accurate without excluding the possibility of previously unthought of data or never-realised local factors emerging. In other words, *the audit will tell you if your intuition is valid and give you a basis from which to start future curriculum planning.* So a curriculum audit is an excellent starting point for curriculum change. Though the task may seem daunting, the rewards are well worth it.

What Factors will you Investigate?

Malcolm Skilbeck has devised a rather useful list of factors, that are external and internal to a school, for inclusion in such an exercise. The audit team should select from these the factors that relate to the specific problem that has initiated the audit, e.g. to improve student literacy K-6 or to cater for the increasing number of students staying on in Years 11 and 12 who are not tertiary bound. A total curriculum audit would address all the factors.

Situational Analysis Factors: that constitute the situation[7]

External factors to the school

- *Cultural and social changes and expectations*: This includes major changes to society, such as unemployment patterns, societal values, economic growth and family relationships. Parental, employer and community expectations of schools are included (e.g. the need for improved literacy and numeracy).
- *Educational system requirements and challenges*: Includes systemic influences such as policy requirements, inquiry reports, external examinations, major curriculum projects and significant educational research.
- *Changing nature of content*: The subject matter taught in schools requires constant revision to update it in accordance with developments in the outside world. Examples include new knowledge acquired, technological developments and new literature.
- *Teacher support systems*: A variety of external systems can contribute to enhancing teaching/learning strategies, content updates, evaluation techniques, audio-visual material and other resources. Support may come from tertiary institutions, educational institutions, local teacher centres, curriculum consultants/advisory teachers, inservice courses and subject associations (e.g. Science Teachers' Association).
- *Resources*: Curriculum developers need to be aware of the availability and flow of resources into the school. These may come from Commonwealth sources, State education departments, the community and business organisations.

Internal factors to the school

- *Pupils*: Significant data that may be gathered on students include abilities, physical and psychological development, aptitudes, emotional and social

---

[7]   Skilbeck, M. (1976), 'School Based Curriculum Development and Teacher Education Policy' in *Teachers as Innovators*, OECD Paris, pp. 80–1 quoted in Print. M., (1987) *Curriculum Development and Design*, Sydney, Allen and Unwin, p. 84–5.

development, and educational needs. An accurate understanding of the nature of students allows for effective curriculum planning.

● *Teachers*: What are the skills, experience, teaching style, values, and special strengths and weaknesses of school teaching staff? Special strengths may broaden curriculum offerings (e.g. aeronautics, horticulture, meditation) and allow for curriculum enrichment and extension.

...special strengths broaden curriculum offerings...

● *School ethos*: The school climate/environments is a significant factor influencing curriculum, and includes Principal involvement, power distribution, social cohesiveness, operational procedures and professional cohesiveness.
● *Material resources*: What exactly does a school possess in terms of buildings, equipment, resources (books, curriculum materials), land and vehicles, as well as financial resources for future purchases? Knowledge of resources facilitates curriculum planning (e.g. can we offer horticulture, rowing and photography?).
● *Perceived problems*: Major stimulus for curriculum change emanates from a perception of needs or problems. Curriculum planners ascertain these from parents, teachers, students and the community. Needs-assessment techniques may be used.

Data Collection

Your audit team should select data collection methods that best suit the nature of the problem that initiated the audit. These might include a mixture of a variety of techniques — such as interviews, or analysis of exam results, school records, questionnaires, student/staff community profiles, inventories and surveys.

The main steps in developing a questionnaire are to:

● decide the objectives of the questionnaire
● decide the most user-friendly method for the particular audience
● develop the questionnaire
● check the sense/unambiguity/validity of the items (test it on other teachers)
● pilot the questionnaire using a small but representative sample
● make any necessary adjustments to the items
● administer the questionnaire.

What Should be in the Parent and Community Survey?

It is very important that parents participate in the audit. Not only does this enable them to understand educational processes more fully and encourage them to be more supportive, but it also enables you to identify the range of skills that can be provided by parents. Parent participation generally leads to improved student learning — intellectually, socially and emotionally. There may be questions you wish to ask about social factors, such as the nature and composition of the family, and the parental expectations of children and the school. The following list provides some general starting points for developing a parent questionnaire. The questionnaire should include:

- an explanation as to the purpose of the questionnaire
- an outline of the mandatory curriculum
- a brief overview of any trends in education relating to curriculum
- a brief outline of the school's main curriculum goals
- a series of open-ended curriculum related questions, e.g.
    — What do you think should be the main purposes of schooling?
    — Name three curriculum areas you think this school does well.
    — Name three curriculum areas you think could be improved.
    — Is there anything you think is missing from this school's curriculum that you would like to see included?
- questions on assessment and reporting practices.

For a specifically targeted issue, questions should be developed to throw light on the factors being analysed.

What Should be in the Staff Survey?

A staff survey provides you with an opportunity to investigate the climate for curriculum change as well as the understandings of current curriculum trends and initiatives. Undertaking curriculum development provides experienced teachers with an opportunity to clarify their own philosophies of education and young teachers with an opportunity to develop their philosophies. Since teachers must both design and implement the curriculum, the factors to consider in this survey are those influencing the development and implementation of curriculum. These could include teacher strengths and weaknesses in both curricular and extra-curricular areas, teacher likes and dislikes, teacher interests, teacher expectations of student performance, willingness to engage in professional development in/out of school hours, major areas of dissatisfaction with the existing curriculum, attitudes to curriculum development and innovation, and preferred teaching styles.

Questions on the survey could include:

- What do you think is the main purpose of this school's curriculum?
- Do we meet the needs of our students? . . . all students?
- Are our community's expectations realistic?
- Which of the given mandatory curriculum areas do you feel are being implemented well, adequately, poorly?

- Which areas need more resourcing?
- What factors influence the curriculum we offer?
- Do we need to alter the school day?
- What factors about this school do you think present the biggest problems in implementing curriculum change at this school?
- What do you think will be the biggest obstacles to implementing curriculum change at this school?

Provide a list of curriculum features that could include latest educational trends/initiatives, programming; desired student outcomes; learning theory, classroom organisation, broad curriculum organisation, teaching spaces and resources, community links, courses by outside providers, process of curriculum change, assessment, reporting, timetabling, gifted and talented student programs, teaching practice, internal school organisation, etc.)

Staff could be asked to use the list to help them answer the following questions:

- What are the strengths of this school's curriculum?
- What are the weaknesses of this school's curriculum?
- Tick the areas in which you would like more professional development.
- What are the three greatest curriculum problems facing this school?
- What do you see as providing a solution for each problem listed?

Even in a small scale audit, such questions will help develop significant data from and about the staff. Appendix D provides a sample staff survey to determine assessment purposes and priorities, while Appendix E provides a staff questionnaire on reporting (see pages 221 and 223).

Should we Include Students in the Audit?

Students, as learners, must be given the opportunity to be active, responsible and engaged in their own learning. If students are involved in initiating and reacting to curriculum, their attitudes to school and learning are enhanced, as is school climate. As consumers or clients of education they have expectations and opinions that can provide valuable data. They can also help gather data from each other in the form of research projects.

Climate

The tone, ethos, atmosphere or organisational climate of the school is largely dependent on the supportiveness of the Principal. Since climate is all pervading, it must influence all aspects of curriculum planning. A study covering all aspects of school education in Australia stressed the importance of the Principal in facilitating change:

> ' . . . Poor schools are lifted markedly by a good Principal; good schools sag with a poor Principal. The Principal is the focal point of the effort by the school community to create an adaptive school.'[8]

---

8   From *Schooling for 15 and 16 year olds*, Schools Commission Canberra, November, 1980, p. 62.

So the curriculum planner needs to include the climate of the school in the curriculum audit. Questions could be asked about what the school is trying to achieve, communication within the school, on what aspects of education the school places greatest value, its traditions, its standards, whether teacher-student relationships are the kind that contribute best to the school's purpose, whether teaching-learning methods are appropriate, etc.

Some principles that are helpful in creating a climate for enhancement of instructional effectiveness include:[9]

- participative decision making being utilised within the school
- all staff being encouraged to assume appropriate leadership roles
- public recognition being given to staff for both organisational and educational achievements
- staff being encouraged to work cooperatively to encourage both confidence and competence
- time demands on teachers for their involvement in the wider school organisation being realistic, in consideration of the primary task of teaching
- there should be provision of as many curriculum and professional resources as possible within the school.

...appropriate leadership roles...

Issues for Reflection

♦ *Decide which of the factors above you feel are successfully operating in your school. Appendix F (see page 224) provides a sample climate analysis.*

---

9 Connors, B. and Schoer, B. (eds.) (1988), *Towards Effective Teaching: a guide for supervisors*, NSW Department of Education, Metropolitan East Region, Sydney, p. 19.

The School Itself

The school will have a limiting or enhancing influence on what students and teachers in it are able to achieve. Items to be considered include:

- use of time and structure
- space, equipment, facilities and the use of them
- the availability of subject resources
- procedures for selecting new materials
- money for materials and equipment
- quality of the library
- availability of professional development resources.

Audit's Over — What Now?

Analysis, Feedback and Recommendations

The final phase of the audit is analysis of the data collected, presentation of results and recommendations. The audit will have reflected the school community's view of educational purpose and needs, and students' abilities. It will also have revealed teacher strengths, resources needs, current curriculum strengths and perceived weaknesses. The analysis of this data will have led to a series of recommendations that will form the basis for the school's curriculum policy and curriculum development plan.

Once the audit team has developed the list of recommendations, these recommendations need to be presented to the staff. In fact, all participants in the audit require feedback — a summary of the findings and information about the uses to which the information gathered will be put. Some focussing will need to be done to relate the results of the audit to the curriculum purposes that initiated it. Remember, the impact of your findings will vary according to the way they are reported.

On the basis of the audit results, conclusions need to be drawn concerning the following:

- What educational purposes should the school seek to attain, either overall or on this particular issue (depending on the purpose of the audit)?
- What is the quality and relevance of the current curriculum?
- What educational experience can be provided to supplement or adjust the current curriculum to enable it to attain these purposes?

Prioritising

The recommendations need to be ranked in a priority order by the whole staff. They then form the basis for developing an overall curriculum policy and a series of action plans.

The following proforma will help prioritise your school's recommendations.

Curriculum Priorities		
Maintenance (*requiring active planned strategies to renew understanding and refine practices*)	Improvement (*identified as important but weak*)	New (*any new mandatory requirements*)

The staff should be asked to work in small groups to assign the curriculum issues listed by the curriculum audit committee into one of the three columns on a larger version of this proforma. Each group should then be asked to give an approximate priority to each issue by assigning a 1, 2 or 3 to each one (1 = highest priority, 2 is second highest, and so on).

The results can then be used by the curriculum committee to develop an overall priority when developing the curriculum plan for the immediate and long-term future of the school.

Some of the curriculum issues listed for attention could be:

● Evaluate post-compulsory initiatives elsewhere to cater for Year 11–12 retention.
● Basic skills focus is needed.
● Review curriculum in light of NESB population.
● Improve learning environment/climate.
● New syllabus is not yet fully implemented.
● Use of small group work insufficient.
● Review assessment procedures; are they meeting needs?
● Review homework policy.
● Reporting to parents needs updating in the light of outcomes.
● Investigate gender issues.
● Students to be more responsible for their own learning.
● Do we cater adequately for the gifted and talented?; investigate vertical timetabling and classroom strategies to cater for total and partial acceleration.
● Inservice needed in classroom practice and curriculum content.
● We are very good at Performing Arts. Maintain/expand this program.

Issues for Reflection

♦ *On the previous page, there are a number of sample issues that may have been suggested as needing attention or investigation as a result of a general audit, or upon which an issue specific audit may have focussed. Choose ten that could be relevant to a hypothetical school where you are the hypothetical curriculum manager.*

♦ *Work through the curriculum prioritising exercise discussed (on pages 74–5) using the ten issues that you selected. Using the 'Curriculum Prioritising' proforma on page 75, place the selected issues under the three headings, then give them a priority rank.*

Action Planning

The next step will be to use the results to assist future curriculum strategy planning. Planning is important because:

● it facilitates forward thinking
● it develops a coherent and organised approach to managing curriculum
● it assists the identification of all the components involved in any curriculum management issue
● it prevents duplication of effort
● it identifies who is to take responsibility for the implementation of action strategies
● it facilitates budgeting
● it establishes a timeline for action
● it establishes indicators of successful achievement of the outcomes of the plan.

The audit committee has completed its work. This should be publicly acknowledged. The next job is to form a *curriculum committee*.

The Curriculum Committee

Using the diagram on the facing page as a discussion starter, explain to your curriculum committee the process of strategic improvement.[10]

The first tasks of the curriculum committee will be to develop:

● a set of educational principles for the school, addressing the common curriculum — issues, questions, knowledge and skills that all students should address
● a criteria by which any course and curriculum offering might be evaluated
● a five year curriculum vision

---

[10]   Blum, R. E. and Kneidek, A. W. (1991), 'Strategic Improvement that Focuses on Student Achievement', *Education Leadership*, Vol. 48, no. 7, April, pp. 17–21.

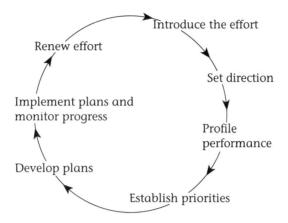

- a series of goals statements or strategies based on the issues raised by the audit, e.g. 'We will actively pursue the involvement and support of parents, non-parents, business and community leaders' or; 'We will integrate technology into every aspect of our school community'.
- an overall priority for the goals statements, according to the staff's prioritising. This will need to mesh ongoing and new needs. This task may also involve some culling of lower priority items. An excluded item would be one that does not have a great gap between existing and desired practice, will not cause great harm if the gap is left untouched, and is less important than other needs. The proforma on the next page provides a useful overview that ensures balance, and is easily published and understood (see page 78).
- a plan of action. You will decide how many issues can be dealt with in the immediate semester, year, two years, or five years. It is desirable to develop five year curriculum plans, even if the priorities change several times during that time to meet emerging needs. The proforma below provides an 'at-a-glance' timeline, for recording your plan of action. Make your own, larger, version of this. List your tasks in the space on the left-hand side.

Curriculum initiative	**Year 1**	**Year 2**	**Year 3**	**Year 4**	**Year 5**

Overview of priorities

To improve outcomes for students at _____ School, the
following issues need to be addressed:

Curriculum content	
Teaching and learning	
Resources	
Staff development	
Student support	
School organisation/ climate	
Parent/ community	

● a working party for each initiative listed. Each working party can be composed of people outside the committee, to utilise expertise across the whole school. Action plans are not written by the core planning group. Rather they are written by members of the staff and the school community who have volunteered to serve on action teams. Action teams — one for each curriculum initiative — are charged with the responsibility of ensuring thorough, clear and concrete action plans, ensuring that the initiatives will become a reality. There should be about 6–8 people on each action team and these should be people who have both a stake and expertise in the initiative that they are working on.

Caldwell and Spinks explain this model of two different types of action groups (curriculum committee and working parties) and provides guidelines for their operation:[11]

● There are two different action groups. The *policy group* (e.g. School Council) sets the policies and priorities. The *program teams* (e.g. the Mathematics team) prepare program plans and budgets that must be approved by the policy group.
● The use of these teams enables teachers, Principal, students and community all to be participants.
● There is, inevitably, some overlap between the tasks of the policy group and those of the program teams. Some persons may be members of both groups.
● There are strict maximum writing limits for statements, plans, reports, etc.
  For example: Policy statement: 1 page (maximum)
                  Program plan: 2 pages (maximum)
                  Evaluation report   1 page (maximum)
● All planning and evaluation reports must be written in non-technical language that can be easily understood.
● School communities should work on completing a small number (e.g. 3–5) of policy-making, program planning and budgeting activities in each *calendar year*, with a systematic plan in subsequent years for the evaluation of existing programs.
● Each school community should plan for a period of 3–5 years to complete most of their planned changes.

What is an Action Plan?

An action plan is a detailed step-by-step specification of how the goals or strategies are to be achieved. Such plans are orientated towards short term results and structured to assign responsibility, state timelines and estimate budget. (See Chapter 4, on program budgeting.) Each program team is to use the questions on the next page to assist in the planning process.[12]

---

[11]   Caldwell, B. J. and Spinks, J. (1986), *Policy Making and Planning for School Effectiveness*, Education Department of Tasmania, Hobart, quoted in Marsh, C. (1988), *Spotlight on School Improvement*, Allen and Unwin, Sydney, p. 186.
[12]   Cunningham, W. G. (1983), *Systematic Planning for Educational Change*, Mayfield Publishing Co., Mountain View, California, p. 10.

- Where are we?
- Where do we want to go?
- What resources will we commit to get there?
- How do we go there?
- When will it be done?
- Who will be responsible?
- What will be the impact on human resources?
- What data will be needed to measure progress?

This can be presented in diagrammatic form as shown on the facing page.

The following proforma will help with establishing an action plan. Make your own, larger, version of this.

Action Plan

Initiative: _____

Manager: _____

Current situation: _____

Brief description of where we want to go:

_____

Action	By whom	When	Resources needed	Performance indicators	Outcome achieved

---

If an issue is likely to be controversial, the action team should gather a few alternative proposals, each supported by practical examples, for presentation to the curriculum committee, then to the staff as a whole for collaborative decision making. The Principal's role throughout, in monitoring progress, encouraging, providing advice and initiating each new step, is crucial.

The planning process[13]

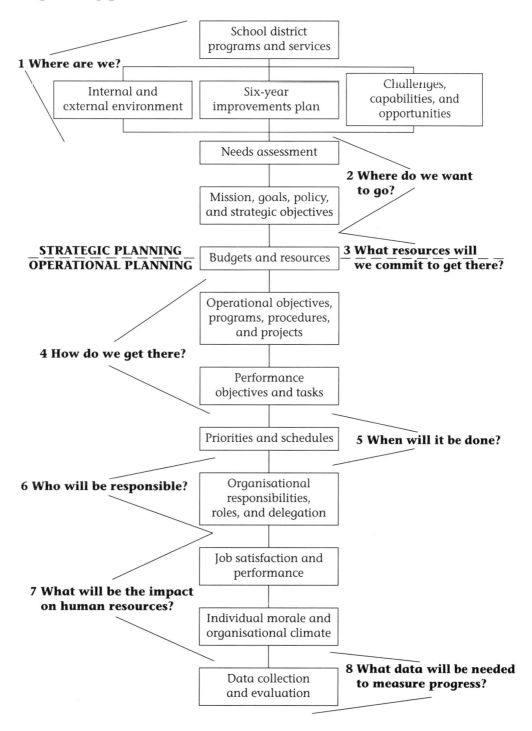

[13]   Cunningham, Ibid, p. 11.

Implementing the Plans

When the curriculum committee (in consultation with the staff as a whole through a consensus process) has accepted the action plans, the formal strategic planning process has concluded and implementation begins — the *process* of change begins. The implementation of the plan is the *action* moment of the action plan. If the planning has been good, the implementation will be a success.

The implementation phase should seek to bring about improvement of practice, of understanding and of the overall situation. It should focus on process, people and people's concerns. Implementation will involve descriptive information sessions by the developers (who, having a stake in making the curriculum work successfully, can explain the changes in detail) with the staff who will implement the plan and the rest of the school community who will benefit from it. These strategies will encourage ownership and also commitment. Special professional development needs of teachers, both individual and in groups, will be catered for to develop new and positive attitudes, knowledge and skills. This will include opportunities for ongoing consultation, reinforcement, monitoring and evaluation to take into account any problem areas that emerge — building by expertise and confidence.

The implementation phase aims to take the individual teachers through Hall's Stages of Concern and Levels of Use. The chart, adapted by Colin Marsh,[14] that follows on page 83, shows the need to allow time for teachers to work through each of the stages of concern about curriculum change, and time for them to progress through the levels of use as they move towards proficiency in implementing the curriculum change.

As participants develop greater understanding, confidence and expertise the success of implementation is enhanced. This is crucial, because the effectiveness of implementation determines how well the curriculum change will succeed.

Issues for Reflection

♦ *Think of three curriculum innovations that you are involved in implementing. Refer to the chart on the next page to match your 'stage of concern' and level of use to each one. The following table format will help.*

Innovation	My stage of concern	My level of use
1 2 3		

---

[14] After Hall, in Marsh, C. (1988), op. cit., pp. 196–7.

The teacher's 'stages of concern' about an innovation	'Levels of use' of the innovation: typical teacher behaviour at each level
6 *Refocussing*: The focus is on an exploration of more universal benefits from the innovation, including the possibility of major changes, or replacement with a more powerful alternative. The individual has definite ideas about alternatives to the proposed existing form of the innovation.	**(vi)** *Renewal*: The user is seeking more effective alternatives to the established use of the innovation.
5 *Collaboration*: The focus is on coordination and cooperation with others regarding use of the innovation.	**(v)** *Integration*: The user is making deliberate efforts to coordinate with others in using the innovation.
4 *Consequence*: Attention focusses on the impact of the innovation on students in his/her immediate sphere of influence. The focus is on relevance of the innovation for students, evaluation of student outcomes including performance and competencies, and changes needed to increase student outcomes.	**(ivb)** *Refinement*: The user is making changes to increase outcomes. **(iva)** *Routine*: The user is making few or no changes and has an established pattern of use.
3 *Management*: Attention is focussed on the processes and tasks of using the innovation and the best use of information and resources. Issues related to efficiency, organising, managing, scheduling, and time demands are uppermost.	**(iii)** *Mechanical use*: The user is making changes to better organise the use of the innovation.
2 *Personal*: The individual is uncertain about the demands of the innovation, his/her inadequacy to meet those demands, and his/her role in regard to the innovation. This includes analysis of his/her role in relation to the reward structure of the organisation, decision-making, and consideration of potential conflicts with existing structures or personal commitment. Financial or status implications of the program for self and colleagues may also be reflected.	**(ii)** *Preparation*: The individual is preparing to use the innovation.
1 *Information*: A general awareness of the innovation, and interest in learning more detail about it, is indicated. The person seems to be unworried about himself/herself in relation to the innovation. He/she is interested in substantive aspects of the innovation in a selfless manner, such as general characteristics, effects and requirements for use.	**(i)** *Orientation*: The individual is seeking out information about the innovation.
0 *Awareness*: Little concern about or involvement with the innovation is indicated.	**(0)** *Non-use*: No action is being taken with respect to the innovation.

Evaluation — Reflecting on the New Practice

A system for periodic reviews of the implementation of each initiative must be developed — involving communication of results, and annual updating and revision. Curriculum evaluation involves measuring the degree to which the performance of students meets objectives and judgements about the curriculum and about the ongoing processes involved in its development and implementations.

Institutionalisation and Curriculum Maintenance

Once the new practice has been implemented, and evaluation has indicated that the innovation has been accepted into the school, it warrants further financial and administrative support. Plans need to be made to ensure that the change becomes consolidated into normal practice, i.e. *institutionalised*. At this time, it should become part of the curriculum maintenance program.

Issues for Reflection

♦ *Try to recall a change you have been involved in that did not survive into institutionalisation. Can you identify the factors that contributed to its failure to continue, e.g. teacher transfers, drop in funding and consultancy support, or new students involved?*

Only by positive support from the school, and by its inclusion into the school's curriculum maintenance program, will an innovation reach the desired state of institutionalisation into the school's curriculum. The whole change process has been summarised by Fullan as follows:[15]

Education Change Process

Expressed need, problem

Uncertainty over choices. Seeking information.

Initiation/adoption

Diffusion/dissemination activities.

Developing expertise. Building up confidence.

Implementation/use

Evaluation activities.

Building up resource base. Building support role.

Institutionalisation/ continuance

---

[15] Fullan, M. in Marsh, C. (1986), *Curriculum an Analytical Introduction*, Ian Novak Publishing Co., Sydney, p. 103.

Play the Curriculum Game

Curriculum development has been likened to a board game or jigsaw puzzle, in which all the pieces can be fitted together in many ways. Any number of people can play, and the 'game' requires imagination, strategies, problem solving and many false starts. Like a game it gives a feeling of pleasure, can build on cooperation and can also lead to conflict. Some of the pieces in the Curriculum Development Game[16] are:

- sequencing principles
- educational philosophy
- teacher training
- teacher attitude
- student interests
- student ability
- financial constraints
- theory of subject
- administrative structures
- change theory
- time constraints
- evaluated outcomes
- view of society
- materials
- school facilities
- objectives
- societal constraints
- leadership
- unanticipated outcomes
- planning

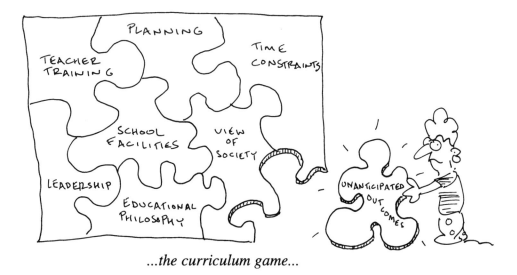

...the curriculum game...

---

[16]   Purves, A. (1975), 'The Thought Fox and Curriculum Building', (after D. Duffy) quoted in Marsh, C. and Stafford, N. (1984), *Curriculum — Practices and Issues*, McGraw Hill, Roseville, NSW, p. 11.

Playing the 'game' involves taking into account all the game pieces and moving from 'Start' (developing a vision) to 'Finish' (successful institutionalisation of curriculum change).

Curriculum development is not an activity that is undertaken once in a school and then concluded, never to be repeated. Knowledge and insights are continually being fed back in to provide a fresh starting point for further development. The following diagram reminds us of the tasks and steps, the frustrations, and the need for a sense of humour in managing curriculum change.[17]

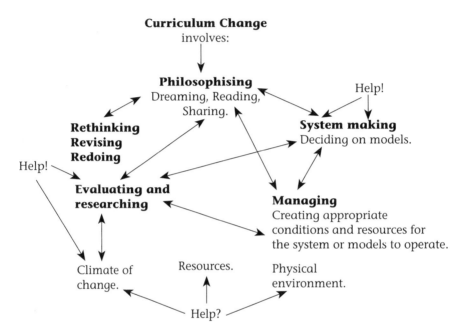

See also Appendix C, 'Who Controls the Curriculum?' on page 220.
    Remember:

> 'A school which is standing still in terms of its curriculum is in fact going backwards.'[18]

[17] Duffy. D. (1970), *Teaching About Society*, Rigby, Adelaide, reproduced in Marsh and Stafford, Ibid, p. 11.
[18] Nicholls, A. and H. (1972), *Developing a Curriculum: a practical guide*, George Allen and Unwin, London, p. 104.

CHAPTER 4

Financial Issues in Educational Administration

Ken Curran, Cath Laws, Terry O'Brien

In 1979, J. Lloyd Trump predicted:

> 'The schools of the future will eliminate uneconomic procedures so that available funds can go further . . . Expenditures will be applied to the more functional and important type of learning. Relatively unimportant school activities must qualify after honest appraisal of their value'.[1]

Trump's 'future' is with us *now*. Increasing numbers of school Principals have:

> ' . . . the authority to make decisions about the composition of their resources and the flexibility to manage them within the context of appropriate policy and guidelines, in order that the school can best meet the educational needs of its students.'[2]

Since desirability exceeds availability, resources must be allocated intelligently to obtain from what is available as much as is possible (making the educational dollar go further) with some desired alternatives sacrificed. In NSW this is called Global Budgeting; in London, Local Management; and in Edmonton, Canada, School Based Budgeting.

Whatever the name, the new financial management in education can be defined as planned acquisition, use and control of financial resources to meet predetermined educational goals and objectives. Without planning, money will not be available

---

[1] J. L. Trump quoted in Cunningham, W. G. (1983), *Systematic Planning for Educational Change*, Mayfield Publishing Co., Mountain View, California.

[2] NSW Department of School Education, Schools Renewal Task Force, 'School-Based Budgets', *Departmental Bulletin*, Vol. 11, no. 1, August 1990.

when it is needed. Without control to ensure what should be done is done, money will not be available to meet long term goals.[3]

...money will not be able to meet long term goals...

Issues for Reflection

♦ *In the light of the quoted information on the previous page, note three things that you think a good financial manager of a school should do.*

Three things that are important for good financial management are:

● ensuring that there are effective financial policies and procedures operating in the school
● planning educational programs in financial terms (i.e. budgets)
● ensuring that there are measures in place to monitor and control finances.

These are the three areas that this chapter will look at in detail.

Financial Management Opportunities

Schools are gaining greater freedom to add to income, or expand or contract expenditure according to their own perceptions of their local needs. This means that schools are in a position to adjust budgeting to make gains or losses that suit the targets for any school program, provided that they can maintain the relative parity between overall income and expenditure for the period. Decentralisation of responsibility for management of finance has opened many new opportunities for the funding of

---

[3]   Adapted from the NSW Department of School Education Metropolitan East inservice notes *Financial Management and Global Budgeting for Directors of Schools.*

programs at schools. Now that Principals are free to explore ways of generating funding and of applying funds as they believe best suits the needs of the schools, they need to be much tighter in the recording and monitoring of those funds through the budgetary process. There are guidelines and, sometimes, policy settings for the general framework of budgeting in schools, but these are increasingly widened to leave the school managers with broad flexibility to meet their own needs.

So, one of the increasingly important roles of the Principal is to ensure that the school's financial resources are efficiently and effectively applied towards the achievement of educational outcomes. An intelligently administered budgeting procedure can compel planning, promote communication and coordination, and provide performance criteria. Educational priorities of the school can be identified and educational programs can be linked to financial programs. Individual teachers feel they have a say in decision making, while faculties or project teams are forced to think about their relationship to the school as a whole. Good educational management, visible to the parents and teachers, is promoted.

Issues for Reflection

♦ List five advantages of the Principal being involved in financial management.

Developing an Educational Philosophy

The first step the Principal must take is the development of a *personal budget philosophy*. Responsibility for the budgeting process is not a task that can be delegated.

> 'Budgeting is a function of top management and, unless this is recognised, the company will be denied the full benefits of a budgeting procedure. It has to be top management inspired and motivated . . . the aim of every company should be to prepare its budget meticulously, systematically and factually and as an instrument of management control.'[4]

The Principal should develop and display an explicit approach to budgeting that lays the foundation for a whole school approach to financial management — all those involved in the implementation of the budget should have the option to be involved in its compilation and the utmost care and consideration should be taken in deciding and approving budgets.

Issues for Reflection

♦ Do you have skills? Make a list of the skills you have already in managing the school and its resources.

---

[4]   McAlpine, T. S. (1976), *The Basic Arts of Budgeting*, Business Books Ltd, London.

The list of skills you have just compiled should have included such skills as organising student time around the curriculum, and deploying staff and materials to deliver the curriculum, e.g. timetabling and class allocations. Skills such as these can be applied with equal ability to financial management. If you remember that financial management means much more than merely managing money (an attitude implied by the 'One Bucket Approach') you will realise that you already have many of the skills required.

The One Bucket Approach[5]

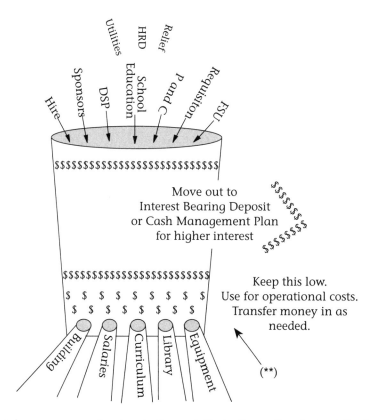

Financial management extends these skills to the exit points at the bottom of the bucket (**) so as to plan, prioritise and control what the institution does in allocation and deployment of financial and other resources, using economic as well as educational criteria.

As you see, budgeting does not exist in isolation. It is impossible to discuss budgeting without discussing planning, because the school budget is *an expression of the school plan in fiscal terms*. Planning lays the foundation for an effective budgeting system, yet any plans that have not been budgeted will seldom be started and, if started, are unlikely to succeed. The budget, therefore, adds the dimension of feasibility to the strategic plan. The budgeting process fits somewhere between strategic objectives and operational objectives.

---

5   NSW Department of School Education (1992), *Met East InforMER*.

Issues for Reflection

♦ *Note the place of budgeting in these two planning models:*

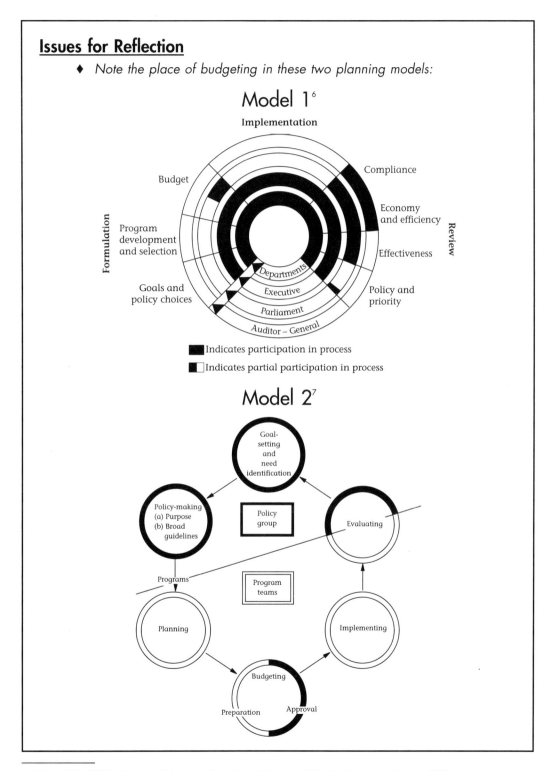

Model 1[6]

Implementation

Budget

Compliance

Economy and efficiency

Formulation

Program development and selection

Review

Effectiveness

Goals and policy choices

Policy and priority

Departments

Executive

Parliament

Auditor – General

■ Indicates participation in process

◨ Indicates partial participation in process

Model 2[7]

Goal-setting and need identification

Policy-making
(a) Purpose
(b) Broad guidelines

Policy group

Evaluating

Programs

Program teams

Planning

Implementing

Budgeting

Preparation   Approval

---

6   Harrold, R. (1982), *Economic Thinking in Education*, University of New England, Armidale, p. 285.

7   Caldwell, B. J. and Spinks, J. M. (1989), *The Self-managing School*, Falmer Press, London.

The School Plan

It is critical that your school management plan — the intent of the school to demonstrate its educational outcomes — be the driving force in setting targets for your school's programs. The budget should not be the driving force behind the school plan. The budget is there to support your school's plan, not the reverse.

...the budget is there to support your school's plan...

Then and Now

While schools have had written management plans for many years they have usually been in the following format:

- What do we want to do?   (aims, goals or objectives)
- How are we going to do it?   (strategies)
- Who will do it?   (responsibilities)
- How will we see how it went?   (evaluation)

Current changes in accountability and general management principles require a different way of making sense of planning.

A current school plan might focus on the following:

- What do we want students to have/be doing?   (outcomes)
- How are we going to get there?   (strategies)
- What funds will be allocated to this?   (budget)
- Who will be involved?   (responsibilities)
- When should it occur?   (timeframe)
- How will we know if outcomes are achieved?   (success indicators)

Specifying outcomes, outlining strategies, deciding on indicators of success and including costing in planning, all need to be part of your school's plan.

The formulation, monitoring and evaluation of your plan will need to be done in consultation with your staff, and key players (School Council, parents and students) in your whole school community. Consequently, it is important that all these interests are represented when formulating the budget priorities in relation to the school's plan.

Financial Committees

Once the school plan has been formulated, the funds necessary to implement the plan can be identified. First, a financial management body ought to be set up to translate the school's finances into effective funding support for those programs specifically outlined in its management plan, as well as those aspects necessary to its regular operation. In the best interests of financial management and accountability it is no longer appropriate for any one person to be responsible for framing budgets and for the control of school finances.

Schools are now responsible for much greater sums of money than before and, often, these funds represent the money needed for the school's total operation of administration and educational programs. Schools are also responsible to the general public for the way in which they manage their funds. So it is in everyone's best interest to include a broad spectrum of participants on this committee.

Modern personnel management and plain good sense suggest that those schools using staff and parent participation in appropriate decision making have the best chance of creating a positive school climate, where staff and parents feel they are valued partners in the operation of the school. Most schools operate at their optimum when staff have a preparedness to commit themselves above and beyond their professional responsibilities. Staff who feel that their contribution is valued are best placed to make that kind of commitment. Budgeting can be used as a tool for staff motivation, improved communication, and improved cooperation, staff development and staff morale. This must be true participation and not 'pseudo-participation'.

Issues for Reflection

♦ *Make a list of the advantages of allowing those who will be responsible for performance under a budget to participate in the decisions by which that budget is to be established. This will consolidate your ideas and attitudes towards the formation and functioning of the budget committee.*

The selection of a budget committee is crucial if the school community is to respond in a positive way to the budgetary decisions, and if commitment to the budget is to be fostered.

While there may well be only one person maintaining the necessary records of funding, an advisory body should be formed to reflect the overall budgetary strategy for the school. Some Principals will prefer to limit this to members of their own staff and limit the group to a small number (2 or 3). The group ought to comprise more participants than this, and should include members of the wider school community. Other schools may find that their school council, or a sub-committee of this, will form its financial committee.

Issues for Reflection

◆ *Compile a list of possible members of your budget/finance committee.*

You may wish to call for nominations from staff and community members to form a budget committee. You could then select your committee from these nominations, keeping in mind the importance of having a wide representation across the staff (including non-teaching representatives). You could have school-wide elections, within school or within the parent group, for committee members. The decision about who is on your management committee rests with you, as you are the person ultimately accountable for the management of the school's finances. It is important to remember that the budget committee has an educational role and needs to make *recommendations* to the school's council or management committee.

A possible schedule of meetings for the budget/finance committee follows:

- *September*:   AGM
                Election of Committee.
                Tabling of 1992–93 Report — discussion.
                Draft format for 1993–94 presented for discussion.
- *September*:   Budget submissions from faculties presented.
                Discussion of method to be used to allocate funds to faculties.
- *October*:   Setting of fees for 1994.
                Allocation of funds to faculties for 1994.
                Final budget approved.
                Submissions for initiatives funds to be invited.
- *November*:   Initiative submissions presented.
                Process for prioritising discussed.
- *November*:   Prioritising initiatives.
- *February*:   Review of initiatives spending.
                Submissions for initiative funds (Round 2) to be invited.
- *March*:   Round 2 initiatives presented.
                Discussion of how to prioritise.
- *April*:   Prioritising of Round 2 Initiatives.
- *May*:   Review of whole budget expenditure to date.

Preparing a Budget

The NSW Department of School Education[8] describes the budget committee as having five main tasks. These are:

- to express the school plan in financial terms
- to identify and place school programs in priority order
- to estimate school income from various sources
- to allocate income to programs in priority order
- to monitor progress of actual performance against budget.

The following sequential steps will aid you in preparing a budget.

- Form a budget committee.
- Determine a timeline.
- Towards the end of Term 3 set the deadline dates for submission of programs for the following year. These include educational, administrative and capital programs.
- Programs are submitted, approved and ranked.
- Identify likely income.
- Allocate funds to those programs that can be afforded, matching expenditure to income.
- Prepare cash flows.
- Publish the budget, invite comment and amend if necessary.
- Monitor the budget implementation using a commitment register, cashflow, OASIS.
- Evaluate and report.

We will now examine five main tasks related to five of the steps listed above.

1 Expressing a School Plan in Financial Terms

The idea that budgeting should focus on the results of educational plans, rather than on resources, has great appeal to educators who value program structures as a basis for budgetary decision making and recognise both the importance of identifying organisational objectives and relating these to the budget as well as analysing the long range impact of budgetary decisions. For these reasons, program budgeting is deemed to be a superior structure for educational institutions. The link between resources and results gives the budget process the ability to shape and direct resources towards the achievement of specific desired results.

A program is any school plan, effort or project that will involve the spending of money.

---

[8] NSW Department of School Education (1991), 'Managing the School's Financial Resources', *Certificate of School Leadership and Management Module*, HRD Directorate, Sydney.

...financing school programs...

Types of *educational programs* could include:

● key learning or syllabus areas
● student welfare
● Aboriginal education
● girls' education
● sports
● computers
● environmental education
● multicultural education

Administrative programs could include:

● school maintenance
● office operations
● casual relief
● utilities, electricity, water, gas and sewerage supplies.

Capital programs could include:

● computer hardware
● office machines
● furniture renewal
● reserves for long term asset purchase
● general reserves for future budgeted expenditure.

It is important for all school programs to be presented to the committee with an estimate of costs that will be incurred for each program — allocate the amount expected to be expended over an identified amount of time, and establish monitoring and evaluation mechanisms. Consultation with staff and community is critical at this stage, so that everyone has an idea of the logic behind allocations and of the constraints to the budget.

It is the *school management plan* that should be continually referred to at this time.

This will identify the school's educational priorities for the year and indicate where the bulk of funding should be directed. Clearly, all schools have ongoing service charges to be met and these will also need to be assessed. There are also ongoing commitments to be made to capital programs. This may require funds to be set aside within the budget towards future purchase of major plant and equipment. Account must also be taken of the depreciation of items, and funding should be set aside for the eventual replacement of equipment, etc. Any new initiatives will need to be given attention and the school budget committee will have the responsibility to determine which of these are likely to be supported.

Approaches to Budgets

Two approaches to budget setting could be considered. It may be possible to sort through the preferred expenditure for the year and, having done so, to then consider how to raise the necessary income to match those targets. It is more likely that you will use a process that, first, determines the level of anticipated income for the year and then refines the expenditure to match those levels. This can be best achieved by requiring a budget for each type of program.

Program Budgets

A program is considered to be a plan of action based on a particular objective. Key learning areas are generally not considered programs, as there may be more than one subject and more than one program within each key learning area. Most programs are divided into sub-programs or stages and these relate to more specific objectives within a program. For example, Student Welfare might be considered to be a program and it might comprise sub-programs including Girls' Education Strategy, and School Reward Systems. On the other hand, a Girls' Education Strategy might be considered a program in itself and sub-programs could relate to initiatives in cooperative learning and computer education.

When your management plans are drafted, each of the parties that vie for funding ought to submit a budget that would support that program. Each submission should ensure that the level of funding applied for is the optimum for that program to run effectively. This will still be likely to mean that all applications add to more than double the available funding, but it is a starting point. The program submissions should also be careful to indicate whether the programs will be capable of generating funding for the school through the presentation of their activities. Some do and others do not.

Program Submission

Some examples of areas where program submissions would be required could include:

- Training and development
- Student welfare
- Each curriculum area and any subset of these, that should then be amalgamated for that key learning area
- Paper and printing

- Textbooks
- Library
- Support and/or specialist teaching
- Special programs
- Administrative programs
- Capital programs

and so on . . .

The specific number of program areas will vary from school to school, and will change according to the way in which you decide to amalgamate or separate areas to recognise their individual priority. A caution is that, if you are recording in cash books, you might like to simplify book-keeping by limiting the number of overall dissections you use. Computer spreadsheets usually allow for extensive dissections to be easily managed.

Issues for Discussion

♦ *Brainstorm the list of programs or 'activities that cost money' now operating in your school, under the three headings 'Educational', 'Administrative' and 'Capital'. Keep the list of programs resulting from your brainstorming. You will refer back to it later (see page 108).*

To link each program in the school to the school management plan, a proforma needs to be developed linking programs to the school plan.

A program plan should be about two pages in length and requires the identification of an *objective* that is fundamental to education, *planning for implementation* that is fundamental to the pursuit of the objective, and *focus on student outcomes and development*. Elements in the plan should be arranged in *order of priority*. A listing of *resources* and a *plan for evaluation* of this program are required. The program plan and the proposed pattern for resource allocation to implement the plan, together, constitute the *program budget*.

This approach promotes a whole school approach to education and resource allocation. Staff are sensitised to the realisation of limited resources and, therefore, a consideration of alternatives at all levels for all programs. The very act of creating programs has the positive effect of identifying who is responsible for various areas of activities and orientating policy makers towards making decisions on the basis of results to be achieved instead of simply on the price of items.

Examples of program submission proformas appear on pages 100–103. The first proforma is for a primary school (pages 100–101), the second sample proforma is for individual initiative programs, and the third proforma is for a large high school. You will need to include aspects of all these forms to develop one that suits your own needs.

The three worksheets referred to in the third sample proforma are provided following that proforma (pages 104–106).

Before you examine the three proformas that follow, an explanation of some terms may be necessary.

Explanation of Terms

- *Program area*: This is the area, be it educational, administrative or capital, in which you are proposing a program to operate.
- *Specific title*: This title will specify the program or part of the program with which you are dealing.
- *Outcomes (student/other)*: These are often best generated using de-clouding wheels or other brainstorming techniques. The outcomes should be definite statements that are expected to be achieved. While they should be stated as student outcomes, there are many times when the connection to students is quite indirect.
- *Strategies*: For each outcome the strategies or tactics to be used to achieve them should be listed.
- *Budget*: This requires the listing of the resources that need to be made available to support the programs and their cost. 'Resources' includes not only physical but also human resources. You must ensure also that infrastructure costs — phone, post, printing, etc. — are factored into the budget as these, and many consumables, are often overlooked. The budget should also show any anticipated income from any activity that the program may operate. If this activity is to generate income, it can help to offset the overall costs of the program. Some programs may even produce profit, however, their income must be shown to be included in the school's budget sheet for the year.
- *Timeframe*: The budget could also show the *timeframe* for the program, so that the timing of the expenditures on resources can be shown. This may be of some significance in avoiding major expenditure before the school has generated sufficient income to support these costs.
- *Ratings*: You might ask program coordinators to indicate the priority of the program, or priority of items within the program. You might ask them for a rating of 1 to 5, or one of 'Essential', 'Very important' or 'Desirable'.

...priority ratings...

- *Funding source*: You might also ask proposers to propose a funding source for the program, such as annual requisition, government grants, general funds, or special fees to students or community members.
- *Success or performance indicators*: These answer the question, 'How will we know if our program has operated successfully?' They form an important part of the monitoring and evaluation process.

Proforma for a program submission

_____ Primary School   Year _____

Program area _____

Specific title _____

Head of Committee _____

Committee members _____
_____

Outcomes _____
_____
_____
_____
_____
_____
_____
_____
_____
_____

Strategies   Success/indicators

_____   _____
_____   _____
_____   _____
_____   _____
_____   _____
_____   _____
_____   _____

Income
Activity   Amount/timeframe

_____ $ _____
_____ $ _____
_____ $ _____
                                    Total cost $

Expenditure
Resources   Cost/timeframe

_____ $ _____
_____ $ _____
_____ $ _____
_____ $ _____
                                    Total cost $

Proforma for a program submission (continued)

199 ____

Program area ____

Program strategies

Strategies	Coordinator	When By?	Resources

Proforma for application for initiative funds

_____ High School   Year _____

Name of initiative _____

Committee/person responsible _____

Educational purpose of this initiative (student outcomes)

_____

Indicators of success of initiative

_____

_____

Plan for implementation (what, who, when, where)

_____

_____

_____

_____

Resources required to implement this initiative:

_____

_____

_____

_____

_____

Funding requested $
Level 1: (minimum possible)
Level 2: (more effective implementation)
Level 3: (most effective implementation)

Signature: _____   Date: _____

Committee use only: Priority: H   M   L
                      Funding approved: 1   2   3
                                Amount: $

Note: All applications must relate to school priorities and be accounted for in terms of a program.

Signature: _____   Date: _____

Proforma for preparing your budget submission

Financial year 19____ – 19____

1 All purchases for the budget year must be **completed by September 7**.
2 All monies expended and committed (orders placed but not delivered or paid for) will be calculated by .... and included on your summary sheet. (There is no need for you to complete this section.)
3 Projects authorised by the finance committee as forming part of the budget, but for which no orders were placed, will have their funds returned to the school's accounts.
4 Should you still wish to go ahead with these projects (i.e. Point 3 above), new submissions will need to be made for the 19 __ — 19 __ financial year.
5 In preparing submissions for the 19 __ — 19 __ budget please follow these steps:
   a Read the information concerning the school's aims and objectives and school priorities.
   b Re-read your 'Three Year Plan' in the light of this information, to determine your own priorities.
   c Complete **Worksheet 1**. (This is where you argue your case for the particular project. A separate sheet needs to be completed for each project in each budget area. The budget areas are as follows: Textbooks, Other books/resources, Furniture, Equipment, Teaching aids, Maintenance, Functions, Expendable items and Miscellaneous.)
   d Select/elect a project coordinator. This is the person who is proposing the project and who will be authorised to make orders.
   e Complete **Worksheet 2**. This is a summary sheet and should be as accurate as possible.
      (i) For each project, summarise:
- the items to be purchased.
- the number required.
- the cost per item.

      (ii) The *expenditure* level indicates if the project is:
- E (essential for your area)
- D (desirable)
- VI (very important)

      (iii) The *activity* level indicates if the project:
- A, *maintains* the present situation.
- C, is a *new* project.
- B, *extends* the present situation.

      (iv) The *source of finance* indicates from where you believe the funds for your project will come.
- G1 (Annual requisition)
- G2 (Government grants*)
- F (General school funds)
- S (Special fees**)

*Government Grants include: ESL (Resource), Art grant, Cash grant, Textbook grant, Drug education grant, Special education grant
** Special Fees include Art fees, Home science fees, Computer studies fees, etc.

      (v) For each project, please indicate *when* you would like to make your purchases. (We need to know this in order to *manage our cash flow*.)
- Term IV (1990)
- Term II (1991)
- Term I (1991)
- Term III (1991)

      (vi) Indicate the total amount for that project.
      (vii) Indicate your order of priority for the projects you are preparing. Rate those that are *essential* first, then those that are *very important*, etc.
      (viii) The cumulative total is found by adding the total for each project to the previous (cumulative) total.
   f Complete **Worksheet 3**. This sheet aims to give the committee an idea of the cost individual students are likely to face in the next financial year in regard to excursions, sporting events and the like. These projects are of a 'contra' nature. The funds will be collected for the specific project and will cover goods used or consumed by the students (e.g. in Art, Home science or Computer studies) or services received (transportation, entry to galleries museums, or accommodation). Please remember that none of these activities is to run at a loss. Surplus funds will be used for the rest of the budget.

Codes to be used in completing worksheet 3

Expenditure level	E	essential	*Source finance*	G1	annual requisition
	V	very important		G2	government grants
	D	desirable		F	general funds
				S	special fees
Activity level	A	maintenance	*School term*	IV	Term IV
	B	extension		I	Term I
	C	new		II	Term II
				III	Term III

Worksheet 1

School financial year 199___ – 199___

Faculty/area: _____

Expenditure level: Name of project:

_____   _____

Project coordinator:

_____

Objectives of project: _____
_____
_____
_____
_____

Area of school aims and objectives that the project aims to fulfil:
_____
_____
_____

Criteria for inclusion at this expense level:
_____
_____
_____
_____
_____

Benefits and shortcomings arising out of this level of expenditure:

Benefits	**Shortcomings**

If nothing is done: _____
_____
_____
_____

Worksheet 2

Faculty/area: _____   Budget area: _____

Name of project	Items to be purchased	Unit cost	Number to be bought	Expenditure level 1	Activity level	Source finance	School term	Amount $	Priority rank	Cumulative total

Worksheet 3

School financial year 199___ – 199___

Faculty: _____

Income from special fees, etc. (Includes excursions)

Detail	School term	Amount $

Issues for Reflection

● *Carefully examine the proformas and worksheets provided on pages 100–106. Identify the headings that you think you could use to develop a program budget proforma. Make a list of them, or design a rough proforma to suit your own purposes.*

● *Choose a program with which you are very familiar. It might be one that you have initiated yourself or are currently implementing. It might be a cross curriculum perspective or a key learning area. Fill in the program budget application for this program — use either the ones provided on pages 101 or 103–6 or the one you designed yourself as suggested above.*

The goal of the above exercise is for the total program efforts to be included. Faculty heads, Year teachers or program managers — in fact, managers of any school project that will spend money — are asked to think through the total budget implications of their plans for the following year. For some, this may be the first time they have been required to justify or detail their activities. Brockman gives this example:

> 'What will the art program need to accomplish its curriculum objectives next year in terms of staff, textbooks, materials, equipment, supplies, library support, hardware, facilities, transportation and equipment maintenance?'[9]

2 Identify and Place School Programs in Priority Order

Program managers should present up to three levels of funding. Levels set can vary but one Principal described those at his school as:

● The core — what you can't function without.
● Phase 1 — what you'd like to have for starters.
● Top level — what you'd only be likely to get in a 'pink fit'.

Depending on the priority given to each program in relation to the school management plan, the most expensive alternative may be chosen in one program and the least expensive in another. Budget decisions are based on the hard data provided about individual program outcomes and the formal weighing up of the costs and benefits of alternatives that might be selected to achieve the school's overall objectives.

Once all the program budgets have been received, they must be prioritised and ranked. In some schools this is done by the planning committee, or council, or executive. In other schools, the prioritising is done by the finance committee or budget committee. The following brief exercise will give you an overview of the

---

[9] Brockman, F. J., 'Program Budgeting: Implications for Secondary Principals' in Levacic, R. (ed) (1989), *Financial Management in Education*, Open University Press, Philadelphia, Chapter 9.

prioritising, ranking and allocation of funding phases that will be described in more detail later.

Prioritising

Issues for Reflection

♦ *Locate or redo the list of programs that you prepared on page 98. Give each program a priority (H = High, M = Medium and L = Low).*

♦ *Rank all the Highs, all the Mediums, and all the Lows using a number system (1 = highest, 2 = next, and so on).*

♦ *Imagine you have totalled the cost of all these programs and have an amount of money that will enable only 75% of these projects to be funded. The order in which you will allocate the funds has been determined by the priority and the ranking. Tick those that would have been funded.*

...ranking...

The activity you have just completed is, in essence, program budgeting. On the next page is an example of a summary of program submissions once they have been prioritised. The next step is to rank them. Each submission must relate to school priorities and must be accounted for in terms of a program.

Ranking

Issues for Reflection

♦ *Pretend you are the budget committee at the school that produced the summary of submissions on the next page. Complete the prioritising for each program, using H, M or L to indicate High, Medium or Low. Then rank all the High priorities (1 = 1st, 2 = 2nd, and so on), rank all the Medium priorities and then rank all the Low priorities.*

♦ *Use a calculator. If this school had $36 000 to spend, decide how many programs would receive funding and how many would miss out or be deferred?*

Summary of submissions

From	Type	Program	PR	Costs	Rank
Art	Faculty	Filing cabinets	H	93	
Computers	Whole	10 × Optima computers + 4 printers	H	17 790	
English	Fac/Whole	Textbooks and reference books — Drama new subject	H	820.14	
English	Faculty	Whiteboard	1M	160	
History	Faculty	Computer and printer	H	2421	
IA	Faculty	2 × secondhand computers	H	400	
IA	Faculty	3.5" disk drive	1M	99	
IA	Faculty	XY plotter	1L	1300	
IA	Faculty	Radial arm router	1L	700	
Language	Faculty	Filing cabinet		93	
Language	Faculty	Portable double-sided whiteboard		153	
L/T	Whole	Mobile whiteboard		362.60	
L/T	Whole	Toyota bus		35 953	
Library	Whole	Fiction books for wide reading	1H	2000	
Library	Faculty	Portable bar code reader	2M	849	
Library	Whole	Compact Disk — 1990 Time Magazine	3L	299.95	
Library	Whole	Compact Disk — Science and Innovation	1L	139.95	
Maths	Faculty	Staffroom and classroom computer		2052	
Principal	Whole	Funds for 1993 School Musical	1H	3500	
Principal	Whole	Expenses for playday	2M	500	
Science	Faculty	Staffroom and classroom computer	1H	2052	
Science	Faculty	Blinds for Lab 5 (replacement)	2M	1000	
Social Science	Wh/Cur	Textbooks Yr12 Business Studies	1H	625	
Social Science	Wh/Cur	Resources Yr12 Retail Skills Kit and Consumables	2M	650	
Social Science	Wh/Cur	Resources Yr12 Business Studies	3L	800	
SRC	Whole	Subsidy for SRC group development session 2 day	1H	600	

The following is a blank of the 'Summary of Submissions' for you to adopt or adapt. Provided is a *bottom line* for you to note the number of programs funded and not funded.

Summary of submissions 199__

From	Type	Program	PR	Costs	Rank

Funded ...   Not funded ...

3 Identify and Estimate Income from Various Sources

Buckets of Money

Today's funding regime can be likened to two buckets balanced on a scale. Into the first bucket goes all the school income from all sources. This includes the funds carried forward from the previous year, reserve funds, fees, excursions, transport, central funding and funds generated by the school programs themselves. This bucket becomes a projection of funding for the year, from all anticipated sources.

The second bucket contains the school's expenditure. It will hold the expenditure on all programs for the year, funds committed for the payment of due or unpresented accounts, and the new level of reserve funds that can be increased or decreased each year. The only necessary connection between the first bucket and the second bucket is that the two buckets must balance.

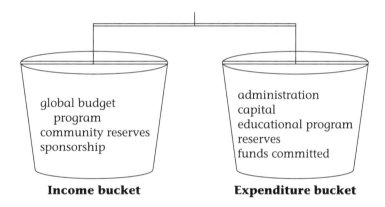

| **Income bucket** | **Expenditure bucket** |

Income

The budget committee, probably with extensive background work by the Principal, will need to ascertain the likely levels of income from the normal operation of the school. The flow of funds estimated from historic data (projected forward and modified by percentage increases and numbers of students in the school, special funding etc.) will need to be tabulated to provide a best estimate of income projection for the year. It would be wise to err on the conservative side, because any unexpected bonus will make more funds available to either upgrade the budget at a later stage of the year or, as is more likely, to provide a larger fund pool for the ensuing year.

When determining likely income:

- consider every possible source — such as grants for students, maintenance, staffing, professional development utilities as well as donations, and links with business (including materials such as paper and cash grants)
- be realistic about the amount you will have, especially those donations and sponsorship funds available from private organisations
- use the previous year's income and expenditure as a guide

- consider possible impacts on the school, such as socio-economic changes resulting in parents being able to contribute less
- consider non-cash areas, for example donated equipment. Estimate investment interest.

Following is a sample table involving projected income.

Projected Income

1 Funds carried forward from the previous year **less** any funds committed for unpaid accounts.
2 Global or Government grants
3 School fees
4 Funds provided for special programs, such as:
   - computers in schools
   - support teaching for learning difficulties
   - support for non-English speakers
   - school special initiative programs
   - special education programs.
5 Funds generated from school educational programs that might include:
   - sport
   - excursions
   - Maths
   - English
   - Science
   - Music and Drama
   - Art and Craft
   - concerts
   - various fundraising '-thons'
   - other curriculum programs
   - Student Council activities
6 A variety of other sources, such as:
   - rentals from community groups using the school premises
   - interest on accounts
   - sale of school goods and equipment
   - proceeds from marketing initiatives.
7 Miscellaneous (some income is unexpected and doesn't fit your other dissections neatly).

...projected income from school excursions...

Combined with all the dissections of possible sources of income for your school, these elements will add to provide you with a projected income for your year.

It is wise to next ascertain the level of reserve funding that you will want to keep — probably in an investment account — and, after subtracting this figure, you will be left with the level of income available for expenditure for your year. Having obtained this figure, you can then begin, through your finance committee, to refine the requests for funding until the figures add up to a balanced budget. You also need to consider asset reserves for major new assets to be bought, replacement reserves for replacement of existing assets and general reserves to cover emergencies.

Issues for Reflection

♦ *Estimate your school income (to the nearest ± $500) on the following income worksheet.*

Income worksheet	Sample school	My school
Balance c/f	100 000	
Global/Government grant	180 000	
School fees	19 500	
Subject fees	17 500	
P and C contribution	10 000	
Special programs staying on	21 000	
Facilities hire	3 000	
Sponsorship	2 000	
Fund raising	2 000	
Interest	6 000	
Total	368 500	

Other Forms of Income

Community Funding

Many schools will have in place some mechanism to integrate the community fundraising with that of the school. This usually occurs through school councils. However, many communities, even with school councils, still prefer to maintain separate funding and to apply this to elements of the school that require their support. Ideally, it will benefit the school if the community groups can be persuaded to at least integrate their *budgets* with that of the school.

This is best done by giving the community the opportunity to determine which of the school's programs it wishes to fund and then to leave it with exclusivity for that funding (within reason). This will allow the community to feel responsible for funding sections of the school's operation — ideally those areas seen as directly benefitting the students themselves. The school can then apply its own funds to the remaining areas of need.

Pooling funds

If the community can be persuaded to pool its funds with those of the school, this will increase the potential income and make the funding of school programs more straightforward. If the funds can be integrated with the school's (i.e. the funds remain separated from the school's but payments are made to support those programs from the school management plan that have become the community's responsibility), this can be equally effective. It will also give the community a purpose for their funding and avoid the feeling of a loss of control of the proceeds of their lengthy fundraising efforts. Community organisations are likely to feel more productive than if they simply handed over their funds to the school.

Schools that still need to approach communities as each individual need arises will find it more difficult to coordinate expenditure but coordination can still be achieved by identifying those areas likely to seek funding before they arise. Either of the two approaches outlined above is preferable to the constant need to approach the community for further funding.

Community Use of School Facilities

Schools are prime properties and are usually situated in areas where there are people and families. The potential exists for you to gain income through hiring out your facilities. While the amount that can be charged will vary due to time and place, it is clear that school systems are moving for you to gain income from this opportunity. A few things need to be taken into account if you are thinking of promoting the use of your school facilities.

- Check your system's current guidelines and see if limits apply to the amount you can charge for renting out your facilities.
- Check if your system has exempted certain groups from charges.
- Think about the types of groups you want to use your premises.

- Weigh up the costs and benefits of particular groups using your facilities. Evening colleges or night classes may make financially attractive offers but you will need to also think about the impact involved in your teachers' rooms being used at night, security and organisational issues. If your school is to be used for evening classes you might think about keeping a part of the school 'off limits', where you can keep school-related things.
- Even if your system's policies allow you to charge fees for hiring out your facilities, you might think about not charging some groups. For example, you may not want to charge for the local Safety House committees meeting at your school because the benefits that you get from close liaison with police may be worth more than the potential income.

...close liaison with police...

Sponsorship Agreements

In difficult economic times, companies generally want their money's worth. While they may be tempted to get involved with your school parent associations as a registered charity (for reasons that are obvious), negotiating agreements with companies on behalf of the school is not always easy.

You really need to think about what the company does and what the implications are for you if you become associated with that particular enterprise. Goodwill and the respect of the community are difficult to build up and are highly desirable for a company so don't undersell your potential. On the other hand, don't expect the world. The bottom line for companies is more clients and, therefore, better profits. If you want to negotiate with a company, and there are many excellent companies with which you would be happy to be associated, you need to think about what they will get out of it as well as what the school will get out it.

You may be asked to sign an agreement with a company detailing the obligations of both parties. If you are entering into a contract with a company, think carefully that it covers everything you want, and that you are able and happy to meet your obligations. It's wise to consult the legal advisers of your system before you sign the contract or agreement.

You might also be approached by companies to rent part of your premises — particularly if your school is an ideal location. As well as considering the benefits this offers, you need to think through all the possible costs associated with this — the lack of space, being associated with the company, security risks, etc. You might enter into such an agreement on a twelve month basis to see how it goes. Consult your system's legal advisers about the leasing contract.

Issues for Discussion

♦ *Brainstorm ideas for generating funds by renting facilities, sponsorship and P and C activities.*
♦ *Estimate the likely income of each of the activities you thought of.*

Rent of facilities	Sponsorship	P and C
e.g. hall, tennis courts, graffiti remover	e.g. newsletter, sports team	e.g. fete

Likely income

Rent of facilities	Sponsorship	P and C
$	$	$

---

4 Allocate Income to Programs in Priority Order

This process needs to focus on the school's established priorities. It is usually the strategic planning committee, or school council, or executive who are responsible for establishing the priorities for the school's year — although it could also be the whole staff. Once these priorities are known, the allocation of funds for expenditure purposes should begin, by focussing on those priorities and ensuring that they receive adequate funding to ensure that targets for the year are realistically met. These priorities, or areas for school emphasis, have been carefully determined by staff and parents and must be supported for the process to have credibility with its audience.

Funds should then be allocated for recurrent education programs — those programs which continue on a yearly basis and can be fairly well estimated from past experience. The school band may continue at the same level, the athletics carnival, the education week expenses, and so on. Those submissions which continue ongoing and valued school programs should be funded at manageable levels.

Next might be a focus on special programs. These could be other school initiatives, English language, support teaching, computer education, etc. Necessary funding needs to be allocated to these as well. The list continues with the essential funding for utilities maintenance and staff related expenses. Separate categories are likely to be staff development costs, capital expenses and stock expenses. All of these, and the other elements specific to your school, will generate a table of expenditure similar to that following.

> **Projected expenditure**
> 1 Priority expenses, such as student welfare programs or the school assessment program.
> 2 Recurrent programs, such as Maths, English, Sport, Music, transport and excursions and Student Council.
> 3 Special programs, such as computers, English language teaching, support teaching and special education programs.
> 4 Service cost of utilities, such as telephone, water, sewage, gas and power.
> 5 Staff related expenses, such as casual relief, staff development and ancillary.
> 6 Capital and stock, such as machinery, stationery, textbooks and printing.
> 7 A wide miscellany of expenses that relate to your special organisation, e.g. marketing costs, fees and rentals.
> 8 That inevitable 'miscellaneous' column for those surprise expenses that always crop up, but which are too small to merit their own dissection.

Beare calls this a process of reconciliation 'with estimates of expenditure adjusted in the light of estimates of revenue'.[10] The decisions are made in terms of the total school organisation, rather than on the basis of ideas presented by vested interests. Overlap between programs can be identified and a check made that all programs reflect school priorities. This process also enables adequate recognition of the total costs of the school's management plan. A school that is unable to carry the costs of its plan either must find ways to raise funds or must revise its plans. Resource considerations, therefore, inject realism into planning. To approve a single program requires the committee to make decisions on feasibility, resource demands and timing — possibly not only for the future year but, in some cases, involving commitments for many years into the future.

The Principal's role in this procedure is that of *facilitator*. The Principal must encourage deliberation, differing opinions and disagreement — insisting that people who voice an opinion also take responsibility for supporting that opinion with facts, and presenting alternatives. The Principal must ensure that the school's strategic objectives are kept in mind and that time is not wasted arguing over priorities. Since it is highly likely that the request for funds will exceed the resources available, programs ranked high (whether for political, economic or merit reasons) are going to be funded, while the reverse applies to those ranked low. Greatest discussion should focus on those programs in the middle, around the decision point or affordability level. Decision making procedures should follow the 'KISS principle' (Keep It Simple, Stupid), so as to avoid 'entanglement in mental gymnastics'.

Issues for Reflection

♦ *What do you think your role would be in the budget decision making process? Take the time to write a description of what you see your role to be.*

---

[10] Beare, H., Caldwell, Brian J., and Millikan, Ross H. (1989), *Creating an Excellent School: some new management techniques*, Routledge, London, p. 145.

Hartley provides a list of 20 criteria (listed below) that are commonly used in setting budget priorities.[11] Decide which of the criteria listed you think might be a useful tool. Make your own list of those useful tools you wish to encourage, and another separate list of elements you'd like to avoid.

The Criteria

1 Subjective judgement
2 Past practice
3 Legal requirements
4 Quality of program
5 Test results
6 Number of students
7 Parental pressure
8 Needs assessment
9 Staff recommendations
10 School Council priorities
11 Staff seniority factors
12 Collective bargaining
13 National curriculum trends
14 Effect on matching funds
15 Non-instructional services
16 Least opposition
17 Accreditation recommendations
18 No other options available
19 Total program costs
20 Local politics

Hartley also suggests a method for ranking, involving the development of several categories (essential, desired, marginal) in order to assign relative values to the competing programs, and the preparation of a ranking sheet on which the programs are ranked in priority order with costs and personnel alongside and the cumulative cost specified at each level in the ranking. Pattillo recommends vigorous examination only of those programs that are at the funding margin or 'cut off point'.[12] He suggests a voting process based on the number of evaluation criteria that can be qualitative, quantitative or both. After a vote is taken, the differences are discussed and final ranking established by another vote. Pattillo also raises the very important issue of adequate feedback being provided to the program 'owners' on the reasons their programs were accepted or rejected.

Cheek suggests that a decision card system to assist consolidation of ranking decisions as they change and gradually consolidate.[13] He provides a useful proforma 'decision card' that summarises the proposed program, its goals and the recommended approach for one level of effort. The detailed program is kept nearby for ready reference. Decision cards are ranked and a schedule created by photocopying them, overlapping with headers only showing. This mechanism provides a working tool that is easier than scribing and erasing on an overhead projector or whiteboard, and cards can be re-ranked quickly as priorities and objectives are discussed.

Harrold[14] suggests the use of an 'efficiency advocate' when making any resource decisions. This efficiency advocate is required to participate in the budget decision making with no authority other than to comment and criticise proposed policies and

---

[11] Hartley, quoted in Levacic, R. (ed) (1989), *Financial Management in Education*, Open University Press, Philadelphia, Chapter 10.
[12] Pattillo, J. W. (1977), *Zero-Based Budgeting — A Planning Resource Allocation and Control Tool*, National Association of Accountants, New York, Chapter 1.
[13] Cheek, L. M. (1977), *Zero Base Budgeting Comes of Age*, Amacon, New York, pp. 82–9.
[14] Harrold, op. cit, p. 133.

suggest alternative or more cost effective solutions. It is then up to the decision maker (committee) to balance the efficiency viewpoint against educational and other considerations.

The following shows an example of a budget summary for a high school. Each entry on the expenditure pages is supported by a program.

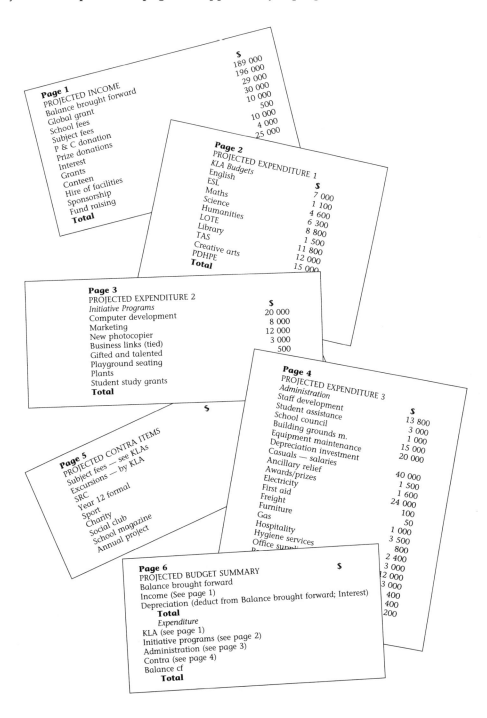

Page 1
PROJECTED INCOME
Balance brought forward
Global grant
School fees
Subject fees
P & C donation
Prize donations
Interest
Grants
Canteen
Hire of facilities
Sponsorship
Fund raising
Total

$
189 000
196 000
29 000
30 000
10 000
500
10 000
4 000
25 000

Page 2
PROJECTED EXPENDITURE 1
KLA Budgets
English
ESL
Maths
Science
Humanities
LOTE
Library
TAS
Creative arts
PDHPE
Total

$
7 000
1 100
4 600
6 300
8 800
1 500
11 800
12 000
15 000

Page 3
PROJECTED EXPENDITURE 2
Initiative Programs
Computer development
Marketing
New photocopier
Business links (tied)
Gifted and talented
Playground seating
Plants
Student study grants
Total

$
20 000
8 000
12 000
3 000
500

Page 4
PROJECTED EXPENDITURE 3
Administration
Staff development
Student assistance
School council
Building grounds m.
Equipment maintenance
Depreciation investment
Casuals — salaries
Ancillary relief
Awards/prizes
Electricity
First aid
Freight
Furniture
Gas
Hospitality
Hygiene services
Office suppli

$
13 800
3 000
1 000
15 000
20 000

40 000
1 500
1 600
24 000
100
50
1 000
3 500
800
2 400
3 000
12 000
3 000
400
400
200

Page 5
PROJECTED CONTRA ITEMS
Subject fees — see KLAs
Excursions — by KLA
SRC
Year 12 formal
Sport
Charity
Social club
School magazine
Annual project

$

Page 6
PROJECTED BUDGET SUMMARY   **$**
Balance brought forward
Income (See page 1)
Depreciation (deduct from Balance brought forward; Interest)
    Total
Expenditure
KLA (see page 1)
Initiative programs (see page 2)
Administration (see page 3)
Contra (see page 4)
Balance cf
    Total

Prepare a similar summary for yourself, estimating the likely figures from last years expenditure.

Page 1 PROJECTED INCOME　　　$	**Page 2** PROJECTED EXPENDITURE 1 *KLA Budgets*　　　$
Page 3 PROJECTED EXPENDITURE 2 *Initiative Programs*　　　$	**Page 4** PROJECTED EXPENDITURE 3 *Administration*　　　$
Page 5 PROJECTED CONTRA ITEMS　　　$	**Page 6** PROJECTED BUDGET SUMMARY　　$

5 Monitoring the Progress of Actual Performance Against Budget

The Principal must realise that the budget task does not stop with the final allocation of funds. It becomes the task of the school staff, under the Principal's leadership, to deliver the programs to students, with each program team responsible for its own operations. Final delegation to sign for expenditure must be made and a list published and filed. An example follows:

Financial Delegation for 1994

In force from 29 March 1994. The following people have authority to sign orders, **up to the limit of their budget** as set out in the budget statement. This includes money allocated in 1993 for 1994, including requisitions, retained funds and global allocation.

Records of expenditure authorised will be maintained by both the authorised delegate and R. Rogers with monthly reconciliation.
J. CRAIG — General, Principal
S. TRACEY — General, Deputy Principal
(NOTE: General includes programs such as office administration, marketing, computer development.)

Principal and Deputy Principal only sign orders for KLA budgets on request of authorised delegate or on evidence of delegate's approval of expenditure.

H. EDMOND — English, ESL, Drama.
J. JACKSON — Mathematics.
R. HAWKINS — Science.
M. POWELL — Humanities.
J. JONES — Technology and applied studies, including Computing studies.
A. VASILOU — LOTE, Library, STLD, ESL, Careers.
M. NGUYEN — Creative arts.
P. BAKER — PD/H/PE.

Subjects that collect material costs are:

Art, Design and technology, Food technology, Textiles and design, Computer studies, Music, Photography, LOTE, Drama, Careers, Sports.

Delegation extends in the appropriate KLAs to cover those materials used **up to the limit of their fees collected to that date**.

Excursions:
Delegation extends to appropriate KLA. Excursions are not intended to make profits. Any profits will be diverted to the relevant KLA excursion fund for an excursion subsidy.

JULIE CRAIG
Principal

The Principal's role as facilitator continues, with:

- close involvement in the *implementation* of the programs that have been budgeted
- supervision
- providing support
- staff development
- judging efficiency and effectiveness.

Revenue and expense are monitored, with program teams and the budget committee receiving regular financial statements. The Principal must ensure that appropriate systems of program accounting and accountability are developed. The remainder of this chapter will deal with this.

A monitoring process must be established by the Principal, so that educational goals and programs will not be placed in jeopardy due to poor management of finances. At least once a term, the expected budget cash flow must be compared to the actual performance of the program. The Principal must also appreciate the need to account to the school community for the stewardship of financial resources entrusted to the school.

The following sheet shows one way a program manager can monitor spending on any one program. If computerised reports are generated monthly (see page 123) the program manager can compare and check the manual records to identify any data entry errors or outstanding orders. Adapt these ideas for your own purposes.

.... High School

Faculty/initiative:

Global budget: $

Date	Details	Texts	Equipment	Equipment repairs	Requisition	Petty cash	Other	Total remainder

Date: 4/09/92

Budget expenditure performance report

Dissection code name	Subdissection code name	Budget	Payments	Unpaid orders	Net transfers	(Refunds)	Balance	Budget remaining	% used
Human resources Dt	Staff Development	7000.00	6762.06	0.00	0.00	(0.00)	6762.06	237.94	97
	Dissection totals:	7000.00	6762.06	0.00	0.00	(0.00)	6762.06	237.94	97
Staying on	General	21000.00	7407.30	2717.50	0.00	(0.00)	10124.80	10875.20	48
	Dissection totals:	21000.00	7407.30	2717.50	0.00	(0.00)	10124.80	10875.20	48
Student assistance	General	4930.00	2490.11	0.00	−898.00	(0.00)	3388.11	1541.89	69
	Dissection totals:	4930.00	2490.11	0.00	−898.00	(0.00)	3388.11	1541.89	69
School council	S/Council Gen.	0.00	170.63	0.00	0.00	(0.00)	170.63	−170.63	****
	Dissection totals:	0.00	170.63	0.00	0.00	(0.00)	170.63	−170.63	****
Admin and office	Awards and prizes	2000.00	545.71	0.00	0.00	(0.00)	545.71	1454.29	27
	Bank charges/errors	0.00	12.00	0.00	0.00	(0.00)	12.00	−12.00	****
	Electricity	25000.00	18007.85	0.00	0.00	(0.00)	18007.85	6992.15	72
	Equipment	11000.00	1451.00	0.00	0.00	(0.00)	1451.00	9549.00	13
	Courier freight	100.00	28.60	0.00	0.00	(0.00)	28.60	71.40	29
	Gas	12000.00	7064.72	0.00	0.00	(0.00)	7064.72	4935.28	59
	General	5200.00	6457.43	5.80	20.40	(0.00)	6442.83	−1242.83	124
	Hospitalities	1000.00	753.62	0.00	0.00	(0.00)	753.62	246.38	75
	Petrol/oil	2000.00	1042.78	0.00	0.00	(0.00)	1042.78	957.22	52
	Dup/paper/toner	18000.00	10898.31	1680.00	0.00	(0.00)	12578.31	5421.69	70
	Postage	300.00	0.00	0.00	0.00	(0.00)	0.00	300.00	0
	Stationery	6000.00	3795.68	147.12	0.00	(0.00)	3942.80	2057.20	66
	Telephone	6000.00	5582.17	0.00	0.00	(0.00)	5582.17	417.83	93
	Waste disposal	3000.00	1344.56	0.00	0.00	(0.00)	1344.56	1655.44	45
	Calmic	500.00	550.62	0.00	0.00	(0.00)	550.62	−50.62	110
	Water8000.00	4497.94	0.00	0.00	0.00	(0.00)	4497.94	3502.06	56
	Petty cash	1000.00	173.34	0.00	0.00	(0.00)	173.34	826.66	17
	Dissection totals:	101100.00	62206.33	1832.92	20.40	(0.00)	64018.85	37081.15	53
Building maintenan.	Insurance	2771.10	6187.85	156.00	0.00	(0.00)	6343.85	−3572.75	229
	Maintenance build.	7000.00	8286.95	140.00	0.00	(0.00)	8426.95	−1426.95	120
	Dissection totals:	9771.10	14474.80	296.00	0.00	(0.00)	14770.80	−4999.70	151
Ground maintenance	Maintenance grounds	7000.00	4721.70	250.00	0.00	(0.00)	4971.70	2028.30	71
	Dissection totals:	7000.00	4721.70	250.00	0.00	(0.00)	4971.70	2028.30	71
Salaries	Casual teachers	35500.00	29948.93	0.00	0.00	(0.00)	29948.93	5551.07	84
	Dissection totals:	35500.00	29948.93	0.00	0.00	(0.00)	29948.93	5551.07	84
Equipment maintenan.	Insurance	0.00	1205.00	0.00	0.00	(0.00)	1205.50	−1205.50	****

Accountability

Finance committees would be well advised to consider end-of-term monitoring meetings as the minimum required to ensure that the school budget is on track — monthly meetings are preferable. Regular reporting to community bodies or to school councils should be standard procedure. This will clearly demonstrate the integrity and professionalism of the school.

Frequent monitoring will signal an early warning if finance expenditure exceeds expectation. You will need to know how your income and expenditure reflects the budget, so that you can revise budgets and/or school plans. Monitoring will also give you a good idea of when funds may be available for investment so that these opportunities are not lost.

A useful suggestion, assisting committees responsible for maintaining their own records of expenditure and keeping track of outstanding deliveries and accounts, is to take either a spare copy of the order voucher or a photocopy and to store this in a folder, filed under the particular dissection.

...take a photocopy of the order voucher...

An excellent tip is to ensure that an order voucher is written for *every* transaction, no matter how small. This will ensure that paper work directly supports all expenditure. The record folder can carry a running record of expenditure in each dissection. This is more current than the 'books', as they tend to be written up and reconciled after each month's trading.

The 'books' only represent the cheques written and do not indicate outstanding deliveries and accounts. Although this information is obtainable from the order system, you will usually have several order books in action at any time and it would take a detailed search of records to find the outstanding information.

Cash Flows

Most often budgets are monitored by means of *cash flow*. In simple terms, this is a plan and report of your expenditure for each month. Your actual expenditure will either be in excess of or fall short of your anticipated expenditure. At the top of the next page is a sample cash flow for one area of the budget.

Cash Flow Report for the Month of . . . .

Area	Anticipated expenditure	Actual expenditure	Variance
Staff expenses			
Casual relief	$1448.00	$11 055.00	+$393.00
Human resource development	$400.00	$600.00	–$200.00
Computers	$2376.00	$2376.00	$0.00
Admin staff relief	$100.00	$300.00	–$200.00

You might have planned your major 'computer' expenses close to the end of the financial year, to gain benefits from sale prices.

While 'cash flows' may seem unnecessary and you may think it better to wait until you see what you spend, this will mean that you cannot plan the whole year and you may miss opportunities for investment. It really does not matter if your actual expenditure differs from what you anticipate (except of course if you are overspent each month and look like being overspent all year!). Cash flows will give you a progressive idea of how you are going.

Budget Performance Indicators

Performance indicators provide a way of assessing and evaluating programs and actions within an organisation. They are useful for gaining an idea of how things are going, whether a change of direction is needed, and where to go next. Indicators need to be:

- valid — that is, they must measure what you say they are measuring
- reliable — that is, if you did it again would you get the same results?
- relevant to your programs
- acceptable to the school community
- simple and complete
- practical
- cost effective
- related to the outcomes you want to achieve.

The following are some of the types of performance indicators:

- Workload indicators are raw figures. They could be used to refer to the number of students choosing to go on a particular excursion.
- Productivity indicators are expressed as a rate or a percentage. They could be used to refer to the percentage of parents attending meetings.
- Output indicators are expressed as quantities related to objectives. They could be used to refer to the number of school developed resources sold to other schools.

● Efficiency indicators are expressed in terms of ratios of input to output. They could be used to refer to the dollar versus teacher cost when looking at professional development.

● Effectiveness indicators are designed to measure whether or not a program is successful. They could be used to refer to the number of students who improved their scores on a specific rating as a result of a specific program.

● Cost indicators compare actual costs to budgeted costs. They could be used to compare the original budgeted cost, the actual cost and any variance between the two comments.

Within your budget projections you will need to indicate how you intend to measure your desired outcome and evaluate whether or not the expenditure was worthwhile. The above indicators will be helpful in this process.

Issues for Reflection

♦ *Make a note of any points you wish to remember about accountability, cash flows and performance indicators.*

Audits

Whenever you take over as the Principal of a school, it is wise to ask for an audit so that you have a clear perspective of the financial management of the school. It is also a good idea to prepare a financial statement for an incoming Principal before you finish at your school. You should, in turn, be able to anticipate this courtesy from your predecessor at your new school. An audit still remains a sound idea. You would be wise to maintain a regular external auditing program, in order to provide valuable assessment updates of school records. An audit will serve to monitor the activities of your administrative staff, as well as to check on the efficiency of the management procedures that you have developed for your school's finances.

In a school that has reasonable financial efficiency, an audit is a relatively painless procedure. You do need to be careful, however, as the auditor may not be a school system specialist but could be an agency auditor employed to check on schools. If this is the case, the auditor's focus in regard to your records may differ slightly from in-house appraisers. One of the more common criticism of schools made by auditors is the infrequency of banking. Because of the heavy pressures on time it can be difficult to get to the bank as regularly as recommended, but common sense should apply, and you should not leave large sums of money in the school overnight.

...don't leave large sums of money in the school overnight...

The following documentation should be readily available and up-to-date to assist the auditor.

- Staff list
- Cash books (both a/c)
    — OASIS: reconciliation
    — Cancelled vouchers
    — Cancelled cheques
- Bank statements
- Deposit books
- Cheque books
- Payment vouchers
- Investments held
- Register of financial items
- Attendance books
    — Ancillary
    — Teachers
    — Casuals
- Record of teachers' leave
- Equipment register
- Condemning register
- Loans register
- Cash register: Daily 'Z' report (last five months).

Financial Statements

Most systems require an annual reporting mechanism. This should be readily available from the figures compiled throughout the year. At the end of the prescribed financial period, the school will be able to report its state of finances and will also be able to comment on areas where either income or expenditure differed significantly from projections. These reports should be made available to all interested bodies — the community, school council, staff and system, as required. A written synopsis usually assists understanding and can be used for verbal reports.

The three forms following show:

- the format required by the Department of School Education in NSW (below)
- a primary school financial statement following this layout (page 129)
- a report for a high school, generated by OASIS Finance, also following this format (page 130).

OASIS Report

Income

Global grants	230 935.94
Fees general/elective	31 243.95
P & C	10 000.00
Interest	2 662.44
School activities	65 396.76
Hire facilities	1 539.00
Extra curriculum	43 675.82
	385 453.91

EXPENDITURE APPLIED TO:

Educational programs

Initiatives	–25 582.83
Computer education	–5 884.73
Extra curricula	–53 199.17
School programs	–64 185.85
Human resource development	–8 047.31
Special programs	–64 486.27
Student assistance	–4 152.61
	–225 538.77

Administrative programs

Casual salaries	–47 550.78
Telephone/fax	–7 487.47
Trade waste	–2 412.17
Rates	–7 309.29
Energy	–34 957.07
Office supplies	–47 813.65
	–147 530.43

Capital

Building and ground maintenance	–25 851.39
Equipment	–17 456.23
	–43 307.62

Miscellaneous

Investments	–100 000.00
Bank discrepancies/charges	–9.71
	–100 009.71

TOTAL EXPENDITURE	–516 386.53
Surplus/deficit for year	–130 932.62
Retained earnings	138 655.00
Funds carried forward	7 722.38

Financial Statement — Primary

PUBLIC SCHOOL — 12 months ended November 30 1992

Funds received from	1992		1991	
Global	$35 415.69		$30 878.13	
Grants	16 168.07		15 210.77	
Service levy	10 221.00		5 796.45	
Library–from parent body	3 000.00		3 000.00	
Educational programs	41 643.39		41 039.91	
Hirings	5 005.00		4 700.00	
Book clubs	3 595.80		2 507.35	
Interest	3 252.49		2 058.45	
Requisition, 1992	10 911.59			
Other	2 631.50	$131 844.53	1 815.13	$107 006.49
FUNDS APPLIED TO:				
Educational programs				
Computers	1 287.95		2 272.33	
Creative and practical arts	2 225.57		577.74	
Library and book clubs	5 855.79		5 907.73	
ESL and STLD	712.88		1 200.08	
Music	4 913.38		5 565.02	
Sport	13 262.06		21 232.26	
Excursions	16 184.50		11 557.58	
Publicity	1 533.32		2 382.88	
Human resources development	6 216.45		3 011.34	
Stock, 1992	10 414.28			
Other	3 026.05	65 632.23	1 415.50	55 122.46
Administration				
Gas and electricity	7 417.84		5 237.80	
Telephone and post	2 072.08		2 281.95	
Stationery and textbooks	8 087.81		6 478.98	
Maintenance	8 045.79		5 576.01	
Water waste and sanitation	7 150.12		7 738.81	
Casual relief	13 034.01		9 787.44	
Other	3 154.67	48 962.32	4 829.12	41 930.11
Capital expenditure				
School equipment		5 864.68		3 007.97
TOTAL EXPENDITURE		120 459.23		100 060.54
Surplus for year		11 385.30		6 945.95
Funds at bank 30/11/1991		9 049.88		
Funds at bank 30/11/1992		20 435.18		
Investments 30/11/1992		20 000.00		

Financial Statement — Secondary

Statement of Receipts and Payments of School Funds, Year Ended 30/11/92

	1992	1991
Income Received From Global grants Fees Donations (principally P and C)		
TOTAL	477 869.00	
Expenditure Applied To Educational Programs (A)		
Total A	193 130.00	
Administrative Programs (B)		
Total B	216 735.00	
Capital Programs (C)		
Total C	51 241.00	
TOTAL EXPENDITURE (A+B+C)	61 106.00	
(Total Income — Total Expenditure)		
SURPLUS DEFICIT FOR YEAR (D)	16 763.00	
ADD FUNDS B/F FROM PREVIOUS YEAR Cash Bank Investment Balances		
TOTAL FUNDS BROUGHT FORWARD (E)	94 283.00	
TOTAL FUNDS C/F to next year (D + E)	111 046.00	

Recording and Book Keeping

For many years, book keeping in schools has been performed by clerical assistants who maintain a basic account of receipts and payments. Initially these were recorded in single entry journals and, later, in records that had columns of accounts. The former were journals in which one page simply recorded income in chronological order and another page recorded payments in a similar manner. The latter was a more comprehensive record in which columns (dissections) were drawn up for receipts and payments. Each income column had to be reconciled with a corresponding expenditure column. It was, therefore, easy to know the particular income being maintained by each dissection, and the balance after expenditure was deducted. Generally, expenditure could not be made unless income was generated for that specific purpose.

Under the current approach to budgeting, it will be necessary each year to establish separate dissections for income and expenditure. This will be relatively easy, because many of the columns will retain the same or similar titles in each year. However, there will be a need to change or introduce new dissections, reflecting the particular income and expenditure initiatives relating to a particular year.

At the end of the preceding year, all money in the school account(s) will have been added together to produce a balance that was then carried forward. This balance is obtained by closing off the expenditure record after, first, ascertaining the amount of funds needed to meet unpaid or unpresented accounts. The amount unpaid/unpresented is deducted from the balance of the account and the residual figure is the balance to be carried forward to the next year as an income (or loss).

Depending on the outcome of your income/expenditure balance, you may have been able to add to your reserves. Alternatively, if expenditure exceeded income, reserves will be reduced. If the school reserve fund has been eroded in a particular year, care will need to be taken in framing the following year's budget to ensure that this deficit does not become a trend. It will not do for the school to run out of funds!

If the record of transactions is maintained manually, it would be wise to establish two separate books — one record for income and one record for expenditure. These books preferably have a number of dissection columns available in them. A double page spread may be enough to contain the average school's requirements but, if not, a second opening may be necessary. If needed, separate accounts for other purposes could be kept, although the downside of this is that it increases the book handling time of clerical staff and reduces the probable interest credits available due to smaller balances being in each account.

Issues for Reflection

♦ *What is your current system of book keeping and what are the changes that need to be made?*

Many schools are switching to computer recorded accounts, or will soon be expected to do so. These have the advantage of speed of entry and they can be programmed to make the necessary calculations for you in a split second. These spreadsheets are slow to set up, unless you have access to a system designed package, or you may wish to purchase a commercially designed program. Either way, the investment of time in establishing these records will be well rewarded with the speed of the calculations and the range of information generated for you by the computer. Printouts are easily obtained and these will be valuable in your monitoring of the finances of the school through your regular finance committee meetings.

OASIS Finances

In NSW, all schools will be on the OASIS system. Many schools are already on OASIS administration. Before considering going on OASIS finance you will need to be on OASIS administration. Below are some points to consider when starting on OASIS administration.

- Think about how many computers you need and the quality of printer you require.
- Decide who is to coordinate the implementation.
- Work out the best place for the terminals and the space required. (Think about Occupational Health and Safety issues.)
- Think about security and where your back-ups will be stored (off the premises!)
- Training of staff is essential. You need to think about training for yourself, your teaching staff and, most importantly, your administrative staff.
- Briefing of all staff. You may want to look at having volunteers to help key in the initial information, but think about privacy and civil liberty issues. You need to consider who has access to the computer in this regard.
- Work out the forms you think you will need — the most useful thing is to start with collecting student information.
- Work out the information headings you will need to put in for all students.
- Enter your data and file it as it is received. Retain a hard copy.
- Accuracy of entry is important or errors will always stay with you.
- Establish daily back-up procedures.
- Your first products will be an admission register, class rolls, other rolls, age and grade information, and census information such as religion, etc.
- You might want to extend this to include a sports roll, extra curricular activities, travel information, family information and ethnic background information.
- You will also have access to attendance information on a daily/weekly basis.
- You might then think about staffing information.
- Decide how the system is to be maintained.

...privacy and civil liberty issues...

Once you have all this established, you will need to have other systems operating before you think about OASIS finance. Some of these include the following.

- Put your equipment register on record. (Establish a room register — size, dimension, floor covering, etc.)
- Do a stocktake and formally write off stock not current or already written off. Then key in existing stock.
- Identify and establish a list of your regular suppliers.

OASIS finance system is a fully integrated accounting system designed for NSW schools. Facilities include an equipment register, a stock register, student invoicing, a cash register, records of purchases and payments, reports (on supplier transactions, student transactions, dissections, budget summaries, and those designed by the school), and budgeting so that the Principal can monitor actual income and expenditure against those expected.

Reports that can be generated in OASIS finance include:

- a budget review report
- a budget report for textbooks
- an allocated, committed and uncommitted report
- a transaction statement report
- a dissection ledger report
- a dissection summary report.

OASIS is a tool and, like all good tools, it requires constant maintenance — to make it a useful tool requires time and commitment.

If not already operating with a complete chart of accounts, OASIS finance means that you will need to develop a chart of accounts. This is very confusing initially. Appendix G contains a chart of accounts for you to use as a starting point (see page 229). While it is a NSW Department of School Education high school chart, it can be easily adapted for a non-government or primary school. On the next page, there is a summary of the requirements of a chart of accounts.

Appendix H on page 239 provides a useful checklist supplied by the Department of School Education in NSW to its Principals. Many of these procedures are common sense and it is clear that the Principal, as financial manager of the school, need not do the actual arithmetic and bookkeeping. What the Principal must have is an understanding of sound fiscal and management procedures. This chapter is a starting point. The best way to learn is by talking with colleagues and sharing ideas. The basic rule is **don't be afraid to ask**.

Issues for Reflection

♦ *Make a note of the names of any other schools you could ask for assistance.*

For those with qualms about the impact of management requirements emanating from school based financial management, the results of a survey of staff in Edmonton, Canada, after three years of school based budgeting, regarding the impact of school based budgeting may be of interest[15]. Fears that time and energy would be diverted from educational programs, and the role of the educator be replaced by that of the bookkeeper, proved to be unfounded. The ultimate conclusion was that 'Johnny would learn better under school-based budgeting' and that the educational role of the Principal was enhanced, particularly in the areas of instructional planning and evaluation. This study also showed that, while the responsibility of the budget rests with the Principal, the formation of the budget is done as a consultative exercise with a committee acting as an advisory body and encouraging appropriate procedures involving teachers in a decision process, producing a greater commitment to goals and budgets, improved morale and generating a sense of belonging. This is worth noting and acting upon.

The benefits from open program based financial management are many. The school and committee are able to share in the management of education. The efforts of the entire school are coordinated and the really important activities are identified — as well as their cost. Once we recognise these aspects, and how they relate to each other and to the broader goals of the school, we have a powerful tool to manage and allocate resources and to achieve the school community's objectives. The focus of this process is on the primary purpose of the schools existence, i.e. teaching and learning.

Chart of Accounts

0010–199	Current assets	
2000–3599	Non-current assets	Statement of financial position (balance sheet)
3600–4099	Current liabilities	
4100–4499	Non-current liabilities	
4500–4999	Equity	
5000–5099	User charges	
5100–5199	Con. fund allocations	
5200–5999	Other revenue	
6000–6399	Employee related	Operating statement (profit and loss)
6400–7899	Maintenance and working	
8100–8199	Depreciation and amortisation	
8200–8499	Grants and subsidies	
8500–8699	Other services	
8700–8799	Clearing suspense accounts	
9000–9299	Extraordinary items	

---

15   Caldwell, B.J. (1980), 'The Principal as Institutional Leader. Impact of school-based budgeting, *Challenge* xx, (i), p. 126, M.E. Sharpe, New York.

The feeling that everyone is working toward a common goal is enhanced. The school is made more effective because the organisational planning and financial planning are integrated.

To maintain the economic metaphor, the 'bottom line' for the educational management remains educational leadership. Management roles exist only to support and complement educational leadership roles. Leaders cannot neglect their managerial roles, but good management is not in itself sufficient. Margaret Nadebaum, Chief Executive Officer of the Western Australian Ministry of Education sees no conflict:

> 'In my view there is no dichotomy at all between our roles as educators and our roles as managers. We must be skilled managers in order to optimise our effectiveness as educators. Our job is to decide about the most effective configuration of resources (physical, financial and human) in order to ensure that the prime function of the school — quality education for children — is achieved.'[16]

---

[16] Nadebaum, M. (1990), 'Noah or Butterfly? The Changing Role for School Principals in the 1990s'. Paper presented to the National Conferences of the Australian Secondary Principals' Association, the Australian Primary Principals' Association and the Australian College for Educational Administration, Hobart, October, 1990, p. 17 of the *Conference Papers*.

CHAPTER 5

Communication, Negotiation and Conflict Resolution

Robyn Johnston

This chapter has been designed to help Principals and aspiring Principals examine the effectiveness of their own communication and of the communication activities and systems of their schools. The chapter focusses on some general principles concerning communication, and provides frameworks for the enactment of some specific communication episodes. It is important to view this information as representing guidelines or frameworks, rather than as recipes for success, because communication effectiveness is rarely achieved though recipes for instant success or quick-fix solutions. This chapter also focusses on some conditions that increase communication effectiveness in groups or work teams and at the broader school or organisational level.

Embedded within the text are a range of Case Studies and Issues for Reflection that, hopefully, provide 'triggers' to facilitate consideration of similar or related situations that have or could occur in your school.

The chapter also includes a series of checklists and proformas. Again these simple instruments are offered as guides to assist you in the process of self-evaluation and assessment of the communication systems currently existing in your school.

The following case studies illustrate diverse aspects of the communication process and communication systems in schools. Among other things, they show that communication is a process involving not only message sending but also resulting in meaning creation on the part of the message receivers.

Difficulties including misunderstandings and disappointments can often arise in any situation involving communication. These difficulties may result from language differences or the provision of too little information. On other occasions, the problems result from meanings that don't match the intention of the message sender being interpreted from the words and actions of the message senders by the various 'audiences' or message receivers.

Case Study: The final visit

Margaret Jones is the mother of four children who have all attended the local community secondary school. She has had contact with the school for 14 years and attended the normal school functions that go with being a parent — parent–teacher nights, occasional P and C meetings, speech nights and canteen duty.

Her final visit to the school follows the Speech Night of her last son through the school. Her son has won a prize for Geology in Year 12. As the prize is a perpetual trophy, it has to be returned to the school for engraving and display in the school trophy cabinet following the presentation at Speech Night.

Margaret goes to the school office to return the trophy and decides that she would really like to thank the staff of the Science Faculty for the support and help they have given her son. She has always felt that the Science staff have been particularly helpful and encouraging to her children. Margaret approaches the clerical assistant to hand over the trophy and tentatively, asks to speak to the Science Head-teacher.

The clerical assistant immediately informs Margaret that third period has 15 minutes more to go and that the science staff are probably teaching. Margaret says that, as this will be her last visit to the school, she would particularly like to thank the Science staff for their efforts. The clerical assistant announces that she will pass on any messages and proceeds to take the trophy from Margaret and put it in the trophy cabinet. Margaret smiles, steps back from the school office counter, wistfully looks around the foyer into which the trophy has been restored, and walks to the door out of the school for the last time.

Case Study: Staff meetings at Longbar Boys' High

Longbar Boys High is a suburban high school with an enrolment of 1000 boys and a staff of 71 (59 of whom are teachers).

The Principal, Malcolm Kennedy, schedules five general staff meetings per year — one at the beginning of the year and one towards the end of each term.

The dates of the general staff meetings are scheduled in the school calendar at the beginning of each year.

Malcolm Kennedy travels a considerable distance to school. He is aware that a large number of his staff also travel some distance to school and that a number of staff have personal commitments after school, so he schedules the termly staff meetings for the 40 minute lunch break, rather than for after school.

On the morning of each staff meeting, Malcolm discusses the staff meeting with his Deputy Principal, William Brown. Together they develop a list of issues they wish to raise at the meeting. These points are typed up to be distributed to staff at the meeting.

Staff meetings usually commence in the staff common room about 10 minutes after the beginning of the lunch break. Staff on playground duty are excused from attending the meeting. The remaining staff settle down to eat their lunch while they attend the meeting.

Malcolm opens the meeting and indicates that he wishes to address the staff on a range of issues. Topics usually include issues relating to student behaviour, school staffing, parental complaints, school finance and forthcoming major events. Sometimes Malcolm uses the staff meeting to issue a general reminder about expectations of staff and the failure of some staff to fulfil duties required. He usually speaks for 10–15 minutes on these issues. If any staff member is leaving or taking extended leave Malcolm takes the opportunity to thank, and wish him or her well. He also wishes all staff a relaxing holiday break at the end of term meetings.

The Deputy Principal, William Brown, then reminds staff about routine administrative duties. Topics usually include completion of returns, student reports, roll marking and security of rooms and equipment during the vacation period.

Malcolm, a strong supporter of the teachers' union, then invites the union representative to talk concerning any matters needing comment. He then opens the meeting to staff questions. Sometimes one or more members of staff raise issues. If these are contentious, Malcolm attempts to deflect the issues by promising to investigate. Usually the meeting ends with no questions, because the lunch break is at an end and the students are returning to their classrooms. Occasionally a staff member may raise an issue that produces a brief heated debate between Malcolm and the staff member concerned. When this occurs, Malcolm returns to his office feeling somewhat upset, as he dislikes conflict.

Malcolm's staff feel that they are frequently denied the opportunity to voice their opinions about important issues in the school. A number of staff members feel that Malcolm only holds the meeting at lunch time to avoid prolonging discussion.

Issues for Reflection

♦ *What messages could the situation in the Case Study about 'The Final Visit' give parents about the school and how the school operates?*

♦ *What messages do you think the meeting described in the Case Study about 'Staff Meetings at Longbar Boys' High' gives staff about the willingness of the school executive to discuss issues or consult with staff?*

♦ *Do you think the hidden messages that parents or staff may take from these sorts of messages are, in fact, the messages the school wishes to send?*

♦ *Have instances of this kind of communication occurred in your school?*

Both of the Case Studies just presented show something about how schools communicate to their 'audiences'. They also perhaps show how communication (through what is *not* said) has the potential to lead to unintended meanings.

Assessing the Communication Effectiveness in your School

Communication could be seen as the life blood of any organisation, whether that organisation is the size of BHP, or is just a small corner shop with two or three employees, a metropolitan city secondary school, or a small one teacher school near Broken Hill. Many organisational and work unit problems are frequently attributed to communication difficulties. *Identifying that communication is a problem, however, is not a solution.* Frequently, what is required is a much deeper analysis of exactly what aspects of communication are creating problems.

...what aspects of communication are causing problems...

If communication is a problem in your school, it may be that the problem resides with individuals who lack key interpersonal skills. It may be that the communication linkages between and within units require attention. It may also be that the way (frequency and manner) information is communicated creates problems.

Sometimes communication 'symbols' used by an organisation are not being used as effectively as possible or they, in fact, send unintended messages to their various audiences. The communication opportunities at both an individual and organisation level may not be being seized. Any of the above conditions may result in the organisation failing to function as effectively as possible and all may become areas requiring examination and evaluation by the organisational leaders.

Schools, like any organisations, may provide quality programs, good working conditions, and have access to the financial support they require but, without key personnel willing to evaluate their own communication effectiveness and that of their school, they will not be maximising their resources.

To begin the task of evaluating the effectiveness of communication in a school, it is necessary to reflect, first, on what you understand of the term communication and, secondly, on what you see as comprising the communication systems that exist or need to exist in your school.

What is Communication?

There are varying definitions of the term *communication* in the available literature and there has also been considerable debate as to what constitutes *effective* communication. What could be seen as emerging from this debate is that:

- communication needs to be seen as a 'meaning creation' rather than a 'message sending' process. As a communicator, the leader needs to strive towards ensuring that the intended meaning has been created by the message receiver, rather than focussing on message sending.
- frequently, the meanings created by receivers of communication do not necessary result from the words or rhetoric of the message sender, but from the actions (or lack of actions) of the message sender.
- communication can intentionally (or unintentionally) be used for a number of purposes. These purposes include informing, persuading, motivating, co-ordinating, controlling, and empowering members of any organisational group. Conversely, communicative and meaning creation can also misinform, demotivate and disempower.

What are Communication Systems?

A school organisational communication system encompasses the mechanisms or structures in place in a school, enabling the staff of that school to communicate with each other and with those audiences outside the school. From a narrow technological perspective the system will include the telephone, fax and electronic mail systems. The organisational communication system, however, should be seen from a much broader perspective. It should be seen as including the various methods of print communication that are used within the school and the education system:

- the daily routine sheet
- the P and C/School Council newsletter
- the memos that are distributed to staff
- the policy documents that emanate from regional office and the centre of the system and federation
- the display of information on school noticeboards
- the school prospectus
- school information directories.

The organisational communication system can also be seen as encompassing the various meeting structures that exist within the school:

- assemblies
- general staff meetings
- faculty meetings
- special taskforce meetings
- some of the informal meetings that are part of the everyday life of a school.

Other components of a school's organisational communication system could be seen as including staff development days, performance review meetings, selection and exit interviews or any formal opportunity that the school leaders set up to discuss professional development with staff members.

The Principal's Role in Communication

The Principal must play a major role in providing both an effective communication model and also mechanisms or structures for communication in the school. Principals must:

- communicate effectively on a one-to-one basis with staff members, students, parents, colleagues from other schools, and personnel from regional and central offices.
- work effectively with small decision making committees, both as a leader and as a member of those groups
- establish and monitor progress of small groups of which they are not members. Such groups often provide the basis of future school policies, programs and initiatives
- establish structures that allow for rapid and accurate communication within and outside the school (reporting back opportunities for small formal task groups, update of committee progress, easy access to school and system policy statements and documents)

...small formal task groups...

- ensure that the image of the school to those outside the school (parents and the community) is that which the school intends
- communicate effectively with large groups (including the students of the school) so that the vision and direction of the school is clearly articulated, understood and shared by those within and outside the school.

Principals expect to spend considerable time evaluating the effectiveness of a curriculum, or a program, or the structure of a timetable, however, they may be less likely to really evaluate and attempt to change or develop the communication patterns and processes of their schools, even though extensive amounts of time are spent communicating with staff, students, administrators and parents. To begin the process of such communication evaluation, it is useful to start by considering the behaviours that are currently used and the systems that exist. This can lead to further questions about the systems and meanings that need to be created.

Issues for Reflection

♦ *Who are the audiences with whom the school communicates (both internal and external to the school)?*
♦ *What are the varying purposes or functions of communication?*
♦ *What are the various communication systems and strategies currently operating in this school?*
♦ *Should other communication systems or structures be implemented in the school?*
♦ *What are my communication strengths and weaknesses?*
♦ *What are the communication concerns of my staff — what do they wish to know more about?*
♦ *What are the communication strengths and weaknesses of my staff?*
♦ *How could I improve the way I communicate?*
♦ *How could the school improve the way it communicates?*
♦ *What are the dominant images that this school communicates to the community, and to its clients (students, staff, the system)?*
♦ *What are the key events that communicate something about the values for which this school stands?*

Interpersonal Communication Skills

Before examining some job specific interpersonal communication skills that a Principal needs to develop and evaluate, it is worth noting that:

● communication competency needs to be seen as a multi-dimensional concept that requires in individuals:
  (i) the ability to comprehend the dynamics of a communication event
  (ii) an interpersonal sensitivity, that includes the ability to perceive accurately one's own internal feelings, the meanings and feelings of others and the demands of the communication situation
  (iii) a repertoire of communication skills
  (iv) an ethical approach to communication. This includes a concern for the wellbeing of all participants and the willingness to share the responsibility of the outcome of the transaction with other communication participants.[1]
● competent interpersonal communication depends not only on the Principal but also on the person(s) with whom he or she is interacting. Communication is about the exchange of meaning and requires the willingness of all interactants to engage in communication.

Thus, competent interpersonal communication is a two-way process. Both the sender of communication and the receiver have a responsibility and an interdependent role in any communication interaction. Both parties, in fact, influence the sending and receiving of messages.

---

[1] Littlejohn S. and Jabusch. D. (1982), 'Communication Competence Models and Application', *Journal of Applied Communication Research*, Vol. 10, no. 1, pp. 29–37.

A competent message sender needs, in the process of sending messages:

- to be sensitive to the non-verbal responses being instantaneously generated by the receiver
- to monitor his or her message sending behaviour, in accordance with how that message is being received and the way the receiver is creating meaning In this way, the message sender is equally a message receiver, and the act of effective communication requires that communicators be sensitive to this process.

Checklist of Communication Skills

The following proforma provides a checklist of some of the interpersonal communication skills Principals must use in carrying out their tasks.

Communication Skills

Skills	Do well	With whom/when	Could improve	With whom/when
Giving instructions				
Delegating				
Giving feedback				
Persuading				
Resolving conflict				
Inspiring				
Negotiating				
Counselling				
Disciplining				
Solving problems				
Being assertive				
Listening				

Consider your own performance using each of these skills. Do you always display these skills well or could you improve? Do you use some skills well in some situations or with some people but, with others or in other situations, frequently feel that you could have displayed a more effective performance? (As well as answering these questions about your own performance you could also consider having your executive complete the proforma about themselves and about you.)

Our Assumptions about People at Work

In reflecting on ways in which we may improve our workplace management and communication, it may be necessary to, first, consider some of the values and beliefs we hold about work and how people should work. These values provide a foundation for the way we behave interpersonally. A self-assessment of our inherent assumptions about people help us know ourselves more clearly and, therefore, assists us to see how we may be understood by others.

A Self-assessment Exercise

The paired statements at the top of the facing page could be seen as representing pairs of extreme positions on a continuum of beliefs about people at work. Each pair contains the opposing extreme positions.

Select, from either Column A or Column B, the position from each paired set that comes closest to your belief about employees in the workplace.

An American organisational theorist, Douglas McGregor,[2] explained the significance of the values and beliefs of managers as a determinant of their management style. He proposed that managers' views of the nature of human beings could be seen as falling into one of two categories. Each category of beliefs, he argued, tended to shape the fundamental personal theories held by managers and applied by them when working with their staff.

...a Theory X manager...

2 McGregor, Douglas (1960), *The Human side of Enterprise*, McGraw Hill, New York.

Column A	*Column B*
1 People really only avoid work because their work is unsatisfying.	**1** It's only natural that people do as little work as possible.
2 People will have better attitudes to work and work more responsibly if they have access to information.	**2** People should really only have access to that information they need to carry out their tasks. Too much information is confusing or unsettling.
3 Asking employees for their ideas broadens their perspectives and provides the organisation with new insights and new energy.	**3** Staff perspectives and ideas are usually too restricted to be of any real use to the organisation because it doesn't take into consideration constraints of the particular school.
4 Staff perform better if they are accountable for their standards and mistakes.	**4** People lower their standards if they are not monitored fairly tightly.
5 Its better to be open with staff, even when the news is painful.	**5** Employees should only be told good news because that's all they are really interested in.
6 If employees set their own goals, they tend to set them higher than a supervisor would.	**6** If employees set their own goals and standards their work output will decline.

One category of beliefs, he claimed, resulted in managers operating, from what he called a 'Theory X' position. Managers who held 'Theory X' type beliefs tended to assume that employees inherently disliked work and would, where possible, attempt to avoid or make a minimal effort at the workplace. For this reason, these managers believed that staff should be coerced, tightly supervised and were unable to exercise self-direction or self-control.

McGregor claimed that, at the other extreme, were managers with 'Theory Y' assumptions about the way people worked. This perspective assumed that employees found work as natural as rest or play, that workers could exercise self-direction and self-control if they were committed to the organisational objectives and that workers had the ability to make innovative suggestions — this prerogative not being solely in the domain of the manager.

If your responses to the self-assessment exercise came mainly from Column A, you could be considered a manager with 'Theory Y' beliefs. This probably means that:

● you have confidence in other people
● you feel comfortable about listening to others non-defensively
● you seek and give feedback reasonably comfortably
● you delegate responsibility.

In some situations, extreme 'Theory Y' behaviour can lead to ineffective managerial performance, because there is a danger of excessive delegation of authority, inadequate coordination of subordinate activities and unrealistic confidence in subordinate ability.

If you tended to believe more strongly the statements in Column B, your beliefs are closer to those beliefs of a 'Theory X' manager. This attitude is likely to manifest in behaviours that communicate that:

- you don't have confidence in others
- you may be unwilling to delegate
- you are concerned with close monitoring and control of your staff
- you are probably less concerned to share information with them and to seek information from them.

McGregor certainly realised that many managers displayed behaviour that would place them away from the extreme ends of the continuum and closer to a central position.

School leaders should consider the beliefs underlying their managerial behaviour. They should also reflect on their actions, because it is these actions that communicate messages to staff, students and the school community. Sometimes Principals may believe that they are displaying 'Theory Y' type behaviours when, in fact, their staff would consider that their behaviour was closer to that of a 'Theory X' type leader.

Issues for Reflection

- *Which of the above characteristics apply to your own behaviour?*
- *Have you ever worked for a 'Theory X' boss?*
- *Do your executive staff show 'Theory X' or 'Theory Y' tendencies?*
- *Are there some situations in which you adopt a 'Theory X' position and others in which you would seem to be applying 'Theory Y' beliefs?*

Some Frameworks for Enhanced Interpersonal Communication Skills

Listening

In 1981, researchers completed a study that attempted to examine how people spend their time in communication activities (Barker et al.)[3] The following pie chart shows the participation percentages for each major type of communication activity in which individuals participate.

---

[3] Barker, L., Edwards, R., Gaines, C., Gladney, K. and Holley F. (1981), 'An investigation of Proportional Time Spent in Various Communication Activities by College Students', *Journal of Applied Communication Research*, Vol. 8, pp. 101–9.

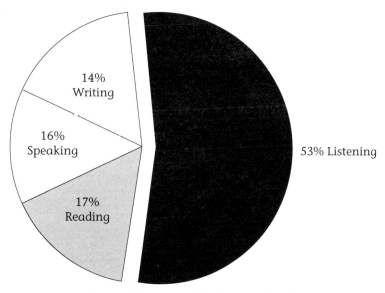

Types of Communication Activities

This pie chart shows the importance of the skill of listening. The listening category has been broken down into listening to mass communication messages (radio/television/public address/lectures) and listening to face-to-face messages. The former category accounted for 32% of the subjects' communication, whereas the latter accounted for 21% — still more than any other type of non-listening communication activity.

Interestingly, we receive little training in listening, and probably spend little time evaluating or refining our listening behaviour or practising our listening skills — unlike the time we spend in reworking our writing or rehearsing our public speeches.

Studies of management activity have also shown that those in leadership positions may spend up to 60% of their time listening (W. F. Keefe)[4] and it is, therefore, important that we focus more of our attention on the way we listen.

Some Common Misconceptions About Listening

- *Listening is hearing:* Hearing, barring illness, injury or ear plugs, cannot be stopped. Our ears pick up sound waves and transmit them to our brains, whether we like it or not.
- *Effective listening is natural:* Sometimes we deliberately do not listen. Instead of paying attention, we block out what we hear because it is irritating, we think we have heard it before, we do not want to know, or we do not think it is important. We have all had the feeling of not being listened to!
- *All listeners hear the same meaning:* Physical and psychological factors, social roles, cultural backgrounds individual interests and needs, all can influence and distort the raw data so that we create different meanings for what we have listened to.

---

[4]   Keefe, W. F. (1971), *Listen Management*, McGraw Hill, New York.

Poor Listening Behaviour

Poor listening behaviour can result from many factors. The message may be boring or difficult, the medium may be inappropriate, or the environment in which we are situated may not be conducive to attentive listening. The fact that we all can think more quickly than someone can speak (our brain is capable of handling a speaking rate of about 4 times the speed of the average speaker), produces an excess of thinking time that can become a source of poor listening behaviour. Any of these factors can produce one or some of the following poor listening behaviours.

- *Pseudo listening* or imitating the real thing: Pseudo-listening occurs when we give the appearance of being attentive but, behind our polite facade, we are masking thoughts that have nothing to do with what is being said.

    Another version of the pseudo listener is the 'I'm in a Hurry' listener. This person never slows down enough to allow you to finish the conversation. This person listens while shuffling papers or opening mail, and sometimes takes phone calls in the middle of your conversation. More often than not, the speaker in this situation tends to hurry his or her conversation and walk away.
- *Stage hogging:* Stage hogs are really only interested in expressing their own ideas and don't really care about what the other person is saying. They are able to rapidly turn the focus of the so-called discussion to themselves or their views, rather than really listening to the perspective of the other.
- *Selective listening:* All of us are selective listeners at times. We screen out TV or radio commercials, listening really only for the time, weather or traffic condition reports. Selective listeners often only listen for the part in which they are interested and neglect the major meaning intended by the person sending the message.

...selective listening...

Sometimes the selective listener takes the position of listening carefully for fact, and interrupts to point out any error of fact even if not essential to the message.

- *Assimilation to prior messages:* We all have a tendency to interpret messages in terms of similar messages remembered and valued from the past. The phenomena is called assimilation to prior messages. The danger of the process arises when we go overboard and mutilate current messages to gain consistency with what we have heard and believed in the past, e.g. negative reports of a teacher's performance in the past may predispose us to really only listen for negative comments about the present.

- *Defensive listening:* This occurs when we take often innocent comments as a personal attack and, thereby, rapidly begin to defend ourselves — sometimes aggressively. This occurs because we can begin formulating mental arguments to counter what is being said instead of genuinely listening to what is being said. There is a great danger of this occurring during interactions that involve discipline or negative feedback.

- *Insensitive listening:* Insensitive listeners fail to listen beyond the words of the speaker. They accept what is said at face value. It is sometimes easier than really listening and the listener often misses the real meaning of the message. These listeners often neglect the non-verbal messages that accompany message sending.

Issues for Reflection

    ♦ *Do you display any of the poor listening behaviours?*
    ♦ *Are you aware of your staff displaying some of these behaviours?*
    ♦ *Do you have any strategies to help you overcome these behaviours?*

Effective Listening

Effective listening is active rather than passive. It requires you to get inside the speaker's mind so that you can understand the communication from his or her point of view. It requires you to suspend your own thoughts and feelings, and adjust what you see and feel to your speaker's world.

Active listening also requires listeners to listen with their ears, their eyes and their minds. They take in the objective information by listening to the literal words that are spoken. However, every message contains more than words. Speakers also communicate subjective information — their feelings and emotions — through other vocal sounds and nonverbal signals.

No matter how good you are at listening for total meaning, there still remains the potential for misunderstanding. That is why effective listeners verify the completeness of their understanding by asking questions. The asking of questions can minimise distortions and clarify misunderstandings.

A Framework for Effective Listening

- *Be motivated:* As a listener, be willing to make the effort to listen and understand. No amount of advice is likely to improve listening effectiveness if the listener is not really willing to make an effort or to examine the way he or she listens. This can involve picking a time and place that are conducive to listening.
- *Make eye contact and maintain a natural level of eye contact:* People judge if you are listening by looking at your eyes. Making and maintaining eye contact (without staring) focusses your own attention and encourages the speaker.
- *Show interest:* Use a relaxed natural posture and gestures. Use your body to communicate interest. Make use of simple encouragers, such as smiles, head nods, etc.
- *Avoid distracting actions.*
- *Be emphatic:* Don't project your own needs and intentions on to the speaker. Put yourself in the speaker's shoes and reflect the feeling he or she is expressing. Listen to both what is *said*, what is *not* said and *how* it is said.
- *Paraphrase* or restate what the speaker has said in your own words: The effective listener uses phrases, such as 'What I hear you saying is ...'. This mechanism allows you to check that you have understood what the speaker is saying. Clarity checks are vital when critical decisions must be made.
- *Don't interrupt:* Let the speaker complete his or her thoughts and words before you respond. Avoid second guessing or assuming that you know what the speaker is going to say.
- Retain the *confidentiality* of what you hear.

...don't interrupt...

Providing Feedback

As discussed earlier, in any communication episode, the receiver of a message, provides the sender with at least *some* non-verbal feedback about his or her response to the message that he or she is receiving. This is one level of *feedback*.

Feedback can, therefore, be seen as *any* communication to a person, giving that person information about an aspect of his or her behaviour and its effect on you.

As a Principal, you are expected to provide feedback to staff and students about their performances, and to parents about the performances of their children. Sometimes the feedback will be a face-to-face communication experience. At other times the feedback will be provided in written form (e.g. reports, newsletters, letters). The provision of feedback, in any form, is an important task that can have significant consequences for the functioning of members of your school.

Research shows that *effective feedback* leads to *increased employee performance. Feedback can help subordinates set and achieve goals.* Adequate provision of feedback from a trusted superior also seems to be related to both the *level of communication satisfaction* and *workplace commitment* felt by employees.

Giving positive feedback is usually a pleasant experience. This type of feedback is readily accepted and perceived as accurate, because it tends to fit what people wish to hear and already believe about themselves. Conversely, giving negative feedback can be uncomfortable. The fear of offending or having to cope with the various forms of recipient defensiveness often means that negative feedback tends to be minimised or glossed over. Negative feedback is more likely to be accepted in situations when it comes from a person with high status and credibility. However, negative feedback which in any way appears subjective, and unsupported by facts or specific examples, is less likely to be received well. This is a particular problem for less experienced Principals, those from lower ranks of the organisation or those whose reputations have not yet been established, e.g. Principals who have recently arrived in a school, or have come from another region may have difficulty providing negative feedback to members of staff who have been long entrenched in the school.

Feedback provision has become particularly important in those working environments in which Principals have a greater responsibility for the promotion of staff. Feedback about performance will not only be necessary to justify some promotion decisions but will also play a role in shaping future career moves by staff.

Similarly, in a work environment where there is more delegation of responsibility to subordinates, Principals will need to be able to give feedback to staff members and seek feedback from their supervisors in terms of performance in regard to newly delegated activities.

A Framework Giving Effective Feedback

The following behaviours can make your provision of feedback more effective.

- Focus on specific behaviours rather than on general impressions when giving either positive or negative feedback. Avoid statements such as:
  — 'I'm really happy with the good job you did.'

— 'You need a little more experience.'
— 'I am not happy about the way the foyer area was cleaned.'
— 'You weren't quite ready for the role. I am sure next time will be different.'
  Specific statements should be used to tell the recipient *why* you are being critical, or complimentary, or what is expected of them in the future. An example of a specific statement may be:
— 'The instructions you gave to the children about dress and behaviour on the excursion were very good. They now know what the school expects of them.'
— 'The way you included the new staff members in the curriculum review by having them talk about what they did on the topic in their past school really allowed them to feel part of the process and that they were contributing to the new program.'

● Keep the feedback job-related and never criticise someone personally because of an inappropriate action. The moment the feedback becomes personal or able to be attributed to a personal quality, rather than a work behaviour or action, it is likely to provoke an emotional reaction and the reason for the negative feedback is likely to be overlooked. You may be attempted to tell someone they are lazy or not putting in enough effort (which may well be true). However, this type of comment becomes personal. You are better to suggest, 'Your programs have been incomplete the last two times I examined them.'

● Keep the feedback goal/task/behaviour orientated. Feedback should not be given in order to dump your own anxieties on someone else, e.g. 'I am fed up with having repeatedly to ask...'

● Choose the time for giving feedback carefully. The closer in time the feedback is provided to the action/behaviour requiring feedback, usually the more effective the feedback. Immediate feedback, however, can be a disaster if either you (as feedback provider) or the recipient is angry or upset. In these situations, delay may be required in order to ensure the focus is on the specific behaviours and actions.

● Make sure the feedback is understood. Ensure that your feedback is concise yet complete, and that the recipient understands your meaning. Establish checks for clarity. Encourage recipients to rephrase your message and future expectations to check that the meaning is complete in face-to-face situations. If you are providing written feedback, consider providing opportunities for your recipients to clarify this feedback, if necessary. Invite your audience to contact you or reply to your comments where appropriate.

● Adjust your feedback to fit the person. You should always consider the recipient's past performance, areas within his or her control, and his or her future potential when providing feedback. Do not neglect to provide positive feedback for high or consistent performers. Everyone likes to be acknowledged and feedback provides such acknowledgement. For poor performers, particularly those whose work may be deemed unsatisfactory or who are unjustifiably seeking promotion, feedback should be frequent and very specific. It is important, in situations that may result in an unsatisfactory decision, that the connection between acting on the feedback and the negative sanctions should be made explicit.

Case Study: Feedback on a selection interview at Woodsville Primary School

Woodsville Primary School is a large inner city primary school. Of its school population, 79% came from a non-English speaking background, including a small percentage of Aboriginal students.

The Principal, Maria Broughton, advertised for a Deputy Principal. The job advertisement listed among the essential criteria a demonstrated ability in the leadership of staff, skills in curriculum implementation and the professional development of staff, sound understanding of multicultural and Aboriginal perspectives in the curriculum, and understanding of the welfare needs of the students in a multicultural school.

David Brown, one of the executive teachers at the school applied for the position. David has been teaching at Woodsville for nine years, the last five of which he has held the position of an executive teacher. David sees himself as a strong classroom teacher, even if somewhat traditional in his classroom management practices. A keen sportsman, David has been involved with school sports teams. David has taught a Year 5 class and was the grade supervisor for Year 5 at the time of his application.

There were 17 applicants for the position at Woodsville and six, including David Brown, were shortlisted for interview. The selection panel comprised the Principal, the Principal of a neighbouring school, and the President of the school council. The committee selected Robyn Laverton, a young executive teacher from a nearby school, for the position.

David was rated as unsuitable for the position. Among the reasons given for David's rating was that David was unable to demonstrate a detailed understanding of student welfare needs in a multicultural school. David saw welfare as equating with discipline and strong classroom management skills. While David had completed a B.Ed. degree and had attended a few inservice course over his time at Boxhill, he was not a great believer in professional development activities, arguing that solid teaching of the basics was the major requirement of primary teachers. David was not able to demonstrate a clear understanding of recent trends in curriculum implementation and was not able to demonstrate that he understood the differing needs of students from Aboriginal and non-English speaking backgrounds. Both the President of the school council and the Principal were aware of some difficulties David had experienced with an Aboriginal student in his class.

David was very disappointed when he learned that he had not been selected and indicated to colleagues that he believed that the younger female teacher had been chosen because 'the system' was encouraging Principals to promote female teachers and younger teachers, and that he had missed out because of these factors.

David sought feedback from the Principal, Maria Broughton. Maria told him that he had submitted a good application for the position and that he was well regarded by his colleagues. Maria said that the successful candidate was an outstanding candidate, that it was a close decision but that the successful applicant had a Graduate Diploma in Multicultural Education and had worked as a regional consultant in multicultural and Aboriginal education. She suggested that David might like to go on 'some' inservice courses in multicultural education.

When David was asked by a close friend on the staff about his feedback David replied, 'I didn't learn much, mate. She said I was okay but that the other applicant was better.' He continued, 'I told you they want more women in senior positions, that's what it is!'

Issues for Reflection

♦ *Did the feedback provided by the Principal in this Case Study create the meaning she intended?*

♦ *Would the meaning David gained help him gain promotion in a similar situation?*

♦ *What were some aspects of feedback that should have been provided to David by his Principal before he applied for this position, to enhance his opportunity at interview?*

♦ *In what ways can feedback be seen as part of the staff development process?*

Disciplining

A task that often causes managers as much anxiety as providing negative feedback during any form of performance review is the task of disciplining an employee. Unfortunately, as a leader, it is inevitable that you will need to confront employees and discipline them for unacceptable actions. While in some situations it may be possible to turn a blind eye, hope the problem goes away, or hope the offender seeks an appointment in another school, avoiding confronting disciplinary problems can impact negatively on the morale and behaviours of other staff members. Your lack of action may communicate hesitancy or indifference to other staff members. It can communicate that some issues are not very important or that you, as Principal, favour some staff members over others.

Disciplining both staff and students can be seen as the actions taken by a Principal to enforce the standards expected within the school. It need not be seen as an entirely punitive activity and, in fact, may provide a stimulus for individual professional development.

In taking any disciplinary action, the following factors should be taken into account:

● the severity of the problem
● the time the problem behaviour has existed
● the frequency and nature of the problem
● the employee's previous work performance history
● any factors outside the staff member's control
● appeal mechanisms.

Consideration of each of these factors, before you confront the individual involved, is essential. This will help you determine if disciplinary action is necessary. Once you have decided that some form of confrontation is necessary, the steps discussed under the following heading will form a reasonable basis for your interaction.

A Framework for Effective Discipline

Prepare for the Interaction
Ensure that you have investigated the situation fully, particularly if the problem has been reported to you and you have no first-hand evidence.

Some information you should gather in your preparation includes:

- were there any mitigating circumstances that could justify the actions of the employee?
- is the employee aware that the actions/behaviours were unacceptable?
- has the employee been provided with any warnings in relation to incidents of a similar kind?
- have those warnings been documented?
- has there been any form of contract or undertaking previously given, guaranteeing that the behaviour would not happen again?

Conduct the Discipline Session in Private
Do not discipline employees in public and ensure that you are not interrupted by phone messages, or by people dropping in.

Be Specific about the Problem Warranting Discussion
Even when disciplining over a minor incident, explain exactly the behaviours/actions that are causing you problems.

Be very careful when you are attempting to discipline employees about attitudes. Attitudes move into the personal arena and are only a problem if they manifest themselves as unacceptable behaviour.

After explaining the specific behaviour causing concern, indicate how this behaviour is negatively affecting the individual and school effectiveness. You may also indicate any specific regulation and rules that are being violated, if this is appropriate.

Ensure that the employee is understanding the issue being addressed and your position regarding it, through questioning if necessary.

Listen to the Employee's Side of the Story
Even if you think you have gained all the evidence you need, allow your employee to explain his or her side of the situation. Apply your own listening skills by paraphrasing what the employee has said to ensure that you have understood. Make sure that your non-verbal behaviours indicate that you are listening and that your listening is neither defensive nor selective. If the situation is serious, you should keep a record of the employee's perspective.

...attempts to divert discussion...

Maintain Control of the Direction of the Interaction

Be alert to attempts to divert discussion from the issue being addressed. If the employee wishes to raise other matters, indicate that these issues will be addressed but keep those issues separate so that you can manage them one at a time and not become distracted. If necessary, note down the additional issues so that you can return to them when you are ready.

Establish a Strategy to Prevent the Problem Recurring

This is an important step in disciplinary interviews. Encourage employees to state any plans they have made to prevent the recurrence of the problem. This encourages staff members to formulate their own solutions to the problems.

Conflict Management

Conflict is a natural phenomenon of organisational life. The potential for conflict is increased as a result of contemporary management practices and structures that emphasise coordination, greater self management and autonomy in work groups and schools, increased delegation and responsibility, reduced supervision and central control. Participatory decision making makes conflict unavoidable.

Conflict can have positive dimensions. Conflict between individuals, and between and within groups, can stimulate creativity, innovation and change. Conflict is a mechanism that often challenges us to examine the ways we do things, to find more effective ways of achieving goals or to set new goals.

Conflict, however, can have a negative effect if allowed to fester unresolved, or to escalate to an unmanageable level. As a consequence, the skills of conflict management and conflict avoidance are vital for leaders to ensure organisational effectiveness.

Some of the skills mentioned earlier in this chapter, such as listening, providing feedback, goal setting and persuasion skills, all play a major role in effective management of conflict. The competent display of these skills will often reduce the possibility of false perceptions of other actions, unclear meanings and the distortion of information as causes of conflict.

Conflict Management Styles

Communication is the essence of the way people manage conflict. When communicating, in conflict situations, individuals often resort to a characteristic style of communication, thereby handling every conflict situation in a similar manner. Effective conflict managers are those individuals who tend to have a range of conflict management styles that they adopt according to the situation, those with whom they are in conflict, and the importance of the situation.

Listed below are some typical conflict management styles displayed in conflict situations. No single style is always the best style. It is important, however, for those who manage people to focus on their own repertoire of conflict management approaches and, if necessary, attempt to develop and use different approaches according to the situation.

- *Avoidance/withdrawing:* The style of conflict management involves backing away from the area of conflict. It is the act of disengaging or eliminating the conflict from consideration. On some occasions, avoidance is an appropriate strategy — particularly if the concern is not impacting on the functioning of the school or the quality of work of the protagonists. A typical avoidance conflict behaviour can include choosing not to address an issue with a staff member but encouraging that staff member to seek a transfer, or hoping the issue will resolve itself.

...avoiding conflict...

- *Compromising:* This is solving a problem by mutual concession. Both parties in this situation get something out of the solution, even if this is not either party's first option. While neither party may be completely satisfied, in many circumstances, this may be the best option. It is important that the conflicting parties place some value on the proposed solution. This means that, when the Principal is the third party in a dispute, he or she tests the acceptability of the possible aspects of the compromise with those involved in the dispute.

This will be a frequent method of resolution in processes such as timetabling or allocation of additional duties.

- *Forcing:* Forcing involves the exertion of pressure, or compulsion (using intellectual, physical moral or ethical means) to reach a solution. When the conflict involves the breaking of clearly documented and publicised rules, Principals may find their authority allows, or even necessitates, they use this option in some situations. The danger of using this style of conflict management solely is that the substance of the conflict is not addressed and the mode of resolution may lead to the harbouring of resentment and cynicism in the Principal, the school or the system. This approach allows little opportunity for the protagonists of the conflict to learn or grow productively from the experience.
- *Smoothing:* Smoothing occurs when what is offending or disagreeable is minimised, and the protagonists move on from the conflict situation feeling things aren't as bad as they had first thought. The Principal who employs smoothing will attempt to explain or gain some understanding of the problem and probably present the situation in a different light. False minimisation may produce short-term gain, and potentially sets a pattern for the need for ongoing smoothing and perpetuates lack of resolution of conflict.
- *Confronting/problem-solving:* This means that facing the problem is the basis of the conflict management, rather than avoiding the conflict or smoothing over it. Once individuals are forced to confront problems and recognise the conflict, they can then explore the various elements of the conflict. This can lead to the identification of areas of agreement and potential elimination of at least *some* perceived causes. This may not totally eliminate all causes, but can at least minimise some areas of perceived differences so that compromise becomes possible and manageable.

Consider a conflict situation in which a teacher is seeking the suspension of a student claimed by that teacher to be highly disruptive. The Principal knows the child to be difficult, but also knows that the teacher frequently has fairly serious classroom difficulties. The Principal may avoid the issue by simply hoping it will go away or may say that he or she will investigate and then do nothing. A smoothing approach will involve an attempt to convince the teacher the problem really is not as bad as he or she thinks. A compromise may be reached in that the child may be removed from the teacher's class. A forcing approach may be to tell the teacher to deal with his or her own problems. A confronting/problem-solving approach may be to really address the origin of the conflict and, if it does lie in some of the teacher's management inadequacies, to help the teacher with the development of a strategy that may increase his or her classroom management skills and overcome some deficiencies and the ensuing difficulties. At the same time, some form of behavioural contract with the student (if fault lies with the student) will be negotiated.

Types of Conflict Management

Once you are engaged in a conflict situation, you must determine the stage, intensity and importance of the conflict and determine the strategy you will use to assist in the resolution. Among the decisions you may be required to make is whether you are to be a negotiator, mediator or arbitrator.

Negotiation

This involves conferring with another to arrive at an agreement. Such agreement may be total agreement or a compromise. It will probably involve you:

- determining what you can best hope for or the best possible outcome
- determining your bottom line, the worst-case scenario you are prepared to accept
- recognising that you will probably have to settle somewhere in between.

It is best if these positions are considered before you start the negotiation.

As a Principal, you may be called on to play a *mediation* role. This role involves intervention, your task being to help the conflicting parties reconcile their differences, or at least help interpret their differences, so that they can negotiate a solution. It essentially involves helping the parties reach a compromise between their incompatible views.

Arbitration

This becomes necessary if mediation fails to resolve a conflict. It requires the hearing and determination of a case in question, with the arbitrator acting as a judge with the power to decide. Rules, regulations and precedent can form the basis of some of your decisions.

In whatever approach you are expected to adopt, three outcomes are possible from your conflict management strategy:

- win/lose
- lose/lose
- win/win

In some situations, a win/lose outcome will be inevitable. In this situation, one antagonist is the winner and the other loses. This is not a desirable outcome as, in most situations, the loser will tend to carry a grievance that may be as destructive as the conflict itself.

In other situations, both antagonists may lose (a lose/lose outcome). Once again, the grievances felt from this outcome may be as destructive as the lack of resolution.

The most useful outcome will be a win/win situation. Win/win situations occur when all parties agree on the solution and feel they have gained from the outcome. Achieving this outcome requires the conflict manager to be aware of what will be seen as a gain by each of the competing parties.

Sometimes this result can be achieved by consensus. In consensus resolution, the focus moves to the solution rather than the solving of the problem. Conflict is accepted by all parties as existing, and managing the conflict centres on identifying and analysing possible alternative solutions that satisfy all needs.

An alternative approach to achieving a win/win solution is an integrative approach that requires focussing initially on agreement about a higher order or the 'big picture', and the values involved rather than the solutions to the immediate problem. Once agreement is reached about the 'big picture' or ultimate goals, the search for strategies that both parties are willing to adopt to achieve those goals can begin.

A Framework for Managing Conflict

Prepare for Conflict Management

First, make a decision about whether this is a time when intervention is the most appropriate response. You do not always need to intervene. Avoidance or withdrawal may be acceptable. Not every conflict within the school is worth your time and effort. Sometimes avoidance may be the most appropriate strategy, especially in cases that are either trivial, are not impacting significantly on the functioning of the school, or are between staff members or units who are capable of negotiation themselves. Remember, in some situations, conflicts are unresolvable. This is particularly the case when antagonisms are deeply rooted with neither or no parties genuinely willing for there to be any resolution, or not seeing resolution as being in their best interests. If this conflict is not harming the functioning of the school or the staff involved, it may be best avoided.

Homework

Having decided to intervene, some homework is necessary. Know the players in the conflict, e.g. Who are the people involved? ... What interests do they represent? ... How much support do they have? ... How much personal investment on the part of the conflicting parties is involved? ... How important is resolution to each of the parties? ... What will they gain or could they gain?

Assessment

Assess the source and nature of the conflict. Assess whether the conflict emanates from communication difficulties, structural difficulties or personal differences. Often what looks like a communication problem, or is attributed to a communication problem or a personal difference, in fact, will be a difference of goals and values. Resolution, therefore, needs to come at that level. Encourage participants to share their view points and the reasoning behind it.

...the reasoning behind it...

Strategies

Consider the strategies/styles of behaviour you will use or can use in relation to the protagonists and the situation. Think about possible solutions and alternatives (and the impact of these on the protagonists) appropriate to achieve resolution.

Defuse Emotions

Allowing for 'cool off' time is necessary. People can rarely be rational and act in a thinking mode when their emotions are overruling their logic. If a problem solving win/win approach is tried when participants are in this mood, little will be achieved.

Why, How and What?

Focus your questions in moving towards resolution, on the fundamental differences — the 'why', the 'how' and the 'what'. State the problem as a *problem* or a set of obstacles (rather than immediately imposing a solution) and focus on the issues or behaviours of concern (rather than on the people involved). Search for areas of agreement, including higher order goals and a range of possible solutions. Isolate areas of total disagreement and work on strategies that will reduce these areas.

Expectations

When resolution is reached, conclude with a clear expectation of requirements from the previously competing parties.

Case Study: A question of rooms

Mimosa Primary School is situated in a medium size country town. While there is a regular turnover of a small number of staff at the school, there are a number of staff who have been at the school for lengthy periods of time. Irene Miller has been at the school for 15 years, having grown up in the area and returned to teach in her home district after several years teaching in the city. Irene is well liked by the community. She is regarded by parents as a strong disciplinarian who takes no nonsense from the children, sets high standards and insists on the completion of homework. The Principal and the Deputy Principal are reasonably new to the school. The Principal, John Matthews, has been at the school for three years and his deputy, Susan Askew, is in her second year at the school.

After discussing issues related to school organisation, and wishing to develop a more energetic approach to teaching and a greater enthusiasm towards school initiatives on the part of the staff, John and Susan decide that there should be greater rotation of teachers across the grades, because some teachers have been teaching the same grade in the same room for a number of years.

As the school year is coming to a close, Susan Askew, on John's request, draws up the allocation of classes and rooms for the new school year. She has announced at the previous staff meeting that some consideration of new grade and room allocation is taking place.

In developing the allocation for the next year, Susan has identified that Irene Miller has been teaching in Room 3 for eight years and has been teaching Year 5 every year during that time. Susan decides that Irene should teach Year 3 in Room 8, which is not as spacious. Susan believes that the change of grade and room will assist Irene's professional development and broaden her perspectives about the school curriculum and some new initiatives the school wishes to pursue in the coming year. She also sees this as an opportunity to allocate Year 5 to another teacher. Susan also makes several other room allocation changes, including giving herself one of the older darker classrooms for the following year. Having made her decision, she issues a memo to all staff, detailing the class and room allocations for the next school year.

Irene is very upset when she sees the memo. She is angry that she has not been fully consulted about the change. She is also very angry that she has been moved from Room 3. Over the years, she has made Room 3 'her own'. The room is an attractive learning environment, she believes, for a Year 5 class. She also believes that there are some staff members who are quite envious of her room. She decides to confront Susan and demand that she change her decision. She confronts Susan in her office and tells her that she does not wish to leave Room 3 and prefers to teach the 'older children' who need a fairly firm hand. Susan indicates to her that she doesn't intend to change her decision and it is a decision based on sound educational and developmental grounds, because Irene is probably 'growing stale' teaching the same grade for many years. She tells Irene that the change will be good for her and for the students in the school, and that she can play a very influential role with the Year 3 children.

Irene becomes *very* angry and a heated argument takes place between Irene and Susan. It ends with Irene telling Susan that she feels some members of staff are 'favourites' because they try to be showy about new ways of doing things. She says she will take the issue up with the School Council and the Principal. Irene leaves Sue's office in tears and rushes to the Principal's office, where the Principal is in conference with the local district Superintendent. Irene tells the Principal she is extremely distressed about class reallocation for the following year and dissatisfied with the actions of the Deputy Principal. The Principal suggests that Irene return to speak with him when he has finished with the Superintendent. The Superintendent, in turn, advises the Principal, John Matthews, to resolve the issue quickly because Irene is well regarded in the local community and life could become difficult for the school executive if the matter is allowed to fester.

Issues for Reflection

♦ *What approach could John Matthews use to manage this situation?*
♦ *What information should he seek in preparing for managing the conflict?*

Communication Systems

As well as evaluating and developing your interpersonal communication skills, as Principal you need to ensure that there is a high level of satisfaction with the various communication systems and structures within your school. These systems or structures should provide employees with relevant and timely information, and allow these employees to provide others with relevant and timely information. These 'structures' should enable the coordination of the various activities of the school, and should enhance staff motivation by providing opportunities for participation in decision making.

Research evidence suggests that there is some correlation between communication satisfaction, work satisfaction, morale and employee commitment. Communication satisfaction derives from perceptions of the effectiveness of the various communication structures, mechanisms and relationships in any organisation. It has to do with employees being satisfied with communication with their immediate supervisor, communication with top management, media quality, communication quantity and timeliness.

As discussed earlier, communication structures or mechanisms can be seen as including any systems that have been established to ensure people are able to gain and give information. The communication structures or the communication system of a school would, therefore, include:

- small committee meetings and full staff meetings
- assemblies
- selection, appraisal and exit interviews
- parent teacher meetings
- school newletters
- memos, policy documents and directives
- cluster, zone and regional meetings of specific groups
- noticeboards — for staff and students
- special events/activities, staff development days
- school signage
- school prospectus/induction handbooks
- liaison officers within the school to communicate with outside groups.

The Principal, in ensuring that such mechanisms exist and are effective, could be seen as fulfilling the role of communication manager.

Communicating in Small Groups

Much of the communication that occurs involving schools (between staff members within a school and between schools) occurs in small group settings.

These settings include small informal groups that form when individuals meet together in the common room, at recess and lunch, to talk about both work-related and non-work related matters. Essentially, groups of this kind are informal friendship groups. In evaluating the communication patterns in the school, it is important to recognise that these groups are very important communication networks. Information, sometimes gossip, spreads through these groups much more quickly than through formally constituted groups. Groups of this kind often have access to groups external to the school (other school groups, professional associations and community groups). Information gleaned from such access can bring a vital energy to any organisation. Groups of this kind can be used to maintain an informal 'connectedness' in a school and play a significant role in shaping the culture — the beliefs individuals hold about the school concerning the school. Opportunities, including facilities, for groups such as these to come together may need to be encouraged.

Group communication will also occur in the informal meetings among groups that come together to discuss a particular issue, plan a new activity or approach, or pass on some information. These groups may not be part of the formal meeting structure of the school, however, they may eventually provide the bases for the formation of more formally constituted groups.

Groups will also be formally established to achieve a specific task, e.g. new program committees, school activity planning groups, Occupational Health and Safety committees, staff development committees, union groups, school executive, departmental staff groups, and committees of representatives of a range of schools.

So much of the communication in any school occurs within groups. It is in or through these groups (and the communication that occurs within them) that school staff gain information, become interested and motivated, participate in the school's decision making, develop innovations and coordinate their activities. The communication in these groups also provides guidelines as to what is acceptable and is to be encouraged in the school, and what the expectations of other staff members are.

The level of personal satisfaction staff gain from membership of such groups contributes significantly to the success of these groups, both in terms of productivity and task achievement, and the capacity for the groups to maintain themselves so that they can continue to operate. Additionally, the skills individual teachers learn from the roles they play in these groups will provide a basis for their continued individual development.

Considerations that Apply to all Groups

- Any small group that meets over any period of time develops a culture or a common understanding of the sets of behaviours that are appropriate for the way that group interacts. This culture will, for the most part, determine how participants interact with each other, e.g. the level of preparation with which members come to the group, level of contribution of all members, the degree of domination or aggression of members that others will accept. (Reconsider the case of Longbar Boys' High on pages 137–8. How did the culture of the staff meeting shape the interaction patterns?)
- Each group will also determine the roles that individuals play within that group. A role can be seen as a set of behaviours displayed by an individual in relation to the expectations of the rest of the group. A role is something that evolves out of a trial and error process. The members of the group teach each other which behaviours are appropriate, by rewarding and punishing what could initially be seen as trial behaviours.

One group communication theorist, E. G. Borman,[5] has suggested a stimulus–response explanation for the roles individuals take on as members of a group. He argues that the role individuals play is the result of reinforcement received from the

---

[5] Bormann, E. G. (1975), *Discussion and Group Methods*, Harper and Row, New York.

group's interaction over time. To illustrate more clearly, if a member performs a given role, e.g. makes a contribution of information or starts to joke around, the response he or she receives in terms of approval or disapproval (rejection of the idea, ignoring of humour and a call to get on with the task) will either encourage or discourage that person from making a similar contribution. If the group gives an ambiguous response, the member will generally try the role again. He or she will do so until a clear signal is received from the group about the acceptability of such behaviour.

It should be noted that the process of role development (both functional and disfunctional) can be quite subtle. Often a member may not be specifically aware of a group's reinforcement pattern, or even of a group's expectation for the role. (Think how easily a group can fall into the process of criticism and cynicism that eventually becomes non-productive.) Awareness of the role behaviour and group culture often occurs after the role behaviours have been formed and expectations have been developed.

Work Group/Team Selection

There is no single way to select the perfect work team or committee. Work group selection can be based on a number of criteria. Some groups are self-selecting. Participants nominate themselves on the basis of interest. Motivation is not often a problem with such groups.

Other groups need representation from a range of groups and for this reason representativeness will be a major criterion for selection. Ideally, groups will be constituted of members whose role behaviours complement each others. Some of the role behaviours either needed or frequently found in groups are listed below. When these role behaviours are distributed among members of the groups, or at least some members, the group is likely to be productive. One of the most significant behaviours of the designated leader is in fact to encourage (reinforce) the display of both the task and maintenance behaviours.

In selecting a work team, it is worth considering the effects of role conflict. Role conflict occurs when group member needs and interests are at variance with the needs of the group, e.g. a school Principal may find him or herself in a role conflict situation when the needs of the school are at variance with the broader needs of say the cluster or region. What usually happens in this situation is that the individual enacts the role of greatest personal importance, e.g. the good regional group member versus the loyal to the needs of the school Principal. Principals should consider the competing interest of group members when forming groups to work on projects within the school. The table on the next page lists and describes some of the most significant productive role behaviours required by a group.

If a group needs to maintain itself over a period of time there is a further set of behaviours that must also be displayed in a group. These are known as 'group building and maintenance' behaviours (see the table on page 167).

Both sets of roles given in the tables on pages 166 and 167 contribute to the functioning of any group. They both need to be displayed for groups to be both productive and satisfying to group members. Individuals may contribute by adopting a single set of roles or a number of the roles. When these roles are distributed around the group, the task of leadership could be seen as being shared.

Group Task Roles	
Roles	**Typical behaviours**
1 Initiator contributor	Contributes ideas/suggestions, proposes solutions and decisions, and proposes old ideas in a new way.
2 Information-opinion seeker	Asks for clarification of comments, asks for information or facts relevant to the problem, indicates areas of information needed, and seeks opinions of others.
3 Information-opinion giver	Offers facts, information, relevant generalisations, and opinions.
4 Elaborator-clarifier	Elaborates ideas and other contributions, offers rationales for ideas, and presents ideas or suggestions about how suggested solutions would work.
5 Coordinator	Clarifies the relationship between information, ideas, concepts, and suggests strategies for the integration of ideas and opinions.
6 Diagnostician	Indicates what the problems are.
7 Orientater-summariser	Summarises what has taken place, points out departures from goals, and brings group back to the central issues.
8 Energiser	Prods the group into action.
9 Procedure handler	Handles routine tasks, such as seating, arrangement of equipment, and handing out of relevant papers.
10 Evaluator-critic	Critically analyses the groups accomplishments, and checks that consensus has been reached.

The focus of this point has been on the roles and behaviours that promote effective group functioning. Obviously there are sets of communication behaviours occurring in small groups that can have the opposite effect. Typical self-centred disfunctional roles include aggressive struggles for status by deflating the status of others, boasting, criticising, deserting or withdrawal, remaining aloof, appearing uninterested, engaging in irrelevant side conversations, engaging in irrelevant personal catharsis, using the group to work out personal mistakes and feelings, cynicism or acting solely as a representative of another group rather than focussing on the interests of the immediate group. On occasions a group (or the leader) may need to consider whether these behaviours are dominating the life and task of that group.

Group Building and Maintenance Roles	
Roles	**Typical behaviours**
1 Supporter-encourager	Praises, agrees with, and accepts contributions of others.
2 Harmoniser	Reconciles disagreements, mediates differences, and reduces groups tensions by giving group members a chance to explore differences.
3 Tension reliever	Jokes, or in some way reduces the formality of the situation.
4 Feeling expresser	Makes explicit the feeling of the group, and shares own feelings with others.
5 Standard setter	Expresses standards for the group, may apply standards in evaluating the group process.
6 Follower	Goes along with the movement of the group passively, accepts group ideas, and is prepared to be a sounding board for group members.

A Framework for Leading Effective Groups

The task of leading groups requires the enactment of a range of behaviours, many of which are communication dependent. The following framework provides a brief overview of some essential behaviours. It also can be used as the basis of self-evaluation when reflecting on your own group leadership or that of others.

Preparation for Meetings
- Define the purpose of the meeting. Meetings should not be held if there is no purpose or there are inadequate resources (people or information are not available to achieve desired outcomes). In preparing to hold a meeting, it is necessary to clearly specify the purpose of the meeting in advance and to forewarn participants. This allows them time to consider the purpose of the meeting.
- A specific indication of outcomes sought from the meeting should be planned, e.g. does a plan have to be submitted to the school executive? ... Does a report have to be given to a school staff meeting? ... Does a program need to be communicated to parents? ... and by when? ... Does an indication of the degree of support for an activity need to be gained?
- Establish the starting and finishing times of the meeting, and the place in which it is to be held.
- Notify all members and arrange any special resources you may need for the meeting.

Leading the Meeting

- If this is an initial meeting, make some effort to establish a climate of trust and informality with the group. Some attempt may also be made to discuss expectations of each other and the time required in association with the task, to ensure participants have an understanding in advance about what will be expected.
- Informational and structural handouts may need to be provided, and suggestions or plans for the procedures the group will follow in working on the task. (In some more established groups, or with more complex tasks, the procedures associated with the tasks and future meetings may in fact constitute the content of the entire meeting.)
- Establish any special roles that need to be undertaken by members of the group. You may decide that one group member is to play the role of evaluator-critic or standard setter of the group's activity. Most commonly, the task of recording will need to be established.

Structuring Discussion

- Recognise that in decision making/problem-solving groups a process for dealing with each issue or decision point needs to be adopted. Each issue or problem should be defined, sub-issues should be explored, ideas for managing the problems/issue should be encouraged, and the practicality of these ideas should be tested before a decision is reached. Following the decision, clear allocation of action or implementation responsibilities should be made.
- Keep the group goal orientated in relation to the total task of the group and in relation to the particular sub-issues. Be sure the goals/tasks/issues are clearly understood and accepted by all members. This will sometimes take time. Do not rush this stage of the group's activity, as lack of clarity can cause costly problems much later in the group's life, in terms of group productivity and commitment.
- Summarise, at each major step, in problem-solving discussions and at each decision point. Ensure that the summary is accepted by all members as accurate and complete.
- Make a clear transition to each new step on the agenda.
- If decision making is by majority vote, make use of straw polls to see if there are areas of common agreement. This mechanism saves time because, having established where there is agreement, more time can be spent resolving problems where there is difficulty or conflict.
- Equalise the opportunity to participate. Address your comments to the group rather than to individuals, unless individuals have specific items of information not available to the group. Be sure, as leader, you are making eye contact with the group as a whole. Invite quiet members, or those of less status, to speak — particularly if they may have particular information. Try to control compulsive dominating or long-winded speakers.
- Stimulate creative and critical thinking, by applying the principle of deferred judgment. Use questions such as 'How *might* we ...?' rather than 'How *should* we ...?'. Mechanisms such as brainstorming, or working in smaller subgroups on short tasks for short periods of time on the same issue and reporting back

...invite quiet members to speak...

to the full group, can generate varying suggestions and prevent the group becoming locked into a mindset.

● If the group gets solution minded, quickly suggest more analysis of the problems.

● Encourage group members to evaluate information. Look for contradictory argument, look for the worst possible outcome of the decision. Once again, do not be afraid of conflict of ideas. Conflict is stimulating. Conflict, however, needs to be about *ideas* not about people.

● Bring any discussion to a definite close, ensuring that follow up tasks and implementation plans have been clearly assigned.

Characteristics of a Well Functioning Group

Many writers have developed checklists of characteristics of ideal work groups. Some of these ideas are synthesised in the following profile.

Goals/Tasks
Group goals are cooperatively established. If tasks are imposed by others, the goals or tasks are clarified and formulated in such a way that members can commit themselves to achieving them. Groups are prepared to devote time to clarification of goals and tasks.

Commitment
Group members are committed to the task and to each other. All group members do their best to achieve the group goals and to build satisfying relationships within the team and with other significant groups.

Communication
There is willingness to share information that is of value to the group's purpose. Interpersonal communication is two-way, open and accurate. All members participate and clarify understandings of others ideas. Suggestions and criticisms are offered and received. Members are involved, interested and committed to the work, and have a high degree of confidence and trust in each other and their roles.

Leadership
The designated leader is competent and is aware of and sensitive to the needs of individuals, and to the culture of the group. The leader does not dominate (verbally or non-verbally). Group members do not unduly defer to the leader's decisions and do not feel threatened within the group. Different members of the group are in a position, at varying times, to take leading initiatives and the leader encourages the sharing of responsibility.

Conflict Management
The group is comfortable with disagreement and committed to seeking resolution through open negotiation. Conflict is seen as healthy and as affording opportunities to reach innovative creative solutions and to strengthen groups. Conflict focusses on issues, not on personalities.

Decision making
The group has a repertoire of decision making procedures from which the ones most appropriate for the situation can be selected. Group members are in agreement about decision-making procedures. For important decisions, consensus is the rule — with all members sharing in the process. Full expression of members' opposition, as well as support, for proposals is encouraged. Decision making should be accompanied by an implementation/action planning phase.

Evaluation
The group is self-evaluative. It can and does examine how it is functioning, and how the resources of the group are being used. Criticism is frank but focusses on ideas rather than on personal attacks.

Group Evaluation Processes

With so much of the communication and decision making that occurs in schools taking place in small group contexts, it is important that groups become comfortable with the process of evaluating not only the products of the group but also the processes used in communicating and reaching a decision. In some situations, the group will be self-evaluative. In other situations, the Principal or leader of the group may independently undertake a review of the roles and the contribution individuals are making to groups or the effectiveness of the processes the group is using.

The following proforma may provide a useful instrument for the evaluation of group process. Such structured observation schedules can provide more objective evidence for decision making about the contributions of individuals to groups and those aspects of group decision making that are being either best handled or neglected.

Role Behaviour Evaluation Instrument

This role proforma contains behaviours and space to mark/score both the functional and disfunctional roles being displayed by individual group members. At times individuals may not be aware of the frequency or nature of role behaviour, particularly as it appears to affect and actually affects others or the group as a whole. Self-assessment by a group, or assessment by an invited observer, may provide the basis for more productive analysis of behaviours.

Group _____ Date _____ Time _____

Behaviour	Participants' Names							
Initiating								
Information giving								
Information seeking								
Clarifying								
Elaborating								
Evaluating								
Summarising								
Coordinating								
Recording								
Suggesting procedure								
Harmonising								
Encouraging								
Standard setting								
Evaluating								
Withdrawing								
Blocking								
Recognition seeking								
Dominating								

Proforma for Evaluating the Decision-making Process

Group _____   Date _____   Time _____

Issue

Discussion Process Phases	Phase treated—excellent quality	Phase treated—average quality	Phase treated—poor quality or out of sequence	Phase not treated
Discussion of purpose or definition of problem	_____	_____	_____	_____
Problem exploration / Major issues discussed	_____	_____	_____	_____
Ideas for solution generated	_____	_____	_____	_____
Practical solutions explored	_____	_____	_____	_____
Solution action decision	_____	_____	_____	_____
Solution implementation planned	_____	_____	_____	_____

Separate proforma can be used for each major issue about which decisions must be made or solutions found in the group meeting. Analysis of the decision making/ problem-solving process, using the proforma, may reveal phases that are repeatedly being poorly handled or overlooked. Such information provides an indication of where the group can focus its attention particularly in the decision-making process in future meetings.

Organisational Communication Strategies

As Principal, you are responsible for communication in the whole school. So far, this chapter has focussed on a series of interpersonal skills you will require and, hopefully, model to staff to increase the effectiveness of communication in the school. The chapter has also specified some factors that pertain to encouraging effective communication in the small groups that operate within your school. Your responsibility, however, goes further.

It is important, also, that you establish a communication structure enabling all the stakeholders or audiences to be satisfied with the access they have to information and their opportunity to contribute to the communication in the organisation.

It is also important that you establish mechanisms allowing you to share the vision of the organisation, integrate rather than segment the efforts of staff, allow for intelligent and (in most cases) supported decision making, and sustain an organisation with 'healthy' morale.

Some conditions need to be met to achieve this ideal position. These include:

- the presence of individuals skilled in effective interpersonal communication and encouraged for their display of such effective skills.
- mechanisms that genuinely encourage individuals to participate in the decision-making processes and, thereby, *own* the decisions pertaining to their work life. This includes mechanisms that allow for an effective flow of 'bottom up' communication.
- structures that allow for the integration and dissemination of the efforts of small groups. This involves providing genuine communication opportunities for groups to share and coordinate the efforts of their labours. It is important, in providing these opportunities, to allow for recognition, not only within the school staff but, where relevant, within the cluster, region and community.
- structures that allow all staff, at all levels, to both know about and be sensitive to changes outside the immediate school, e.g. at cluster and regional State level. Mechanisms for reporting back what is happening within the education system are essential. Staff do not like to find out what is happening via the national newspapers, or from friends in other schools, or through colleagues in other departments.
- structures that ensure that everyone knows what is required of them.

A Framework for Establishing an Effective Organisational Communication System

- Ensure that the formal communication channels are operating effectively. In any organisation, a most important channel of communication is that which links superior to subordinate. Superiors, by virtue of their position, should have access to formal information more quickly than subordinates, and part of their role is to ensure that subordinates are informed in a timely fashion about new, relevant and important information. Traditionally, the general staff meeting and the departmental staff meeting are the major mechanisms for spreading formal information. Situations, can however, arise where these do not function effectively for the provision of information. This may result from the limitations of those responsible for these meetings, who can act as gatekeepers and not pass on relevant information — sometimes because of time factors or other work pressures. Principals, in fulfilling their obligations as communication managers, need to evaluate the effectiveness of the communication linkages between superiors and subordinates, in order to ensure that relevant and timely information and feedback is provided to and gained from all staff.
- Information accessibility. It is important that staff have access to official information, e.g. policy documents, updates on regional initiatives, etc. Staff should be aware of where they can easily obtain such information, and information of this kind should be regularly updated.
- Schools should have well-established mechanisms to encourage *upward* communication — from subordinate to superior. In small schools, this type of communication may occur informally, however, in larger schools, some form of upward communication system may need to be formalised, especially where staff have limited access to senior staff members. Some schools have introduced initiatives whereby senior students meet with the Principal for lunch to share information. This mechanism could be useful for staff members as well. Staff may have less access or less voice than students to decision making in the school. While Principals may feel that they are available to staff, the staff may take the real message to be 'only bother me if it is urgent', if the Principal spends most of his or her time in the office.
- Part of the communication system of all schools are the newsletters, noticeboards, and daily memo sheets. As Principal, it is important not to overlook these mechanisms.

    Do they help establish the type of culture you wish to see in your school? Are they simply a reminder of important events and routine messages or do they communicate something more?

    Are they used as a place where excellence or initiative from staff or students can be commended or mainly where one kind of excellence is recognised?

    Are they carrying the type of information that staff and parents wish to know about?

    In managing the communication of the school, leaders need to evaluate the effectiveness of such mechanisms.

Small surveys, or interviews with groups of staff and parents may indicate that they would like different types of information in newsletters. Gathering data of this kind may reveal that parents see the current newsletter as mainly a vehicle for recognising excellence in the sporting events by the school's elite athletes, and for making requests for money. As this may be the major regular contact and communication a parent has with his or her child's school, the newsletter can play a very important part in communication.

...the image of the newsletter...

Similarly, staff may wish to have different types of information in the daily notice system operating in many schools. Discussion with staff of their communication needs using this channel can lead to more effective communication provision.

Newsletters, daily bulletins and noticeboards are significant purveyors and determinants of the culture of the school. They can reflect the degree of energy, pride, interests and key visions of the organisation. They help to establish the organisational image for key stakeholders and school audiences.

Case Study: A new Principal's message in the school newsletter

The following letter, from the new Principal, appeared in a school newspaper:
'Congratulations to Bill Brown and Kristly Dungar for their selection in the Zone Athletics teams. Bill's team will participate in the State Championships. Michael Porter has been selected in the Regional Tennis team. Well done!

Some parents will remember Susan O'Neill (Year 12, 1987). She has been selected to represent Australia in the swimming team to represent Australia in the Olympics at Barcelona.

Fifteen Year 8 children participated in the 1992 Red Shield Appeal collection. My thanks to those students for giving up their leisure time to participate in this worthwhile activity.

Parents are reminded that full school uniform is important to maintain the image of the school. Students are expected to wear the uniform at all times. Black jumpers, sloppy joes and athletics shoes are not permitted. Parents, please ensure that your children come to school correctly attired.

Important upcoming dates:
June 7   Year 11–12 parent-teacher night
June 14   Year 7 Mufti Day
June 19   Year 8 exams
June 26   End of Term 2
July 14   Beginning of Term 3

I have attached a letter from the local Council commending our students' behaviour at a recent visit to the Council. It is gratifying to receive such comments.

Best wishes for a safe and relaxing vacation.'

Issues for Reflection

The letter in the above Case Study is typical of many Principal's messages to parents in the monthly school newsletter. The newsletter is also a communication vehicle for students and staff.

- *Does this example give any indication of the vision or direction the Principal has for his or her school?*
- *Does it do anything to enhance the image of the school for its audience?*
- *What are the major communication functions of this newsletter, e.g. to inform, motivate, persuade, integrate?*
- *How interested do you think the major audiences for this newsletter would be?*
- *In what ways could this newsletter be used to communicate more effectively?*

Vision for the School

Examine the symbolic aspects of your school that could be used to communicate the vision you have for the school. If excellence in academic performance is the image you are creating, what are the mechanisms that you are using to communicate this, e.g. is speech night, as it currently operates, really celebrating and encouraging academic excellence? ... are there other methods and strategies you could use?

If establishing an environment that encourages the growth of all students, what are the mechanisms, strategies and infrastructures you are using to communicate to the staff, students and parents that this is the goal.

As Principal and communication manager, you are also the manager of the symbols of your school and need to approach the management of this aspect of communication as seriously as the management of operational structures. This will involve examination of all the mechanisms you have, so that this vision is embedded. Intentional communication of this kind won't happen by itself.

The task of being the communication manager of a school is complex and time consuming. Every activity of any organisation is dependent on communication, and the effectiveness of the communication pertaining to that activity in part determines its success, or at least the perceptions of success. As Principal, therefore, you need to ensure that there are plans and an infrastructure to support that communication.

This chapter has advocated that effectiveness in communication does not come naturally, even though we have all been communicating since birth. Efficacy of communication depends on a sensitivity to the power of communication, a willingness to evaluate current methods, and a preparedness to seek ways of improvement in terms of the needs of your various audiences, to ensure that the meaning you, your staff and your students are creating in their words, actions, structures, symbols and symbolic events is that which is intended.

CHAPTER 6

Marketing your School

Julie McCowage

Where Do I Begin?

In our current system of change, the days of the 'lamington drive' or 'bring a plate' appear to have taken on a new dimension and meaning in developing our school and community relations. Marketing the school has become a crucial and fundamental aspect of school life, as schools compete for enrolments, funds and sponsorship.

...marketing your school...

The words 'Marketing your School' raise many issues. They can mean:

- publicity for the school
- promoting the school
- advertising the school
- promoting the services and products the school provides
- compiling mailing lists
- gaining sponsorship for the school
- developing a rapport with the media
- identifying areas to be marketed
- developing a marketing plan
- identifying key school personnel to be involved, and their areas of talent and expertise
- identifying community members to be involved
- developing priorities and a time line.

What is Marketing? What is Publicity?

The world of marketing and publicity is often seen as mysterious, magical, glamorous, and something difficult to define.

So what is it? It's all about *communication*. Telling people about your services, events, and achievements; increasing their awareness and understanding; presenting your point of view, gaining their attention and leaving an indelible impression! It's about establishing positive images, and stamping your message on the public consciousness. It's the difference between being anonymous and people knowing you exist.

If you want to achieve a goal through communication with the public, you need to develop a marketing strategy designed to achieve a predetermined positive response from the public. Your aim in your marketing strategy is to gain the active support of your school community and beyond, into local business, prospective parents, government agencies, media and sponsorships. By communicating in a planned way you are developing a marketing strategy!

Developing a Marketing Plan

Why concern ourselves with marketing? Why are we doing this? The obvious response is that we wish to communicate more effectively with our public.

Marketing your school is about providing *quality* education and involves making sure the quality educational programs, provided by the school to meet the needs of the students, are well known by the local and wider communities.

It is essential that, in your communications, you convey the message about the programs and services you offer to those who need to know.

You can never take for granted that your school program/service will have built-in community acceptability.

Therefore your message to your stakeholders must clearly express what you are trying to achieve. It is really about communicating in a planned and thoughtful manner with the community you represent and serve.

Your focus, once again, in this market mix is communication and can be expressed in the following phrases.

- Attract the attention of your stakeholders.
- Create interest in your school and what you are offering.
- Highlight a need for the benefits you offer to your stakeholders.
- Respond quickly to those who have recognised your benefits.

...attract the attention of potential customers...

What do our Clients Think?

In order to develop a successful marketing strategy for your school, it is essential that the market planners have a clear understanding about the demands and expectations of those who use the school, both directly and indirectly.

Schools can acquire information fairly easily and in a number of ways. Decisions must then be made on how the information will be used once collected.

- The first step is to decide what information is needed and why.
- The second step is to arrange the information so that it can be easily understood and assimilated.

Qualitative research is an excellent process to develop and is an area that schools are constantly developing.

For instance, how many schools bother to investigate why parents or children choose their school in preference to another? Even more importantly, how many schools investigate why a particular school has *not* been chosen?

This information is crucial to develop an understanding of the perceptions about your school and can become an excellent starting point for your marketing plan.

Remember this research is invaluable in conveying to your parents and community that you:

- value their opinion, and that you are interested in their concerns and suggestions
- will commence the establishment of a partnership within your school for joint planning, strategies and future events
- are actively using research mechanisms to improve the quality of your school
- note, whenever carrying out research, a 'sampling approach' is always sufficient.

What is the School's Image?

The image of the school is crucial in terms of interpreting client demands, the school's performance and planning for the future.

Renihan and Renihan explain that, '... the image which clings to the school may have an impact on expectations of the organisation and performance by the organisation ...'[1]

To acquire information about your school image, it is helpful to have an instrument that is simple to use, and maximises the response and the quality of the information.

...the image of the school...

---

[1] Renihan, F. and Renihan, P., 'The Concept of Institutional Image: implications for administrative action in schools', *Administrator's Notebook*, Vol. 32, no. 1, pp 1–4.

Kenneth Stott has suggested 'Words' (see below) as one example of a means of surveying community impressions. It is important to note that the school selects the words appropriate to its needs.[2]

When you think of our school, what are the words that immediately come to mind? Write one word in each of the small rectangles, expressing how you feel about the school. Do not be afraid to use words that are critical: you will be helping us by being *entirely* honest. If you can't think of any words, we have provided a few to start you thinking.

old

friendly

drab

vibrant

unwelcoming

happy

boring

exciting

dead

attractive

untidy

formal

trendy

old-fashioned

What's Important to the Community, Students and Teachers?

'Making good decisions means finding things out and that, in turn, means effecting positive actions to acquire data to develop your school's marketing strategy.

---

2   From Stott, Kenneth (1992), 'Marketing your school: finding things out', *The Practising Administrator*, March, Vol. 4, no. 1. Published by ACEA.

Finding out issues that are important to the community, the students and the teachers can be very useful. For instance, information gathered can have a major bearing on the emphasis adopted in publicity material. It also allows for appropriate action to be taken in relation to 'product' improvement.

If the school newsletter contains predominantly 'sports' news, is it communicating the appropriate message and image to *all* parents? Or, if the parents have very strong views on discipline, the school's policy must be clearly set out and communicated to all parents.

You may like to design your own survey. This example has been modified from a design by Kenneth Stott[3]:

When you decided on this school, what were the factors that were important to you in making your your choice? Please indicate by ticking the appropriate column.	Important	Not important
A wide range of extra curricular activities are offered. You heard good things about the school. Friends recommended the school. Appropriate student welfare. The examination results are good. Impressed by the school when you visited. Well maintained. You like the Principal. You liked the appearance of the students. Easy to get to. Please add any more factors you wish to the list.		

Look at those items you have marked as 'Important' and select the three most important. Write the most important in Box 1 below, the second most important in Box 2, and the third most important in Box 3.

1

2

3

Remember to survey the views of *all* interested parties — students, community, parents, teachers — and remember research is an 'ongoing process' that needs to be repeated and updated.

---

[3] Ibid, p. 17.

The Strategies for a Marketing Plan

First, find out what your community thinks, values and wants.

- Taking those ideas into account, the school should prepare a mission statement reflecting the school's philosophy and declaring the school's intent in a succinct statement. The marketing plan can then move from the general rhetoric of intent to the more specific plan of action.
- Your educational goals are then clearly defined and communicated to all.
- A strategic plan needs to be established with a timeline and budget for events/expenses.
- Regularly implement your marketing strategy.
- Regularly review your marketing plan.
- Once your goals have been set, it is a matter of consistently communicating them through the appropriate channels and devising a plan to highlight/enhance or introduce them via the school's programmed events or activities established specifically to introduce them.

Marketing Committee

- It is essential that you identify school staff and community members who have talent/expertise in areas such as public relations, organisation, communication, writing, layout, design, visual art, etc. and it is important to marry each individual's skills with the task — thus forming your marketing committee.
- The committee will need to decide on the market with which they wish to identify beyond the school community, e.g. local shops, businesses, residents, library, local government, etc.
- Your marketing committee will need to decide how to communicate the message, e.g. newsletters, advertising (for instance school items, fridge magnets, pens, etc.) and sponsorship.

What are the Benefits of a Marketing Plan?

A marketing plan:
- provides a framework and guide for the school
- provides and sets specific targets for the school
- provides a means to measure progress
- establishes a base for follow-up planning
- facilitates organised thinking
- highlights strengths and weaknesses for the school to work on
- allows and develops dates and deadlines for all
- provides a working document
- sets priorities, realistic objectives and effective solutions
- provides the staff with a common purpose, helping them develop a better understanding of the worth of the whole school

- increases the knowledge the community has about the school
- provides the school with a wider documented understanding of the perceptions and needs of the community
- provides positive support for public education.

Implementing School Marketing Strategies

What are the major sources of communicating that the school has established? First, establish your major forms of communicating, for example:

- prospectus
- newsletter
- class papers, etc.
- school year book
- flyers/cards/invitations
- posters
- school journals
- key learning areas news
- promotional material
- social club
- parents and citizens.

Try the quick action plan on the following page to get you started.

Implementing the Marketing Plan within the School

Tips for all School Print Media

- Be clear about who your readers are and how much they know about the topic being discussed.
- Be sure to have a range of articles to reflect the 'happenings' of the school.
- KISS (keep it simple, stupid) — simple words, short concise sentences and short paragraphs are the ideal.
- Avoid jargon and buzz words that might confuse rather than inform.
- Be sure your stories explain why something has happened, otherwise you will frustrate the reader.
- A bright, uncluttered, visually appealing layout is essential.
- Remember the school colours.
- Use the school logo.
- Quality presentation is imperative.
- If the school is big enough, establish an editorial committee — otherwise make sure you can get support, stories, information from as many people as possible.

How do I achieve good publicity for my school?				
	Number of publications	**Sponsorship**	**Areas of responsibility**	**Circulation to whom?**
Ways of publicising the school within school publications:				
● the school newsletter				
● the class journal				
● the school magazine or newspaper				
● the report card				
● the letter				
● the certificates				
● the prospectus				
Ways of publicising the school outside school publications:				
● media–local press				
● major newspaper				
● radio				
● TV				
● magazines				
● educational journals				

The Newsletter

The school newsletter is a great way to communicate to your community. Ask yourself:

- what is the purpose of the newsletter?
- where is the newsletter going?
- what stories should be included?
- what is the best format for the target audience and the budget?
- how regularly should the newsletter come out?
- what regular items should be included?
- who can provide articles?

● who can provide photos or illustrations?
● how can regular feedback be guaranteed?
● to whom will the newsletter be distributed in the outside community, e.g. doctors' surgeries.

...to whom will the newsletter be distributed?

Once you have decided the *purpose* of the newsletter, it will be easier to decide its contents. Someone must be appointed the job of updating it. Standard headlines for each issue will help create a warm feeling of continuity.

Try to set objectives for your newsletter and then refer back to those objectives regularly to ensure you are implementing them.

The *name* of the newsletter will give the publication its image, so put a great deal of thought into creating a name.

Layout Tips
● The look of any written, printed material should be clean and contemporary.
● Break up the text copy with photos, illustrations, and graphics.
● Use underlining or put things in boxes for emphasis.
● Use a consistent format in both layout and typesetting.
● Make sure the typefaces used are legible.
● Action photos are better than posed static shots.
● Decide the length and format of the newsletter (number of pages, size of pages, number and position of folds, back page design and acknowledgements text, heading font and size)
● Create a unique, recognisable style.

Frequency of Issues
How often a newsletter should be produced depends on:
● how often interesting, relevant and important material is available
● how long it will take to produce and distribute
● how timely and topical it is.

Budget
- Consider ways to recover costs.
- Consider sponsorship possibilities.
- Plan fundraising activities.
- Utilise in-house production to cut costs wherever possible.

The Prospectus

The prospectus is one of the school's key image-makers. It should include:

- the schools mission statement
- a detailed picture of the range of educational opportunities available at the school
- school policy guidelines, i.e. student welfare policy
- routine and extra-curricula activities
- features specific to the school.

You may wish to make a video to accompany the prospectus.
Editorial material may include:

- children's work
- teachers' material, with information about staff, forthcoming events, and practical advice for parents
- Parents and Citizens Association and School Council material
- outsider contributions, from such people as employers involved with work experience, visitors to the school, ex-students and local personalities.

Layout
The prospectus aims to be:

- attractive
- bright
- glossy

Follow the guidelines of your newsletter layout.

Sponsorship
If you haven't already thought of sponsorship for your school prospectus, now is a good time to start.

The Class Journal

The aim of the class journal is to inform parents of classroom activities. It is prepared by students and teachers working together.

Children's work may be accompanied by a brief explanation of objectives, helping parents understand the educational process.

The Report Card

- Layout must be clear and concise.
- Parents appreciate a report that avoids one line entries such as 'could do better'. They should be given a realistic statement of their child's progress.
- The report should *reflect* the total curriculum, and all codes/symbols should be clearly explained.

The Letter

A letter is always most effective for expressing specific communications, i.e. appreciation or congratulations. A thoughtful letter may be a simple helpful solution when dealing with critical comments.

Have a marketing committee member responsible for letter writing after every function or event. This goes a long way toward building parent and community support. Also remember to thank your staff! The children can design thank-you cards and you can have them printed.

Flyers

Flyers are a great way to publicise events, such as 'school happenings'. Keep them concise, humorous, well illustrated, with use of clear type and layout. Use bright A4 or A3 paper.

The School Magazine or Newspaper

The school magazine or newspaper should:

- be student-centred
- be easy to read
- contain a variety of information, relevant articles and creative items
- include a variety of writing styles
- have a clear layout/format
- encourage as much *varied* student input as possible
- reflect the goals of the school.

Have you developed sponsorship for printing and other costs involved in the school magazine or newspaper? Enlist the expertise of staff, students and members of the local community, e.g. printers.

The Display

By displaying students' work or relevant information about teaching processes in strategically visable locations, you are making a persuasive and positive statement about the school. By taking the school to those places where people spend their time, you are informing them about the happenings in your school. Remember *quality* displays are necessary, with school logo and school colours clearly displayed.

Creating a School 'Atmosphere'

Is your school:

- warm?
- friendly?
- inviting?
- clean and well maintained?
- well signed (can you find the office, the staffroom, the sick bay easily?) with signs reflective of the school community?

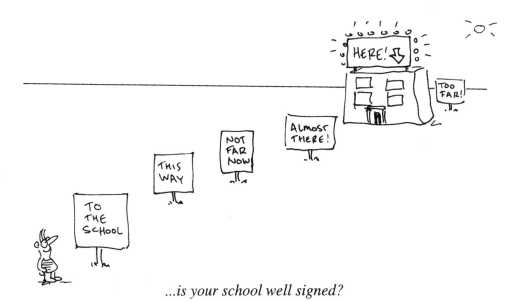

...is your school well signed?

Other areas to be considered are:

- does the reception area of the school reflect the mission statement of the school?
- are there displays of students' work?
- are there *current* copies of newsletters, school magazines, prospectus, and items of interest to browse through?
- is the handling of visitors and/or enquiries prompt and courteous?

Courtesy and Special Days
Prompt and personal attention is always welcoming. Assigning students to greet special visitors and escorting them around the school is one way of displaying a warm welcome and assisting in the development of students.

Telephone Technique

As this is often the first contact with the school, it is essential that the service provided is welcoming, efficient and effective. It is also crucial that messages are communicated effectively and promptly returned. If, due to events, greater demands are placed on staff, they should be supported and situations pre-empted so alternative support can be arranged.

The Community and Parents

The school and community should now be moving forward as one.

The school is a resource in the community and its facilities should be as accessible as possible to that community. Many groups use the school premises and this can be promoted and explored in many ways. These groups using school facilities, are provided with the opportunity to see what 'is happening' in the school by the display of examples of children's work and a cared for environment. They then carry that message back to the community.

Groups from the wider community can also be invited to participate in school events and activities to develop the school–community bond. Members of the wider community can be invited into the school to encourage interaction, for example:

- involving local business people in career forums, resulting in a sharing of expertise
- inviting local personalities to speak on areas of interest
- helping in local charity drives
- participating in local cultural events
- 'adopting' members of senior citizens clubs, residents of aged homes, etc.
- creating opportunities to put the school and its work on show
- promoting special features such as centres of excellence, technology high schools, and environmental areas
- encouraging visits by VIPs and ex-students to enhance the school's reputation and stimulate media interest.

By opening the door to the community, you are also taking the first steps towards gaining sponsorship.

Provide a wide range of activities and invite the parents into the school to view all aspects of school life, demystifying the school environment and developing a rapport with parents.

Sponsorship

Once you have established a rapport with the community, it's time to think about sponsorship.

Think about your community and identify local businesses that could, perhaps, assist you, i.e. printers, businesses you could approach for some contra-deals where you provide a service to them and vice-versa.

Identify parent/community support that will perhaps assist you.

...time to think about sponsorship...

Identify areas of the school that may be of service to the community, i.e. halls, parking areas, signs on corner positions, etc.

Identify businesses that may be interested. Approach various businesses individually (over the phone or in person), outlining your strategy and what you can offer them, e.g. offer advertising in your newsletter, highlighting the readership numbers and distribution details, such as local businesses, public library, doctors' surgeries.

The main points to remember are:

● always go back and deal with the same person
● always follow up your call with further information
● always send the business a copy of what it sponsored or advertised in
● always establish what you will be able to do for them
● don't be despondent if you receive a few rejections
● the key to success is don't give in, and be selective in whom you approach.

Remember to:

● as part of your marketing strategy, identify staff/parents who may have expertise in the area of sponsorship
● establish your own logo on a variety of items for sale or promotional use, e.g. school magnets, key rings, calendars, Christmas cards, thank-you cards, spoons, clothing, badges, etc. Remember to start small and expand gradually.

Mailing List

In developing a community rapport, it is also a good idea to develop a mailing list of people to whom you will send your newsletters, prospectus, etc. Do this gradually and keep building and revising the list over time. Remember to include:

● the local library
● doctors/dentists
● the Council chambers

- local businesses who support you
- local feeder high schools/primary schools.

Because your school is the focus of education for your community, you are in an excellent position to ensure that a positive image, reflecting the tremendous work of your school, is created and that the community, staff and student all receive this positive information.

Remember to refer to the Departmental guidelines in all areas of mass media, and liaise with educational specialists who will always assist, with information or expertise.

Remember to communicate the image of your school and, at the same time, an accurate reflection of the system priorities and you will be on the way to a successful marketing strategy.

Implementing the Marketing Plan Outside the School

The Print Media

The print media is a major form of communication and it is extremely important to identify the area of print coverage for which you are aiming. Your production of a successful press release will depend on this. Decide who you are aiming at and who your audience is. Consider national newspapers, major local papers, suburban newspapers, ethnic newspapers, speciality magazines and educational papers.

The timing of your story is crucial if you wish to make the major papers. The time of the year, the day of the week and the time of day affect the likelihood of the story being covered by the press. Saturday and Sunday (for major newspapers) are quiet news days. Sunday is a good day to approach morning papers for Monday. On public holidays, journalists are normally searching for stories.

...the timing of your story is crucial...

When to Contact Newspaper Journalists

Morning papers:	Journalists work	Deadlines
	12–9pm	1st edition (6–7 pm)
	2–11pm	2nd edition (10–11 pm)
Afternoon papers:	7:30–4:30pm	1st edition (8–9am)
		a lot of editions throughout the day
National papers:	10–6pm	1st edition 6pm Sydney
		4pm other States

For your local papers, you need to know which day of the week they are released and to try and give them plenty of lead time. Often they have a small staff and, if you want media coverage, it is often easier to supply them with press releases including photos. (See pages 198–200 for more information on supplying of photographs.)

Suppose you are having an event or activity at the school and you want publicity. How do you achieve success? The media receives thousands of press releases and hundreds of calls each week. So how do you make yours stand out and successfully obtain press coverage for the event?

There are many steps to producing a printed press release and you need to consider:

- presenting a professional image to the media
- developing a rapport/contact with the journalists/editor
- identifying the angle of the story
- writing a successful press release
- providing appropriate photographs.

It is essential in developing and maintaining a good working relationship with the press to remember that the media work in an extremely competitive, high pressure industry. Therefore, you must make sure your message gets through. The following tips will help:

- be sure of your story and the background *before* you pick up the phone
- provide information quickly and clearly
- have all the facts ready at your fingertips when having a phone interview, and all the information organised *before* a journalist arrives to interview you.
- if you're uncertain about any of the information or facts, have the appropriate people available or try to acquire the information as quickly as possible
- always follow up any queries left by the journalist
- be reliable and accurate
- don't ever give incorrect information
- make sure, when the reporter arrives, that he or she is not kept waiting or 'wandering around' looking for someone
- help — be cooperative and give service
- assist the journalist with any material or setting up that he or she may need, especially if he or she has brought a photographer

● do not leave the journalist to his or her own devices
● remain available.

Try and develop a personal rapport. Ask for the journalist's direct phone line number for future reference. Make sure in your concluding dialogue with the journalist that all questions have been answered and all his or her needs met. Hopefully, you are on the way to developing a good association with the journalist and to having your story published. Remember to thank the journalist after your story is published.

The following list, the 'Cs of Communication', is helpful. Include these in your print communication:

● *credibility:*	the receiver must have confidence in the sender.
● *context:*	the sender must provide for participation and feedback. The receiver must confirm not contradict.
● *clarity:*	the message must be put in simple terms. Words must mean the same thing to the receiver as they do to the sender.
● *continuity:*	repetition achieves penetration.
● *consistency:*	the message must be consistent.
● *channels:*	the sender must use channels that the receiver uses and respects.
● *capability of audience:*	the sender must be aware of the receiver's capabilities. The least effort required to understand the message, the more effective it will be.

A crucial factor in your relationship with the media is the establishment of ongoing contact. You are certainly going to have a greater success rate if you become 'known' by the journalists, and are 'known' for always providing accurate information in a clear, precise and ordered manner.

Once initial contact has been made with the appropriate journalist/editor, always try and re-establish contact with the same person. Make sure you have the correct spelling and pronunciation of the person's name, know his or her office hours and direct phone number (if possible).

Always follow up your press release or initial phone contact — promptly.

After having sent a press release, make sure you are available to have any issues or points clarified, nothing will destroy your 'contact' faster than if you are not available when the journalist wants to talk to you.

As we all know, the diversity of the media is often what appeals to the public most. It is extremely important that, when considering the story you wish to have published, you choose the appropriate *angle* — to maximise its effect and highlight the area of the media that would find it appropriate (especially in regard to the major newspapers). Often, if we are trying to gain press coverage, it is the 'soft news' variety that is our concern — because it equates with human interest stories that are both entertaining and informative.

In finding the angle, be different, be quirky, be original, have a sense of humour, and be visual (use a celebrity, if appropriate).

Sources of News

The following sources of news all provide good material for a school marketing press release:

- school anniversaries, centenaries, etc.; staff and community (P and C) anniversaries, e.g. 20 years of service to the school
- the commencement of something new at the school
- successes of students and community members, and achievements of teachers
- academic areas
- the Arts
- drama
- music
- art
- sporting achievements
- gifted and talented students
- multicultural aspects
- special education
- focus programs
- expansion plans
- new policies
- community service items available
- sponsorship and business links
- new courses
- new equipment
- celebrations — special events, days and carnivals

It is important, when finding the *angle* for your story, to keep the variety of journalists in mind, as some will gravitate towards *particular* stories. The interest in success or talent being demonstrated by an Art student is likely to extend beyond parents, and could be relevant for the art section of a newspaper or even be worth a feature in a specialist magazine. Choosing the right media channels will help you communicate the message.

The Press Release

A press or media release is a way of informing the media of forthcoming events in your school and is the most universal way of contacting any media source.

The Headline

The headline is all important. It must catch the journalist's eye.

The Lead

The first paragraph of an article is known as the *lead*. The lead is often more important than the headline. Remember, your press release is competing with hundreds of other press releases. A quick glance at the lead will tell the editor whether he or she will be able to use your release.

The lead must tell the editor:

- *what*   (happened, or will happen)

- *where*   (it happened, or will happen)
- *why*   (it happened, or will happen)
- *how*   (it happened)
- *when*   (it happened, or will happen)
- *who*   (did it, or will do it)

Hints

- Mention the full name of the school *early on.*
- Attribute statements to a chosen person. The media needs a 'source'.
- Quotations add a human touch. They must, however, be original, interesting, simple and add strength to the release.
- Keep the release short, i.e. always keep it to one page. Use short, 'active' sentences and words. Use punctuation, and make key words bold or put them in capital letters. Avoid cliches, jargon and abbreviations.
- Correctly spell the name of the person to whom you are sending the release.
- Be original, catchy, short, interesting and topical.
- Find the *angle*.
- Remember, when mailing, to make sure the release arrives well in advance of the deadline.
- Make sure the names used are spelled correctly and have the correct titles attached.
- Always follow up with a phone call.
- Use A4 paper, with the school logo, etc. at the top of the page.
- White paper is okay, but coloured paper (bright colours only) is often more effective.
- Type only on one side of the paper, with wide margins and double spacing in between lines.
- The heading should be in bold type or underlined.
- End the release with a contact name and business and after-hours phone numbers, in case further information is required.
- Use the Pyramid Theory — each paragraph should add a bit more information to the release, yet the release should be able to stand on its own for publication with the deletion of paragraphs from the bottom up!
- Aim for quality — one good strong story is worth everything.

Press Release Checklist

- Is it short, sharp and factual?
- Can you cut out anything?
- Has it been carefully proofread?
- Have you avoided repetition, ambiguities and cliches?
- Have you checked your facts?
- Are times, dates and contact numbers correct?
- Is it accurate?
- Always keep your news release to one page.
- Always follow up your release with a personal call to the appropriate person — to clarify or develop further interest.
- If arrangements are made for a journalist or photographer to visit the school, always ring on the day to confirm. Never assume they are still coming.

Think about lead times. Keep looking ahead so that you are always in good time with seasonal features. This may mean holding on to a piece of good news (if it's ageless). There may be a better time to release it.

(If you prefer the information you are releasing to receive low-grade attention, release it late on a Friday afternoon.

Be alert to what's happening around, i.e. if it's Grand Final or Cup Final day, delay releasing your sports story.

Most importantly, if you send out a release and it gets good coverage that, in turn, generates enquiries, make sure the school is geared to handle them. Otherwise, you will have wasted your efforts and your good PR will turn bad.

Prepare a school position paper with policy guidelines so, if two (or more) people talk to the media, the viewpoint is always the same.

Always remember, if your story doesn't come out quite the way you expected, it is common practice for various media outlets to put a different emphasis on the same facts to appeal to their various audiences.

Note that, when an inquiry from the mass media is received in a Government school, it should be referred to the regional office. There will be more information available in that office and there is always the possibility that the matter seeking clarification refers to a wider policy area than relates to one individual school. Refer to the relevant policies and guideline documents that often indicate how the Principal should go about contacting media, and seek parental permission before agreeing to any student interviews or filming/photography involving students.

Photographic Material

Photographs are a crucial aspect in developing the image of your school. Most metropolitan newspapers prefer to use and take their own photographs of an event, but that is not necessarily the case with local press — they often prefer to have a 'black and white' photo sent to them. A good photo will often make the paper even when the accompanying story doesn't.

Tips for Dealing with a Photographer
- Always phone the pictures editor on the morning of the event. (*Note*: this should have been pre-arranged already, through a press release/phone call — even if it was the day before.) Reconfirm.
- When you phone, be prepared to assist in the organisation and setting up of the shot. Discuss the content of the photograph with the pictures editor. So, if they request a prop, person or venue, you can go and organise it.
- Be punctual and reliable.
- Identify yourself to the photographer.
- Discuss with the photographer the theme suggested by the editor. Help the photographer set up. Help with the props. Help with the spelling of the subjects' names. Make sure the photographer has a copy of the press release on the event.
- Offer to set up different photos with different photographers, if necessary.
- Be flexible and be prepared to move to another location.
- Be very, very patient.
- Be enthusiastic, positive, helpful, constructive and inventive.

- Think in pictures — visualise what the photo will be.
- In the case of a social function, identify the personalities or interesting faces who may be present. Take the photographer around. Help set up the photos.
- Remember the photographer's name so that you will develop him or her as a contact as well, especially when they come again to your next event.
- After the shoot is over, make a point of entertaining the photographer, let him/her join the function as your guest.
- Advise him/her if something newsworthy is about to happen.
- Always tell the photographer when she/he arrives what is going to happen during the event, so they are prepared.

...make a point of entertaining the photographer...

Taking your own Photos
- Organise a good reliable photographer.
- Thoroughly brief the photographer on what you want — it'll be too late afterwards!
- Issue the photos immediately to local papers, with appropriate press details. (A press release would have already been sent with all the details prior to the event.)
- Circulate the proofs to others/staff/community so they can be included in newsletters, etc.
- When you send the photos into the newspaper, remember to caption the photograph on an adhesive label stuck on the back. Include the names of all the people in the shot, and the photographer (especially if it is a student).
- Don't use clips or staples on photographs.
- Always send an information sheet with your contact numbers, both at work and at home.
- Don't expect photos to be returned.
- Send different photos to different competing papers — never the same shots.
- Newspapers need glossy black and white prints of a reasonable size (25 cm × 20 cm or 12.5 cm × 17.5 cm)

- Copies of photos used can be purchased from the newspaper photo libraries.
- Act quickly. Remember deadlines — hot news cools quickly!
- News value, human interest and composition are important factors to take into consideration when setting up and circulating photos.
- Sometimes, with major newspapers, there is more chance of the photo being published if the house photographer took the shot, rather than you.

The Celebrity

Using a celebrity in some of your major activities is a great way of developing media coverage of an event.

Checklist of possible celebrities
- Past students
- Sporting celebrities
- Local business people
- Local politicians
- Local artists
- Parents
- Departmental representatives
- Soap opera stars or other television celebrities

Know your parent community. Often we have parents who are celebrities and, if approached, they are usually only too happy to carry out some small function at an 'event'. The local community is a very good place to start as well, community officials, council members, members of Parliament, or business identities are all worth approaching. Once again, if commitments allow, they are usually happy to help. Giving them plenty of notice helps!

...using a celebrity...

Try local sporting clubs. The local football, soccer and netball associations are very helpful. They may have international or State representative players who are able to play a role in your event.

Often having a celebrity can add a dimension to your event, both for the students and the community. It can certainly assist in gaining media coverage in both major and local newspapers — especially if the celebrities are local to the community. Make sure you mention your celebrity (with his/her permission of course) in your press release or any publicity for the event.

Radio Coverage

Radio is immediate, which sets it apart from the other electronic media. If news happens, it will be on radio first. Interviews can be conducted over the phone and broadcast minutes later.

Many radio stations are very supportive of schools and are a great means of communication, announcing special events or cancellations due to rain, etc.

Once again, a press release is an appropriate way to make initial contact, and follow up with a phone call to a specific disc jockey. Remember to keep in mind the image/angle you wish to portray, and know your radio station's image. Stations have rigid formats, so make sure you approach the appropriate one. Breakfast time is when most people listen to radio, after that the number of listeners decreases dramatically.

The format of many shows *necessitates* the announcers to interview guests — sometimes up to four an hour, for three hours a day. These announcers need interview subjects badly. Feel free to phone them — you'll be doing them (and yourself) a great service. Often the announcers will have producers, so be ready with a quick outline of your subject — the topic and angle. Fax through a one-page background, then phone again to confirm the time and date. Always try to do the interview in the studio, live to air — but be prepared to pre-record and, if necessary, do the interview over the phone.

Try calling talkback announcers on air. It works! The talkback announcers are taking calls all the time and, normally, are willing to talk about anything. The music DJs will either talk to you off air, and take down the details to promote later, or some of them have assistants (especially in the breakfast and drive programs) who will help.

Hints
- Prepare your topic.
- Jot down specific points you wish to convey.
- Keep the content interesting and to the point.
- Avoid jargon.
- An articulate and enthusiastic voice will help to attract the listener. Speak slowly and clearly.
- When students are being interviewed, they should also be assisted by a teacher and given every opportunity to clearly identify and prepare their message.
- If you don't agree with the interviewer, say so.
- Be extremely careful of microphones. Don't rustle papers, tap your pen, clear your throat, kick, knock or move around.

● Avoid 'um's and 'er's.
● If doing a phone interview, do it from a quiet place!

If you have been approached by a radio station for an interview, the following paragraphs contain a few points for you to consider. (Remembering of course departmental guidelines!)

Decide whether to do it or not. Ask the radio station:

● who is doing the interview?
● when?
● where?
● how long will it last?

Decide:

● whether you are available or not.
● whether you want to do it.

Ring them back. You'll need to know:

● why are they doing this program?
● why me?
● what is 'the' context?
● will it be live or recorded?
● who else will be on the program?
● what questions will they ask?

Prepare before the interview:

● so you say what you want to say, not what *they want* you to say.
● by planning the message. Make three points (distill them, time is short) supported by three or four sub-points each.

...who else will be on the program?

- to use anecdotes (tell it in stories) and analogies (ring a bell in the listener's minds)
- by learning your brief.

Anticipate their angle. Likely questions can be deduced from:

- what they said they would ask
- putting yourself in their place.

Remember to keep off the defensive. You are going to use their questions to get across your message.

Television

Nothing can match the medium of television for impact, yet it is one of the more difficult forms of media from which to obtain coverage.
Some suggestions to get you thinking follow below.

- When seeking coverage of an event, it is more likely to be successful if the cameras can film lively, original footage at an event ranging from a school spectacular, to a sporting event or fair.
- TV deadlines are more immediate and frequent than those of newspapers.
- If you have a TV story coming up, it's important to work with the TV station so they have the material they need well in advance. It's also extremely important for you to *know* the program that will be covering your story and to become familiar with the different programs on the station and their different approaches.
- Always have a one-page news release/information sheet to send to the station.
- When being interviewed, consider where the interview should take place and choose an appropriate backdrop.

...know the program that will be covering your story...

- TV producers need time to edit and produce a segment before going to air. Remember to allow enough lead time to your event when you distribute your release, and always follow up with a phone call.
- When involved in a news conference — contact all news departments early in the day, when possible.
- Because of the TV medium, questions tend to be 'cut and thrust' and answers need to be short, sharp and instant.
- Personalities change when processed through the media, much of our communication is visual — smiles, frowns, etc.
- TV can be extremely time-consuming. A producer may ask to film a story on your premises and promise that it will only take half an hour. In the end, it might take half a day and the furniture might need to be rearranged 20 times. You need to be prepared for this.
- Be prepared. Arrange your thoughts. Plan what you (students need planning time as well) are going to say and research the facts. Be thoroughly familiar with your subject.
- Look alert. Concentrate on the questions. Answer succinctly. Lean slightly forward in your seat.
- Speak to the interviewer, not the camera. Talk with expression — with your eyes, body and hands. Non-verbal communication counts.
- Don't concern yourself with the microphone — don't fiddle with it. Don't bang on a table or move your chair while on air.
- Make the viewers feel as if you are talking to them personally.
- Be wary of the pregnant pause. The onus is on the interviewer to keep things flowing, don't jump in nervously. Do not hesitate too long in answering a question. No matter how honest your reply, if you hesitate you will come across as indecisive and uncertain.
- If the interviewer makes a mistake, correct it immediately. Don't get sidetracked. Don't be bluffed or intimidated.
- Make your answers short and sharp, but avoid simple 'yes' and 'no' answers.
- Avoid jargon, obscure words and percentages.
- Dress comfortably. Middle tones are better than dark tones. Avoid horizontal stripes or checks that produce a dazzling effect. Make sure your tie/neckline is straight.
- Be positive and assertive. Present your material as fact, not opinion.
- Try to anticipate surprises and if the interviewer does spring one on you, let the viewer know.
- Know when to stop talking.
- Do not rise from your chair at the end of the interview, you will be told when to do so.

Magazines

Australia consumes more magazines per capita than any other nation in the world. Magazines naturally cover a wide range of different interest areas.

Magazines are circulated in many varied timeframes, i.e. weekly, monthly, or even once a year. As opposed to the immediacy of radio, TV and newspapers — magazines have a longer lead time. For example, the *Bulletin* hits the streets every

Wednesday and the deadline for a promotional story is the Friday before. *Woman's Day* deadlines are usually as late as 12 days prior to the 'on the street' publication, day. *Woman's Weekly* works with deadlines around 6 to 8 weeks ahead of publication.

Attention to lead time is essential. Also, as with TV radio and newspapers, make sure you 'know' the style of the magazine before you contact it to try and place a story.

Exclusives and different angles will always be attractive to a magazine, because of their long lead time. All media like exclusives!

Magazines are great for exposure when you have time to plan, i.e. break the story in a magazine then follow on with your general news release to other media.

Reference Material to Assist in Marketing your School

A number of publications are generally available from your Regional Offices of School Education.

Conclusion

Now you have some key elements to commence the development of your school's marketing strategy, and for gaining media coverage and sponsorship, and marketing your school.

Remember this is a dynamic area and requires constant attention, forward planning and review.

Your school is unique, your staff is dedicated and committed, your students are talented individuals, and you are a key provider of services to our community.

Develop your marketing strategy and share your successes with your community.

Bring a plate, discuss key issues with all stakeholders, pass the lamingtons, take a photo and share the story! Happy marketing of your school!

CHAPTER 7

Stress Management

Susie Sharman

What is Stress?

Stress is our physiological and psychological response to demands made on us. Stress is an integral part of everyday life. Within limits, it is beneficial, as it serves to energise us and helps us to achieve our goals. However, 'too much' stress will be detrimental to our physical and mental health (in its extreme form it will leave us burned out).

The stress threshold varies greatly from person to person. It is important for us to be aware of our own optimal stress level.

Stressors

The *source* of stress is known as a *stressor*. It may be externally imposed by others (family, colleagues, friends) or self chosen (expectations, goals, feelings and thoughts). Stressors can be grouped into four main categories:

- threats to our physical and emotional well being (e.g. illness)
- change in our life circumstances (e.g. new baby, promotion, retirement)
- extreme demands made on us
- relationship issues.

However, any given stressful event will generally involve a number of the above categories.

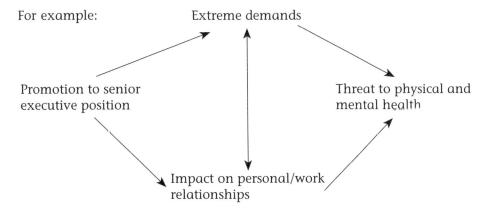

For example:

Extreme demands

Promotion to senior
executive position

Threat to physical and
mental health

Impact on personal/work
relationships

Our stress responses will be a function of both our stress threshold and the severity, frequency and duration of the stressor. Moreover, a *series* of relatively minor stressful events can be just as damaging as a single major stressor.

Symptoms of Stress

Symptoms of stress are clear indicators that we are no longer able to manage our stress. Our body, behaviour and feelings act as a warning system. It is up to us to be aware of our own symptoms of stress.

Self Awareness

Issues for Reflection

♦ *Where in your body do you experience stress? In what way are your feelings and behaviour affected by stress?*
♦ *What do you do when you are stressed? Does this action work for you in the short term? ... in the long term?*

The following self-assessment exercise proforma will help you recognise signs of distress, so that you can continue your management of stress to the point where these signs are greatly diminished. This is *not* a scientific analysis but a self-awareness exercise. Any of these symptoms may be caused by factors other than stress but, if you are suffering them, there is a high probability that stress may be affecting you.

Make a copy of the proforma. Read each item and circle the number that best reflects how often you have had that symptom *in the last three months*, using the following scale:

● 0 = hardly ever
● 1 = sometimes
● 2 = often
● 3 = very often.

You may wish to discuss your assessment with a sympathetic friend or family member to see if he or she is aware of something you have missed. After three weeks of regular relaxation practice, put a mark alongside those symptoms that have improved.

Stress Self Assessment

Mood

I feel nervous, anxious, ill at ease.	.... 0 1 2 3
I feel keyed up, over-excited.	.... 0 1 2 3
I worry excessively.	.... 0 1 2 3
I become confused or forgetful.	.... 0 1 2 3
I have difficulty concentrating.	.... 0 1 2 3
I feel generally irritable.	.... 0 1 2 3
I feel bored or apathetic.	.... 0 1 2 3
Other.	.... 0 1 2 3

Organs

I feel my heart pounding.	.... 0 1 2 3
I breathe rapidly.	.... 0 1 2 3
My stomach becomes upset.	.... 0 1 2 3
I perspire easily.	.... 0 1 2 3
I feel lightheaded or faint.	.... 0 1 2 3
My mouth and throat become dry.	.... 0 1 2 3
I experience cold hands or feet.	.... 0 1 2 3
I need to urinate often.	.... 0 1 2 3
I have diarrhoea or constipation.	.... 0 1 2 3
My face feels flushed.	.... 0 1 2 3
My blood pressure is high.	.... 0 1 2 3
Other.	.... 0 1 2 3

Muscles

My hands and fingers tremble.	.... 0 1 2 3
I develop nervous twitches.	.... 0 1 2 3
I can't sit or stand still.	.... 0 1 2 3
My muscles become tense and stiff.	.... 0 1 2 3
I stutter or stammer when I speak.	.... 0 1 2 3
I clench my jaw or grind my teeth.	.... 0 1 2 3
I develop headaches or eye tension.	.... 0 1 2 3
I experience low back pain.	.... 0 1 2 3
I feel very fatigued.	.... 0 1 2 3
Other.	.... 0 1 2 3

Behaviour

I am short tempered with others.	.... 0 1 2 3
I become withdrawn.	.... 0 1 2 3
I am achieving less than normal.	.... 0 1 2 3
My appetite has changed markedly.	.... 0 1 2 3

(Assessment continued on next page.)

(Assessment continued.)

My sex drive has increased/decreased.	.... 0 1 2 3
I sleep too long, stay in bed.	.... 0 1 2 3
I suffer from insomnia.	.... 0 1 2 3
I have minor accidents/make more mistakes.	.... 0 1 2 3
I increase my medication.	,,,,,,, ... 0 1 2 3
I use more drugs, alcohol.	.... 0 1 2 3
I carry out useless repetitive	
movements, e.g. foot-tapping.	.... 0 1 2 3
Other.	.... 0 1 2 3

Stress Management Techniques

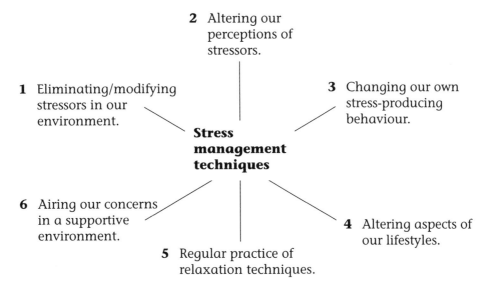

Reducing Stressors in our Environment

Successful stress management is contingent on identification of stressors in our lives. The following exercise focusses on the work environment and demonstrates that many work-related stressors are subject to change.

Spend several minutes thinking about all the things that cause you stress at work. Jot them down, and try to classify them into these three categories:

- E — those stressors that can be eliminated
- M — those stressors that can be modified
- U — those stressors that *appear* unchangeable.

For each stressor you categorised as E or M, list the specific strategies you would use to overcome or minimise its impact. Then select one (or two) stressors from the E/M category and develop an action plan for reducing it (or them).

The Action Plan
- Plan *small* consecutive steps.
- Ensure that each step is *realistic and achievable.*
- Who is responsible for carrying out each step?
- If appropriate, note an approximate time for each step.
- Plan steps that suit your personality style and the environment in which you are operating.
- Don't include in your plan anything you are not prepared to do.

Issues for Reflection

- ◆ *Is there anyone else you can rely on for support? If so, who are they and how can you ensure their support?*
- ◆ *Is there anyone or anything that may jeopardise your chances of success?*
- ◆ *How are you going to celebrate your success (both at the end and during the process)?*

A *holistic* approach to stress management is necessary — one which takes into account stressors in your *whole* life. Many stressors relate to our personal lives — our financial, domestic, health, and social circumstances. These factors will interact with pressures in the workplace lowering our threshold to stress. The above exercise can be repeated with non-work-related stressors.

Modifying Stress Producing Thoughts

Modification of thoughts is a fundamental, powerful technique for managing stress. It allows us to gain control over stressors that appear 'unchangeable'.

It is a commonly held view that events or situations are directly responsible for the feelings we experience. However, it is not the event itself, but rather how we *perceive* it (i.e. our thoughts, attitudes, and beliefs regarding the situation) that determines our emotional reaction. To illustrate:

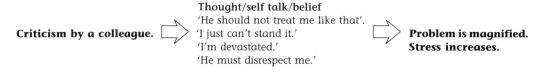

Criticism by a colleague. ⇨ **Thought/self talk/belief**
'He should not treat me like that'.
'I just can't stand it.'
'I'm devastated.'
'He must disrespect me.' ⇨ **Problem is magnified. Stress increases.**

Many of our thinking habits are counter-productive, causing an excessive or prolonged stress reaction. Irrational thinking, that involves exaggeration, labelling or perfectionism, heightens our stress, e.g. 'I *must* get that promotion', or 'People *always* let me down'.

In any potentially stressful situation, we can control the amount of stress we experience by *restructuring our thoughts and self talk* — by replacing exaggerated and unrealistic thoughts with more moderate, rational thoughts. This reframing of process involves *deliberate* effort and practice.

Three key steps are involved:

- *stop* and *listen* to what is going on in your head, so that you can identify what you are thinking and saying to yourself.
- determine whether your thoughts are irrational — whether they lead to negative, unhelpful feelings.
- if so, challenge those thoughts, — replace them with thoughts that are realistic and positive.

Example:

Irrational thought: 'I *must* get that promotion'.

Challenge: 'Are my expectations fair and reasonable? Why *must* I?'

Replacement: 'I would like to get that promotion. I'll be disappointed if I'm unsuccessful, but I'll handle it'.

Stopping Unpleasant Thoughts and Worries

Simply stopping negative thoughts is a useful stress management technique. Nagging thoughts and fears are interrupted using the 'stop' technique. When unpleasant thoughts arise, say 'stop' to yourself, either silently or aloud. Some people find it helpful to visualise a stop sign.

...using the 'STOP' technique...

Modifying Stress Producing Behaviour

Like our thinking mode, our behaviour will be a source of stress to ourselves, but it will also be a source of stress to those around us. Many stress-producing behaviours are self-imposed, arising from our expectations, beliefs, values and goals. In general, they embody perfectionism, extreme competitiveness, a relentless drive to achieve, hostility and aggression.

The following proforma will assist with rating your stress behaviours.

Stress Self Rating

Are the following stress producing behaviours characteristic of you?

	Not at all				Very much
	1	2	3	4	5
a	Always rushed.					
b	Move, walk and eat rapidly.					
c	Finish other people's sentences for them.					
d	Get agitated or angry when waiting in a queue.					
e	Bottle things up when angry or annoyed.					
f	Schedule more and more into less and less time.					
g	Have difficulty finding time to relax.					
h	Forceful or dominating in discussion.					
i	Take over other people's work when you think you can do it better.					
j	Few interests outside work.					
k	Become very aggressive when mistakes are made.					
l	Think or do more than one thing at a time.					
m	Make few allowances for unforeseen delays.					
n	Find it difficult to relax when there is time.					

Many of the stress-producing behaviours listed on the proforma stem from our own unrealistic expectations of ourselves and others. We need to recognise them. The following are some strategies for modifying stress-producing behaviour:

- develop good time-management skills. Decide on priorities, off-load non-essentials. Schedule 10–30 minutes a day quality time.
- have a pleasant sounding alarm to wake you up.
- each time you look at your watch, use it as signal to take a deep breath and relax.
- try to slow down the way you eat, talk and/or drive.
- eliminate behaviours that don't save much time or achieve a great deal, e.g. frenzied lane-changing, 'beating' the traffic lights.
- use breaks to walk, relax, meditate, or to enjoy the present moment.
- print 'R' on small adhesive labels. Stick them on mirrors, the steering wheel of your car, or the fridge, to remind you to relax.
- develop assertiveness skills (attend a workshop if necessary). Focus on the problem, not the person. Express your views effectively, using 'I' statements.
- once a week, give yourself time to do the things you really enjoy.

Relaxation Techniques

Relaxation is a way of producing a quiet body, and a calm but alert mind. Physical and mental unwinding is termed the 'relaxation response' — it counteracts the 'stress response'. Relaxation is an important short-term and long-term stress management technique. It is a practical skill that, once learned, can be carried out at will. Studies have shown that most people can lower their general level of tension by *regular* relaxation practice. For people who live with a high degree of tension (e.g. business executives), this technique has proved invaluable.

Relaxation is a simple, safe and effective way to promote health and wellbeing.

...the relaxation response...

The 'relaxation response' can be achieved:

- physically — by releasing tension in muscles
- mentally — by blocking out thoughts that produce tension, and 'tuning in' to non-stressful thoughts for a time each day (meditation).

A wide variety of relaxation methods exist. You need to experiment in order to find the method that best suits you.

Lifestyle Issues

Nutrition, exercise and sleep all play a crucial role in raising or lowering our threshold to stress. A balanced diet, regular exercise, and adequate sleep will protect us during stressful times.

Issues for Reflection

♦ *List three specific changes you would like to make in relation to exercise/ diet/sleep, so that you are better able to manage stress.*
♦ *For each behavioural change, determine the action steps you would take.*

Communication and Support Systems

Communication can play a vital role in alleviating or diminishing our stress levels. When we are able to 'air' some of our concerns/grievances, in a safe and supportive environment, our stress level is significantly reduced.

Communication is an effective stress management technique because it provides the opportunity to:

- ventilate — it allows some of the emotional energy to be discharged in a safe, healthy way
- affirm — our experiences are acknowledged and validated by being heard we are able to gain a better understanding of what is happening to us, and what options are available to us.
- resolve — a resolution of the problem may be reached.

However, this kind of communication requires a good *listener*. When we are stressed, we do not need to be given instant advice, to be judged, to be cajoled nor to be discounted. First and foremost, we need a good *sounding* board. We need to clarify our thoughts and consider our options. A good listener will facilitate this process.

Our support network comprises good listeners, who may be relatives, friends, peers and/or colleagues. There are times, however, when it may not be easy nor appropriate to approach these people because they are emotionally involved with us. In such cases, there is a range of helping professionals readily available in the community. Psychologists, social workers and psychiatrists have high expertise in dealing with life's stresses. As with other problems, it is important to intervene early to ensure a speedy recovery.

Appendix A

The School as an Organisation

Henry Mintzberg[1] has developed an analysis of all organisations by reference to a model composed of **five key structures**:

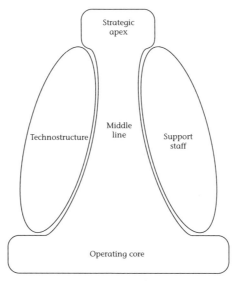

Mintzberg's Five Basic Parts of an Organisation

The 'operating core' refers to those people directly involved in the production of goods and/or services. In schools this corresponds to the classroom teachers.

The 'middle line' comprises those involved in supervising and/or supporting the operating core through directly related sales and marketing, and the management and supervision of operators. Supervisory teachers and subject heads would be in this position in schools.

The 'strategic apex' consists of those who manage the organisation's overall activities, planning and coordinating of the strategies that shape the organisation's future. The school's senior executive body and governing structures, such as a school council, would constitute this group.

The 'support staff' provide indirect assistance for the work of the operating core — including research and development, legal and industrial services, reception, payroll, mail, and the like. In schools, these activities are often categorised as 'administrative support'. Clerical staff and library staff providing resources for teachers fit into this category.

---

[1] Mintzberg, Henry (1979), *The Structuring of Organisations*, Prentice-Hall, New Jersey, p. 20. [See also Mintzberg, Henry (1983), *Structures in Fives*, Prentice-Hall, New Jersey.]

The 'technostructure' contains those specialists who support the design and operation of the organisation and its technical processes used by the operating core. Activities include production scheduling and operations research, as well as strategic planning support. In schools, specialist teachers, consultants and school counsellors may belong to this group. Curriculum and policy committees within the school and external regulatory structures, such as the State Board of Studies and Regional offices, share this function also.

The sort of work that an organisation does will determine how many people are engaged in each set of functions, and what responsibilities they have, thus determining the shape of the organisation. Notwithstanding this diversity, Mintzberg's model indicates that the organisation that emerges can be classified in five key types:

- the simple structure
- the professional bureaucracy
- the machine bureaucracy
- the divisionalised form
- the adhocracy

These are represented in the following schematic diagram.[2]

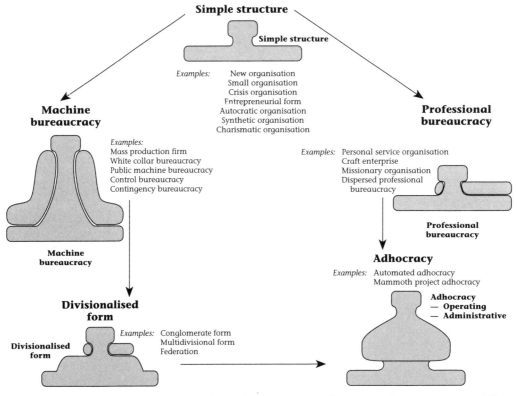

The *professional bureaucracy*, that characterises educational institutions, differs from the machine bureaucracy because of its technology. The work of a professional bureaucracy requires a large number of highly-skilled people at the operating core,

---

[2]   Mintzberg, Henry, op. cit., pp. 470–71.

(compared with the machine bureaucracy, where the operating core is usually less skilled, and production of outputs relies more on mechanised processes determined by technicians who put the technology in place than on high levels of individual decision-making by the operating core).

In schools, this basic difference is what supervisors of teachers have in mind when they talk of the difficulty of actually *getting into the classroom*, of entering into the processes of learning that occur as a result of interaction between teacher and students.

Schools have a very large operating core because learning must take place as a result of teachers' skilled judgments about process, constantly adjusted according to pupils' responses and needs. This reliance, primarily on the learned skills of highly trained people using relatively unsophisticated technology (the blackboard and chalk), is the key characteristic of the professional bureaucracy form. The professional bureaucracy has a small strategic apex, very few middle line positions (typically with dual lines of reporting and supervision — one professional and one administrative), a large support staff to service the large operating core, and a small, specialised technostructure (focussed on curriculum support, counselling services, special education and the like).

This is quite different from the *machine bureaucracy*, where production is much more regulated by mechanistic processes (requiring sophisticated machinery and fewer operators). The operating core has little or no control over the choice of processes to be used. Those in the relatively large technostructure regulate the work of the organisation through their control over its dominant technology (deciding how production will occur). The support staff are fewer, in keeping with the reduced numbers in the operating core that they support.

Mintzberg represents these differences diagrammatically as follows:[3]

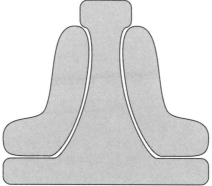

The machine bureaucracy

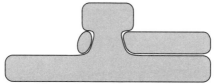

The professional bureaucracy

---

[3] Mintzberg, Henry, op. cit., pp. 325 and 354.

For those schools that operate as part of a system of schools, it is possible to use Mintzberg's model to conceptualise the organisational form at two levels.

The first is *the school itself*. The operating core is the school's teachers. The middle line is its head teachers, or senior teachers exercising supervisory responsibilities. The Principal, senior executive and governing councils constitute its strategic apex. The support staff include those involved in promotion, financial management, enrolments, tuckshop, mail, and the like. The technostructure is its consultants, its counsellors and curriculum planners and its clerical staff. The same staff member may, of course, play a role in more than one structure.

Secondly, it is possible to conceptualise the school as a component of an organisation that is *the educational system*. If we examine a State system, the Minister and the central planning authority constitute the strategic apex, the school teaching staff the operating core, the school executive and any regional staff involved in direct supervision and marketing the middle line, and so on.

Whether applied to a single school or to a school system, Mintzberg's model of the school as a professional bureaucracy generates certain observations about environmental contexts and strategic issues that are relevant to the management of change in schools.

Appendix B

Stakeholders and Other Influences

Schools, more than any other institution in our society, touch the lives of every individual and most of the various groups to which individuals belong. Thus, educational 'stakeholders', those who can claim a legitimate interest in the way in which schools and school systems function, are both numerous and diverse in the demands that they make on schools.

In a pluralist society, and in an era of interest group politics[1] (where government agendas are heavily influenced by the necessity to balance the competing interests of various groups), partisan, conflicting, politically motivated, and sometimes educationally unsound demands may be made on schools, and considerable pressure may be brought to bear to ensure that these demands are met. We might represent some of these stakeholders interests as follows:

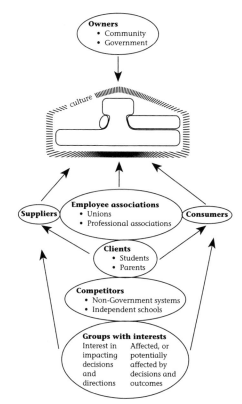

Classification of Interests in the Environment

[1] Marsh, Ian, *Parliament and Consent: collectionist versus pluralist approaches to interest group integration*, Australian Graduate School of Management Working Papers Series, 86–004, University of NSW, Kensington.

Appendix C

Who 'Controls' the Curriculum?

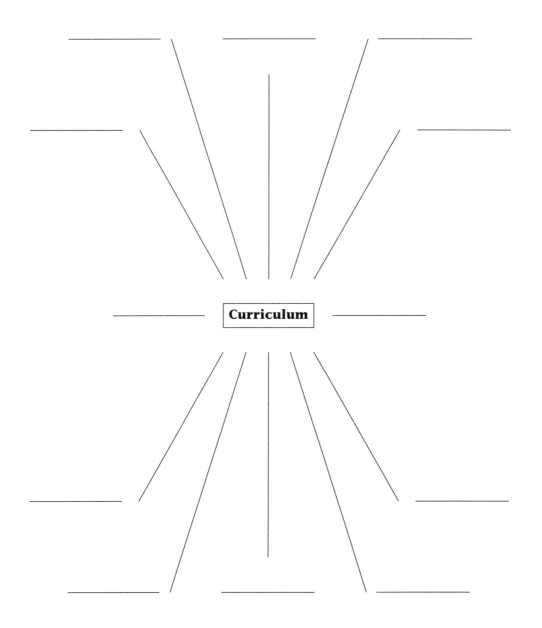

Appendix D

Determining Assessment Purposes and Priorities

Staff Survey

Please consider each of the following statements to decide on their possible inclusion in the school's assessment policy. In each case, decide if the inclusion is one with which you 'strongly agree' (++), agree (+), 'have no opinion' (0), 'disagree (–) or 'strongly disagree' (– –), by circling the selected response.

The school's assessment policy should:

1 Affirm the student and provide encouragement and incentive for further learning. ++ + 0 – – –

2 Provide students with honest and reliable information about their strengths and weaknesses, so that they grow in self-awareness. ++ + 0 – – –

3 Appraise the extent to which the student has met stated *school* aims. ++ + 0 – – –

4 Appraise the extent to which the student has met stated *course* aims. ++ + 0 – – –

5 Provide information for students that will help them plan further educational and vocational choices. ++ + 0 – – –

6 Provide information that could be used by employers to place students in the workforce. ++ + 0 – – –

7 Gather information to assist in placing students in appropriate courses or subjects. ++ + 0 – – –

8 Gather information that will help teachers diagnose learning difficulties. ++ + 0 – – –

9 Gather information that will help teachers meet the needs of individual students. ++ + 0 – – –

10 Gather information that will help teachers develop or modify teaching and learning strategies and the selection of resources. ++ + 0 – – –

11 Provide information to rank student achievement to meet the requirements of the Board of Studies. ++ + 0 – – –

		++	+	0	–	– –
12	Assist in the evaluation of course/program effectiveness by providing information on levels of student satisfaction and achievement.	++	+	0	–	– –
13	Provide relevant information to report to the community, e.g. employers, media.	++	+	0	–	– –
14	Obtain information about the nature of learning in a particular course/program in order to plan curriculum directions.	++	+	0	–	– –
15	Assist students to acquire self-discipline and life skills, such as setting goals, negotiating contracts, meeting deadlines, and becoming self-sufficient.	++	+	0	–	– –
16	Provide a basis for reporting to parents.	++	+	0	–	– –
17	Take into consideration all tasks performed by the student, such as homework and assignments, bookwork, tests, etc.	++	+	0	–	– –
18	Take into account low achievers.	++	+	0	–	– –
19	Take into account students who require special education.	++	+	0	–	– –
20	Take into account the ESL background of students.	++	+	0	–	– –
21	Take into account the extremes of ability range.	++	+	0	–	– –
22	Provide a detailed description of the student's abilities.	++	+	0	–	– –
23	Take into account students who have had prolonged absences.	++	+	0	–	– –
24	Take into account students who have recently arrived at school.	++	+	0	–	– –
25	Encourage the underachiever.	++	+	0	–	– –
26	Place less emphasis on comparative results.	++	+	0	–	– –
27	Be shaped by public examinations.	++	+	0	–	– –
28	Allow room for parent involvement in the assessment process.	++	+	0	–	– –

Appendix E

Reporting

Some Questions to Ask

- Did parents influence decisions about what you report and how you report it?
- Are your report cards just one component of how you demonstrate the achievements of students at your school?
- Do your reporting procedures reflect the many and varied teaching and assessment methods used, or do they focus on only a few, e.g. exam skills?
- Does the information on your report allow the audience to understand what the student can and cannot do? Can the 'codes' be easily understood by the uninitiated? Have you defined clearly the meaning of any labels at the head of each column or in any box?
- Is information about specific achievements provided, or is it lost within a global mark/grade/rank/comment?
- Does the report meet parent needs for information, e.g. what can your child actually do in relation to other students of the same age/ability?
- Have you taken into account the fact that parent information needs vary with the ages of their children?
- Does your report allow you to provide information on student strengths and weaknesses, to celebrate notable achievements and to provide steps to make progress? Are comments significant and based on evidence? Do they avoid personal shortcomings, focussing only on aspects related to achievement?
- Do you report on skills and competencies as well as subject content?
- If a position in class is used, is it clear what standards of achievement have been achieved by the whole group?
- If a percentage mark is used, is it clear what levels of achievement are indicated by each mark?
- If a ranking is used, do you describe the reference group against which the student has been compared, and the nature of the tasks set?
- If specific criteria grades are used, do you describe the objectives/competencies represented by each grade, comment on why a student may have failed to satisfy a criterion, or describe how a student's performance exceeds a particular criterion?
- If you use descriptive profiles, do you detail what was achieved by the student and include comment on the progress and development of the student?
- Do your reports enable you to attract parent support for the school by revealing the hard work of teaching and assessment that led up to the report and the educational business and philosophy of that school?
- Are your reports the sort of reports that a student would be proud to keep for the rest of his/her life?

Appendix F

Sample Questionnaire: School Climate

[This questionnaire has been devised to be completed by small groups of members of the school community.)

Schools are complex organisations within the community. Each school has its own characteristics and its own levels of performance. The following 0–10 scale allows you to measure what is happening in some of these areas.

Circle the number that, in your opinion, best represents the degree to which each aspect is functioning in your school.

When you have completed your responses, work out your score on the score sheet provided (see the last three pages of the questionnaire).

School Climate

1 New ideas are rejected.
0 2 4 6 8 10
1 There is a spirit of innovation in the school.

2 The school is rigid in its systems.
0 2 4 6 8 10
2 There is a flexible approach used in the school.

3 Commitment is fragmented or non-existent.
0 2 4 6 8 10
3 Individual commitment to the school's policy is high.

4 Change is actively resisted.
0 2 4 6 8 10
4 Positive change is accepted enthusiastically.

5 Any change is random and not related to the whole school.
0 2 4 6 8 10
5 Change is planned and organised.

6 There is a lack of acceptance of ideas from outside the school.
0 2 4 6 8 10
6 The school is open to ideas from external bodies.

7 Individual initiative is suppressed.
0 2 4 6 8 10
7 There is an active cultivation of staff initiative.

8 The job is an interruption to the life of staff members.

0 2 4 6 8 10

8 Each staff member enjoys high job satisfaction.

9 There is avoidance of routine tasks.

0 2 4 6 8 10

9 Individuals see themselves responsible for all components of their job.

10 Discussion of flaws in the organisation is avoided.

0 2 4 6 8 10

10 All individuals feel secure in raising matters of concern.

11 All problems are referred to the Principal.

0 2 4 6 8 10

11 Staff have knowledge of their areas, make decisions and solve problems at their own level.

12 Decisions are made by the Principal and announced.

0 2 4 6 8 10

12 Staff are consulted on matters that affect them.

13 Failure is feared and consequences of failure emphasised.

0 2 4 6 8 10

13 Success is emphasised.

14 Excuses and scapegoating are common.

0 2 4 6 8 10

14 Individuals accept responsibilities for their jobs.

15 Individuals are secretive and competitive.

0 2 4 6 8 10

15 There is a high level of project sharing.

16 Problems are shelved or not admitted.

0 2 4 6 8 10

16 Problems are faced and solved.

17 Problems are 'grumbled about' outside school.

0 2 4 6 8 10

17 Problems are investigated and worked on 'in school'.

18 Factions and individuals compete.

0 2 4 6 8 10

18 There is widespread cooperation with others.

19 Policy is hazy and commitment is low.

0 2 4 6 8 10

19 There is knowledge of and commitment to policy.

20 There is apathy about the school's welfare.

0 2 4 6 8 10

20 Individuals are involved in the school's welfare.

21 There is centralised decision making.

0 2 4 6 8 10

21 There is participative decision making.

22 Staff meetings are directive issuing.

0 2 4 6 8 10

22 Staff meetings are involved and sessions enjoyable.

23 The school as an organisation is reactive.

0 2 4 6 8 10

23 The school as an organisation is proactive.

24 Staff are interest only in their own duties.

0 2 4 6 8 10

24 Staff are aware of the range of Principal's job.

25 Communication occurs only between neighbouring teachers and particular friends.

0 2 4 6 8 10

25 Communication between all staff is encouraged or occurs regularly.

Finding your Score

Score boxes are provided below. In the left-hand box each time, show the number of times you scored that particular number. Then proceed to work out your total score.

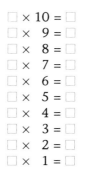

□ × 10 = □
□ × 9 = □
□ × 8 = □
□ × 7 = □
□ × 6 = □
□ × 5 = □
□ × 4 = □
□ × 3 = □
□ × 2 = □
□ × 1 = □

Total score: _____

Scores

176–250   You see your school as highly participative and democratic. Do your group members see it the same way? Check any differences you have.

_____

_____

_____

_____

_____

126–175   Check which areas need attention. What do your group members say?

_____

_____

_____

_____

_____

76–125   Were you lacking information, or is this how you see an efficient school operating? Consult with your group about this result. They may see it differently.

_____

_____

_____

_____

_____

0–75   This may be your perception, but are you being realistic? Check with the other members of your group.

_____

_____

_____

_____

_____

In discussing the results with your group, consider the following items:

1 Are your results realistic?

_____

_____

2 Could the results indicate a need for change?

_____

_____

3 What changes do you and your team feel are necessary?

_____

_____

Appendix G

Sample Chart of Accounts

_____ High School
School Based Chart of Accounts

	Dissection			Subdissection	
No.	**Description**		**No.**	**Description**	
	English			Debating	
				Equipment	
				Excursions – English	
				Equipment maintenance	
				General expenses	
				Photocopying	
				Teaching resources	
				Textbooks	
	ESL			Equipment	
				Excursions – ESL	
				Equipment maintenance	
				General expenses	
				Photocopying	
				Teaching resources	
				Textbooks	
	Mathematics			Equipment	

_____ High School
School Based Chart of Accounts (cont'd.)

| | **Dissection** | | **Subdissection** |
No.	**Description**	**No.**	**Description**
	Mathematics (cont'd)		Excursions – Mathematics
			Equipment maintenance
			General expenses
			Photocopying
			Teaching resources
			Textbooks
	LST (STLD)		Equipment maintenance
			General expenses
			Photocopying
	Science		Equipment – Computing
			Equipment – Hardware
			Equipment – Consumables
			Excursions – Science
			Equipment maintenance
			Equipment maintenance grant
			General expenses
			Photocopying
			Teaching resources
			Textbooks
	Humanities – Social science		Equipment

_____ **High School**
School Based Chart of Accounts (cont'd.)

	Dissection			**Subdissection**
No.	**Description**	**No.**		**Description**
	Humanities – Social science (cont'd)			Excursions – Humanities
				Equipment maintenance
				General expenses
				Photocopying
				Teaching resources
				Textbooks
	Languages			Equipment
				Excursions – Language
				Equipment maintenance
				General expenses
				Photocopying
				Teaching resources
				Textbooks
	TAS – Computer studies			Equipment maintenance
				General expenses
				Hardware
				Software
				Photocopying
				Textbooks
	TAS – Home EC/Food tech			Equipment
				Excursions – TAS

_____ High School
School Based Chart of Accounts (cont'd.)

Dissection		Subdissection	
No.	**Description**	**No.**	**Description**
	TAS – Home EC/Food tech (cont'd)		Equipment maintenance
			General expenses
			Photocopying
			Teaching resources
			Textbooks
			Food items
	Creative arts – Visual		Equipment
			Excursions – Creative arts – Visual
			Equipment maintenance
			General expenses
			Photocopying
			Teaching resources
			Textbooks
	Creative arts – Music		Equipment
			Excursions – Creative arts – Music
			Equipment maintenance
			General expenses
			Photocopying
			Teaching resources
	Drama		Equipment
			Excursions – Drama
			Equipment maintenance

_____ **High School**
School Based Chart of Accounts (cont'd.)

	Dissection		**Subdissection**
No.	**Description**	**No.**	**Description**
	Drama (cont'd)		General expenses
			Photocopying
			Teaching resources
			Textbooks
	PD/Health/PE		Equipment
			Excursions – PD/Health/PE
			Equipment maintenance
			General expenses
			Photocopying
			Teaching resources
			Textbooks
	Sport		Equipment
			Excursions – Sport
			Equipment maintenance
			General expenses
	Special Education		General expenses
			Equipment maintenance
			Teaching resources
	Careers		Equipment maintenance

_____ High School
School Based Chart of Accounts (cont'd.)

	Dissection		Subdissection
No.	**Description**	**No.**	**Description**
	Careers (cont'd)		General expenses
			Teaching resources
			Photocopying
	HT/Adm/Fin HT/Curriculum		General expenses
	Counsellor		General expenses
	Deputy principal		General expenses
			Hospitalities
	Principal		General expenses
			Hospitalities
	Casual salaries – Teacher		Casual teachers salary
	Library		Equipment maintenance
			Equipment
			General business books
	Extra curricula		Charities
			SRC
			Year 10 formal

_____ High School
School Based Chart of Accounts (cont'd.)

| | Dissection | | Subdissection |
No.	**Description**	**No.**	**Description**
	Extra curricula (cont'd)		Year 12 formal
			Gifted and talented
			Staff social committee
			School magazine
	HRD		HRD contra
			School development days
			School priorities
			Teaching resources
			English
			ESL
			Mathematics
			LST
			Science
			Humanities
			Computing
			Languages
			TAS
			Visual arts
			Music
			PD/Health/PE
			Careers
			Library

_____ High School
School Based Chart of Accounts (cont'd.)

	Dissection		Subdissection
No.	**Description**	**No.**	**Description**
	HRD (cont'd)		Welfare
			Counsellor
			Executive
			School assistants
			General expenses
	Special education		General expenses
	Student assistance scheme		General expenses
	Business links		General expenses
	Marketing		General expenses
			Hospitalities
			Printing/publication
			Advertising
			Presentation evening
			Graduation evening
	Administration and office		Awards/Prizes
			Electricity
			Equipment
			Equipment maintenance

_____ **High School**
School Based Chart of Accounts (cont'd.)

	Dissection			**Subdissection**
No.	**Description**	**No.**	**Description**	
	Administration and Office (cont'd)		Gas	
			General business	
			Hospitality	
			Pest control	
			Petty cash items	
			Postage	
			Printing/publication	
			Paper for duplicating	
			Safety/first aid	
			Petrol	
			Security	
			Stationery/office supplies	
			Telephone/fax	
			Waste disposal	
	Building maintenance		Cleaning	
			Equipment	
			General expenses	
	Charities		General expenses	
	Ground maintenance		Equipment	
			Environmental initiatives	

_____ **High School**
School Based Chart of Accounts (cont'd.)

Dissection		Subdissection	
No.	**Description**	**No.**	**Description**
	Ground maintenance (cont'd)		General expenses
	Salaries – Casual ancillary		Ancillary salaries
	Capital – Equipment		Equipment
			Freight charges
			General expenses
			Maintenance
	Furniture		Equipment
			Freight charges
			General expenses
			Maintenance
	Initiatives		School council
			General improvements
	Depreciation		Equipment
	Bank discrepancies		Bank discrepancies
			Bank charges
	Investments		Term deposits 1

Appendix H

Principal's Financial Management Checklist

The following is a summary of the key financial management procedures in schools, to assist Principals in the day-to-day managing and monitoring of financial activities.

Budgeting

Rationale:
Sound financial planning assists a school to achieve its educational plans.

Mandatory Procedures:
a Schools must have an annual budget showing expected income and expenditure programs.
b The budget must be used as a means for monitoring the school's financial performance.

Suggested Procedures:
a Schools should have a budget committee comprising of school staff and community membership.
b Actual income and expenditure figures should be compared to budget on a monthly basis (per term for small schools) and the budget adjusted to reflect any change in circumstances.

Receipting

Rationale:
Receipting controls are designed to enable a school to account in full for public monies it has received in trust.

Mandatory Procedures:
a Official receipt books only must be used.
b Receipts are to be issued promptly on day of collection.
c Cancelled receipts (originals and duplicates) are to be retained in the receipt book.

Suggested Procedures:
a Teaching staff should be aware of the proper procedures for collection of cash, and recording and maintenance of class lists and group receipts.
b Collection/receipting procedures should be adequate to suit the circumstances of the school and the risks involved.

Banking

Rationale:
Banking school funds regularly increases the potential investment interest and decreases the risk of theft.

Mandatory Procedures in NSW:
a   All school bank accounts must be with the Commonwealth Bank.
b   Collections must be banked when cash exceeds $500 or within one week of collection.
c   Collections must be banked intact.
d   An independent person must perform a regular check of the banking to the receipt book(s). (Except in one teacher schools.)

Suggested Procedures:
a   Receipting and banking duties should be performed by different persons.
b   Collection/receipting procedures should be adequate to suit the circumstances of the school and the risks involved.

Purchasing

Rationale:
Purchasing controls are designed to ensure public monies are both wisely spent and subject to a competitive process to ensure value for money.

Mandatory Procedures in NSW:
a   Principals are responsible for obtaining maximum value for goods and services purchased on behalf of the school.
b   Official school purchase orders must be used for all purchases exceeding $100.
c   Purchase orders are an accountable document. Copies of all orders used or cancelled must be maintained, and unused copies secured.
d   At least three written or oral quotations must be invited for purchases from private suppliers, between $1000 and $10 000 per item. Quotations must be in writing for purchases between $10 000 and $50 000. A record of quotations must be maintained.
e   There are no requirements for quotations for goods and services up to $1000 in value, however, the following conditions apply:
   (i)   rates are considered reasonable and consistent with normal market rates for items of a like nature.
   (ii) requirements are not split into components nor is there a succession of orders for the same goods or services.
   (iii) regular reviews are undertaken, including random invitation and documentation of three quotations at appropriate time intervals, to ensure that the exemption is being exercised in the most effective and efficient manner.
f   Public tenders are to be invited for purchases from private supplies of items over $50 000.
g   Sales tax exemptions may only be claimed for goods purchased for use by the school and not for resale.

Suggested Procedures:
All purchases above a designated sum should be authorised, and the order signed by the Principal.

Payments

Rationale:
Payment controls are designed to ensure that public monies are expended only for bonafide purposes and to bonafide payees.

Mandatory Procedures:
a All payments must be authorised by the Principal or delegate.
b All payments must have supporting documentation.
c Cheque counter signatories must be aware of their responsibilities, e.g. sight all supporting documentation and the prepayment voucher before signing.

Cash books

Rationale:
The cash book is the historical record of income received and expenditure made by a school. A properly maintained cash book will assist the Principal in monitoring actual financial performance with budgeted performance.

Mandatory Procedures in NSW:
a A separate cash book is to be maintained for each school bank account (it is strongly recommended that schools operate only one bank account).
b Transactions must be recorded in the cash book at least weekly (except for small schools with 10 or less transactions per month).
c Each cash book is to be totalled, balanced and reconciled with the bank statement at the end of each month (except for small schools, where it must be done at least each term).
d The cash book and bank reconciliation must, wherever practicable, be checked by an officer other than the person responsible for recording and balancing the cash book.

Suggested Procedures:
a Cash book dissections should mirror the expected income and expenditure programs detailed in the school budget.
b The Principal should review the balancing of the cash book and the reconciliation to the bank statement at least once per term.

Asset control

Rationale:
An up-to-date equipment register is essential to enable proper control and security to be maintained over valuable, and often hard to replace, school equipment.

Mandatory Procedures in NSW:
a Equipment valued at $500 or more, and having a life expectancy of at least 3 years, must be recorded in an equipment or asset register immediately on receipt.
b Equipment valued at less than $500 but considered to be at high risk or of an attractive nature must also be recorded.
c Equipment must be marked with an identifying school name and number.
d Details of loans of equipment must be separately recorded.
e Stocktakes of equipment must be conducted annually.
f Adequate details must be recorded of the method and proceeds from the disposal of equipment.

Suggested Procedures:
a Equipment registers may be set out on a school faculty or department basis.
b Stocktakes may be conducted on a progressive basis.

Canteen

Rationale:
A well run canteen may contribute significant sums to the educational programs of students.

Mandatory Procedures in NSW:
a A markup and pricing policy must be agreed upon at the start of the school year including projected trading results.
b Canteen takings are to be recorded in a daily sales book and witnessed by two people.
c Takings must be banked daily and the deposit slip referenced to the daily sales book.
d Payments for goods must not be made from daily takings.
e Stocktakes must be performed at the end of each term.
f Term trading statements must be prepared and the results compared to projected results.

Suggested Procedures:
a Access to canteen trading stocks should be limited to as few people as possible.
b The Principal should commission periodic reviews of the daily sales book to ascertain any unusual variations from expected takings.
c The Principal should commission periodic reviews of the type of goods purchased, and the level of wastage.
d The Principal should commission periodic reviews of the takings to the bankings.

Bibliography

Allaire, Yuan, and Firsiotu, Michaela (1985), 'How to Implement Radical Strategic Change in Large Organisations', *Sloan Management Review*, Spring.

Barker, L., Edwards, R., Gaines, C., Gladney, K., and Holley F. (1981), 'An Investigation of Proportional Time Spent in Various Communication Activities by College Students', *Journal of Applied Communication Research*, Vol. 8.

Beare, Hedley (1989), 'From "Educational Administration to Efficient Management". The New Metaphor in Australian Education', a paper presented at the annual conference of the American Educational Research Association.

Beare, Hedley, Caldwell, Brian J., and Millikan, Ross H. (1989), *Creating an Excellent School: some new management techniques*, Routledge, London.

Beer, Michael (1980), *Organisation Change and Development: a systems view*, Scott, Foresman and Co., Illinois.

Beer, Michael, Spectos, B., Laurence, P. R., Quin Mill, D., and Walton, R. (1984), *Managing Human Assets*, Collier Macmillan, London.

Beringer, Ivan, Chomiak, George, and Russel, Hamish (1986), *Corporate Management, The Australian Public Sector*, Hale and Ironmonger, Sydney.

Blum, R. E., and Kneidek, A. W. (1991), 'Strategic Improvement that Focuses on Student Achievement', *Education Leadership*, Vol. 48, no. 7, April.

Boomer, Garth (1988), 'Some Challenges and Achievements in Australian Curriculum', *Unicorn*, Vol. 14, no. 4.

Bormann, E. G. (1975), *Discussion and Group Methods*, Harper and Row, New York.

Borysenks, J. (1987), *Minding the Body: Mending the Mind*, Addison-Wesley, Massachusetts.

Burack, Elmer H. (1988), *Creative Human Resource Planning and Applications, a Strategic Approach*, Prentice Hall, New Jersey.

Caldwell, Brian J., and Spinks J. M. (1986), *Policy Making and Planning for School Effectiveness*, Education Department of Tasmania, Hobart.

Caldwell, Brian J., and Spinks J. M. (1989), *The Self Managing School*, Falmer Press, London.

Chapman, Judith (1986), 'Decentralisations, Devolution and the School Principal: Australian Lesson on Statewide Education Reform.', *Educational Administrative Quarterly*, Vol. 22, no. 4, pp. 28–58.

Cheek, L. M. (1977), *Zero Base Budgeting Comes of Age*, Amacon, New York.

Clark, Robert (1989), *Australian Human Resources Management*, Mcgraw Hill, Sydney.

Connors, B., and Schoer B. (eds) (1988), *Towards Effective Teaching: a guide for supervisors*, NSW Department of Education, Metropolitan East Region, Sydney.

Costello, R. (1991), 'Government Policy for Professional Development of Teachers', in Hughes, P. (ed), *Teachers' Professional Development*, ACER, Hawthorn.

Cunningham, W. G. (1983), *Systematic Planning for Educational Change*, Mayfield Publishing Co., Mountain View, California.

Drucker, Peter (1980), *Managing in Turbulent Times*, Heinemann, London.

Drucker, Peter (1988), *Education Management*, Heinemann, London.

Duffy, D. (1970), *Teaching About Society*, Rigby, Adelaide.

Duignan, D. (1987), 'The Politicisation of Administrative Reform in Australian Education', a paper delivered to the British Educational Management and Administrative Society.

Dunphy, Dexter C., and Dick, Robert (1982), *Organisational Change by Choice*, McGraw Hill, Sydney.

Ellyard, P. (1990), 'Education in the 21st Century', *Independence*, Vol. 15, no. 1, June.

Eltis, K. J. (1989), *Into the 90s: understanding the curriculum issues*, Sydney Association for Educational Administration, published proceedings of a one-day workshop.

Everard, K. B. (1986), *Developing Management in Schools*, Basil Blackwell, Oxford.

Fombrun, Charles, Tichy, Noel M., and Devanna, Mary Anne (1984), *Strategic Human Resource Management*, John Wiley and Son, New York.

Ford, R. (1989), *Business Administration*, ACAE, Armidale.

Freebairn, J., Porter, M., and Walsh, C. (1987), *Spending and Taxing: national economic priorities*, Melbourne Centre for Policy Studies, Melbourne.

Gamage, David T. (1992), 'School Centred Educational Reforms of the 1990s — an Australian Case Study', *Educational Management and Administration*, Vol. 20, no. 1.

Goodstein, L. et al (1985), 'Applied Strategic Planning: a new model for organisational growth and vitality', *Developing Human Resources Annual*.

Handy, Charles, and Aitken, Robert (1986), *Understanding Schools as Organisations*, Penguin Books, London.

Harrold, R. (1982), *Economic Thinking in Education*, University of New England, Armidale.

Hay, Andrew (1988), 'A Market Approach to Education', *The Professional Administrator*, Vol. 40, no. 3, May-June.

Heath, Robert L., and Nelson, Richard Alan (1986), *Issues Management: corporate public policy making in an information society*, Sage, Beverly Hills.

Jenkins, H. O. (1989), 'Education Managers: paradigms lost', *Commonwealth Council for Educational Administration Newsletter*, no. 51.

Jones, Barry (1983), *Sleepers Wake!*, Oxford University Press, Melbourne.

Keefe, W. F. (1971), *Listen Management*, McGraw Hill, New York.

Kell, Peter (1991), 'Reform and the New Right: observations on reform in NSW education, 1988–90', *Australian Administrator*, April.

Kogan, Maurice (1978), *The Politics of Educational Change*, Manchester University Press, Manchester.

Levacic, R. (ed) (1989), *Financial Management in Education*, Open University Press, Philadelphia.

Littlejohn, S., and Jabusch, D. (1982), 'Communication Competence Models and Application', *Journal of Applied Communication Research*, Vol. 10, no. 1.

Logan, L., Dempster, N., Berkeley, G., Howell M. and Warray, M. (1990) *Teachers in Australian Schools: a 1989 Profile*, Department of Education, University of Queensland.

Majone, G., and Wildavsky, A. (1977), 'Implementation as Evolution', *Policy Studies Review*, no. 2.

Marsh, C. (1986), *Curriculum, an Analytical Introduction*, Ian Novak Publishing Co., Sydney.

Marsh, C. (1988), *Spotlight on School Improvement*, Allen and Unwin, Sydney.

Marsh, C. and Stafford, N. (1984), *Curriculum – Practices and Issues,* McGraw Hill, Roseville.

Marsh, I. (1989), 'Setting the Agenda in Australian Politics: towards regime change through partial realignment', *The Australian Quarterly,* Winter.

McAlpine, T. S. (1976), *The Basic Arts of Budgeting,* Business Books Ltd, London.

McGregor, Douglas (1960), *The Human Side of Enterprise,* McGraw Hill, New York.

McLaughlin, M. W. (1987), 'Learning From Experience: lessons from policy implementation', *Educational Evaluation and Policy Analysis,* Vol. 9, no. 2.

McNay, Henry, and Ozga, Jenny (1985), *Policy Making in Education,* Pergamon Press in association with the Open University, London.

Miles, M. B. (ed) (1964), *Innovation in Education,* Teachers' College Press, Columbia University, New York.

Miles, M. B., Saxl, Ellen, and Lieberman, Ann, 'What Skills do Educational "Change Agents" Need? An Empirical View', *Curriculum Enquiry,* Vol. 18, no. 2.

Mintzberg, Henry (1979), *The Structuring of Organisations,* Prentice Hall, New Jersey. [Abridged version, *Structures in Fives* (1979)]

Nadebaum, M. (1990), 'Noah or Butterfly? The Changing Role for School Principals in the 1990s', ACEA, Hobart.

Nadler, L. (1984), *Handbook of Human Resource Development,* John Wiley and Sons, New York.

Nicholls, A. H. (1972), *Developing a Curriculum: a practical guide,* George Allen and Unwin, London.

Nicholls, D. (1991), *Managing State Finance: the New South Wales experience,* New South Wales Treasury, Sydney.

NSW Department of Education, Services Directorate, *Managing Stress – a workshop for school personnel,* Sydney.

NSW Department of School Education, Human Resource Development Directorate (1991), 'Model 2 – Understanding the Context of Curriculum Management', *Managing the Curriculum* (Unit of the Certificate in School Leadership and Management).

NSW Department of School Education (1991), 'Managing the School's Financial Resources', *Certificate of School Leadership and Management Module,* HRD Directorate, Sydney.

NSW Department of School Education, Schools Renewal Taskforce, 'School-Based Budgets', a Departmental *Bulletin,* Vol. 11, no. 1, August.

Owens, Robert G. (1987), *Organisational Behaviour in Education* (3rd edition), Prentice Hall Inc., New Jersey.

Patillo, J. W. (1977), *Zero-Based Budgeting — a Planning Resource Allocation and Control Tool,* National Association of Accountants, New York.

Peters, Tom (1987), *Thriving on Chaos: handbook for a management revolution,* Pan Books, London.

Pearce, D. W. (1983), *Cost-benefit Analysis* (2nd edition), Macmillan, London.

Print, M. (1987), *Curriculum Development and Design,* Allen and Unwin, Sydney.

Pusey, M. (1992), 'Economic Rationalism', in *Canberra: a nation changes its mind,* Cambridge.

Renihan, F. and Renihan, P., 'The Concept of Institutional Image: implications for administrative action in schools', *Administrator's Notebook,* Vol. 32, no. 1.

Rossett (1987), *A Training Needs Assessment*, Educational Technology Publications, New Jersey.

Scott, Brian (1990), 'School-centred Education: Building a more responsive State school system', *The Management Review*, NSW Education Portfolio, Milsons Point.

Sizer, Theodore R. (1984), *Horace's Compromise: the dilemma of the American high school*, Houghton Mifflin Company, Boston, Massachusetts.

Spencer, J., Nolan, B., Ford, R., and Rochester, J. (1989), *Leadership and Organisational Effectiveness*, ACAE, Armidale.

Stone, James A. F., Collins, Roger R., Yetton, Philip W. (1985), *Management in Australia*, Prentice Hall, Sydney.

Stott, Kenneth (1992), 'Marketing your School: finding things out', *The Practising Administrator*, March, Vol. 14, no. 1. Published on behalf of ACEA by Harcourt, Brace, Javonovich Group (Aust) Pty Ltd, Sydney.

Strike, Kenneth (1982), *Educational Policy and the Just Society*, University of Illinois Press, Ubana.